INDESTRUCTIBLE HULK

S.M.A.S.H. Time

WRITER: MARK WAID

PENCILS: MATTEO SCALERA,
KIM JACINTO & MAHMUD ASRAR

INKS: MATTEO SCALERA & KIM JACINTO

LETTERS: CHRIS ELIOPOULOS & VIRTUAL CALLIGRAPHY'S CORY PETIT
COLOURIST: VAL STAPLES & LEE LOUGHRIDGE

ASSISTANT EDITOR: EMILY SHAW
EDITOR: MARK PANICCIA
EDITOR IN CHIEF: AXEL ALONSO
CHIEF CREATIVE OFFICER: JOE QUESADA
PUBLISHER: ALAN FINE
EXECUTIVE PRODUCER: DAN BUCKLEY

COVER: MUKESH SINGH

Do you have any comments or queries about this graphic novel? Email us at graphicnovels@panini.co.uk Join our Facebook group at Panini/Marvel Graphic Novels

MARVEL
marvel.com
© 2014 MARVEL

TM & © 2013 and 2014 Marvel & Subs. Licensed by Marvel Characters B.V. through Panini S.p.A, Italy. All Rights Reserved. First printing 2014. Published by Panini Publishing, a division of Panini UK Limited. Mike Riddell, Managing Director. Alan O'Keefe, Managing Editor. Mark Irvine, Production Manager. Marco M. Lupoi, Publishing Director Europe. Brady Webb, Reprint Editor. Angela Gray, Designer. Office of publication: Brockbourne House, 77 Mount Ephraim, Tunbridge Wells, Kent TN4 8BS. This publication may not be sold, except by authorised dealers, and is sold subject to the condition that it shall not be sold or distributed with any part of its cover or markings removed, nor in a mutilated condition. Printed in Italy by TERRAZZI. ISBN: 978-1-84653-574-1. LEGO and the Minifigure figurine are trademarks or copyrights of the LEGO Group of Companies. © 2013 and 2014 The LEGO Group. Characters featured in particular decorations are not commercial products and might not be available for purchase.

FSC

MIX
Paper from
responsible sources
FSC® C016466

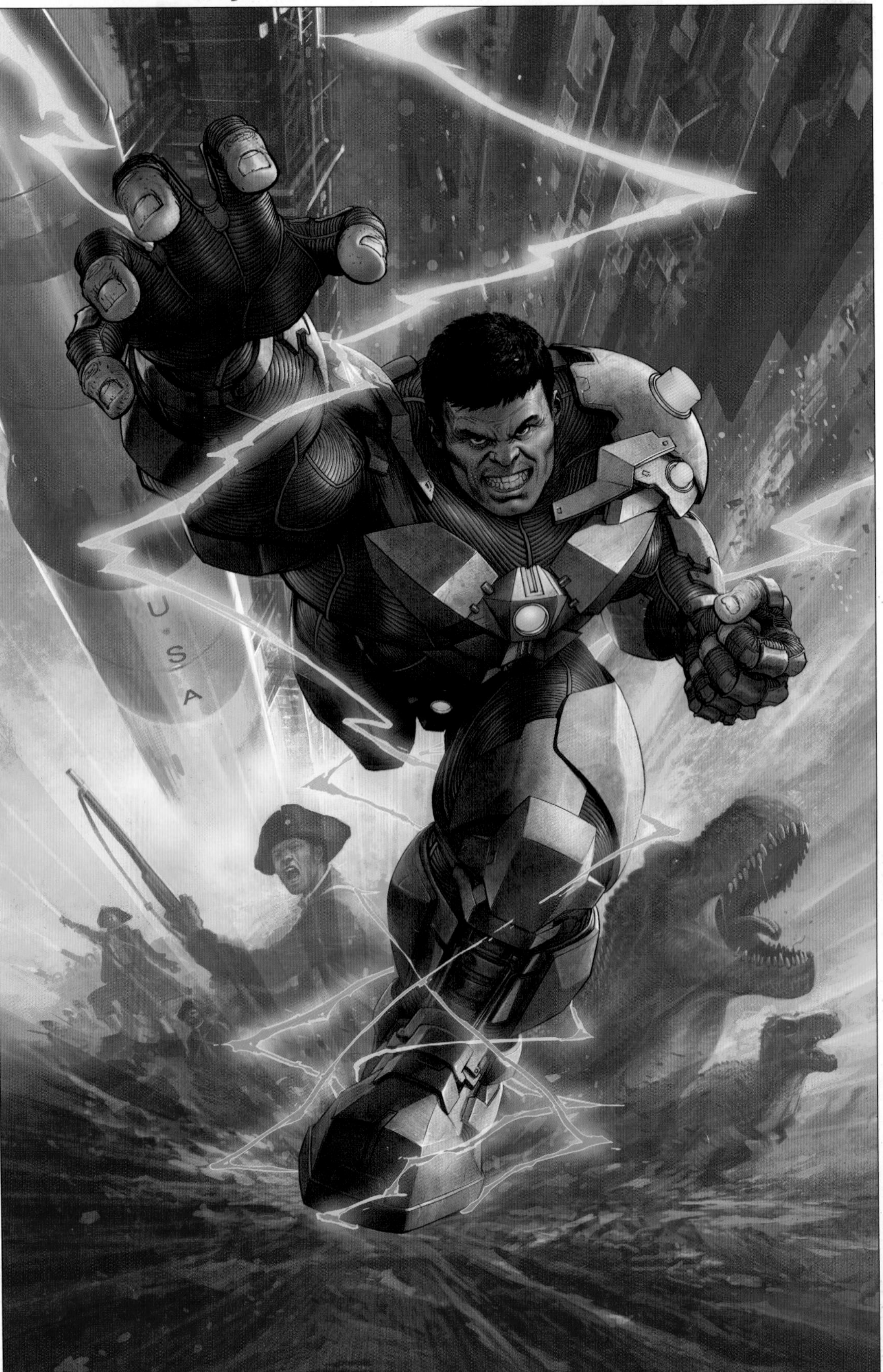
U.S.A

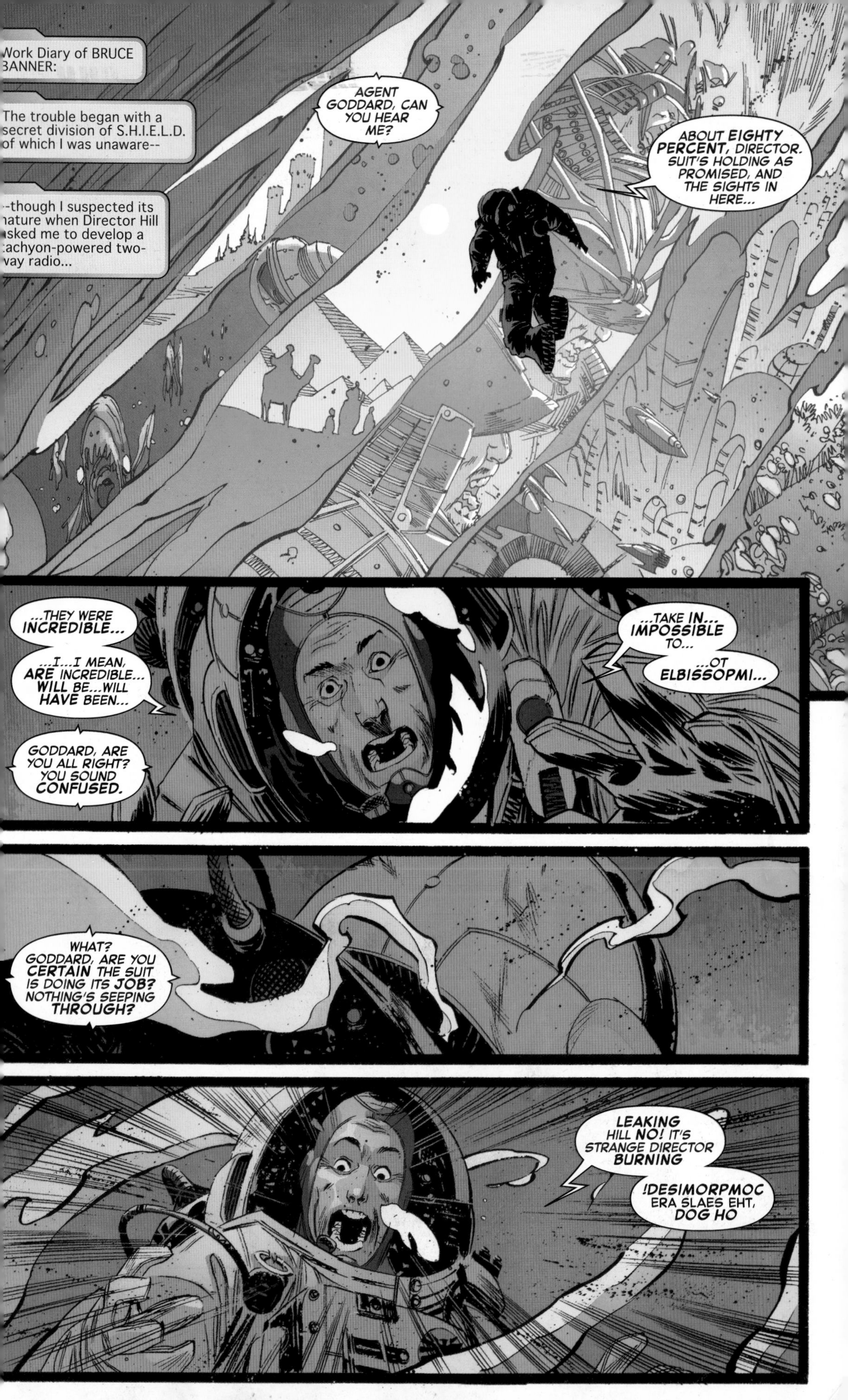
Work Diary of BRUCE BANNER:
The trouble began with a secret division of S.H.I.E.L.D. of which I was unaware--
--though I suspected its nature when Director Hill asked me to develop a tachyon-powered two-way radio...
AGENT GODDARD, CAN YOU HEAR ME?
ABOUT EIGHTY PERCENT, DIRECTOR. SUIT'S HOLDING AS PROMISED, AND THE SIGHTS IN HERE...
...THEY WERE INCREDIBLE...
...I...I MEAN, ARE INCREDIBLE... WILL BE...WILL HAVE BEEN...
...TAKE IN... IMPOSSIBLE TO...
...OT ELBISSOPMI...
GODDARD, ARE YOU ALL RIGHT? YOU SOUND CONFUSED.
WHAT? GODDARD, ARE YOU CERTAIN THE SUIT IS DOING ITS JOB? NOTHING'S SEEPING THROUGH?
LEAKING HILL NO! IT'S STRANGE DIRECTOR BURNING
!DESIMORPMOC ERA SLAES EHT, DOG HO

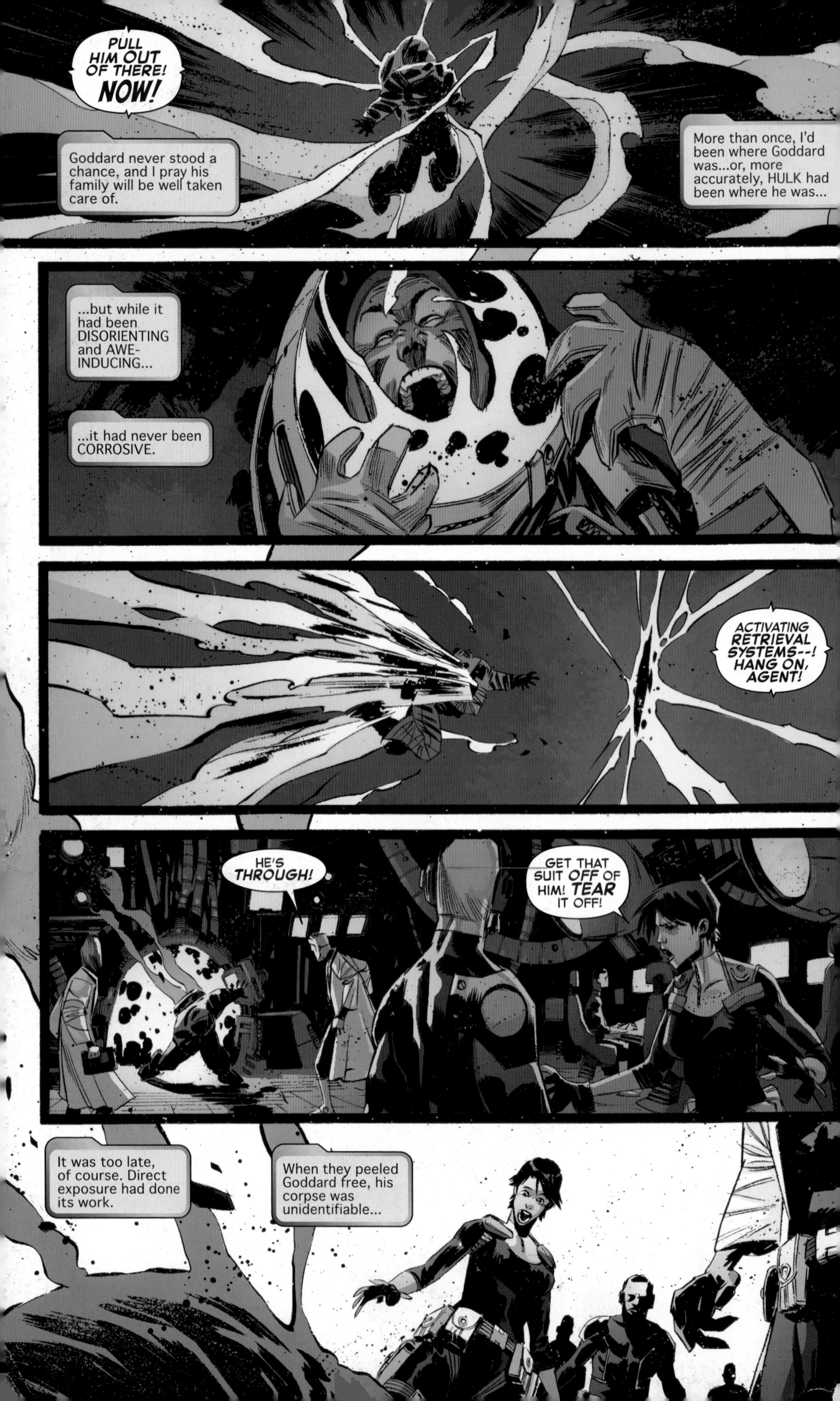

PULL HIM OUT OF THERE! NOW!
Goddard never stood a chance, and I pray his family will be well taken care of.
More than once, I'd been where Goddard was...or, more accurately, HULK had been where he was...
...but while it had been DISORIENTING and AWE-INDUCING...
...it had never been CORROSIVE.
ACTIVATING RETRIEVAL SYSTEMS--! HANG ON, AGENT!
HE'S THROUGH!
GET THAT SUIT OFF OF HIM! TEAR IT OFF!
It was too late, of course. Direct exposure had done its work.
When they peeled Goddard free, his corpse was unidentifiable...

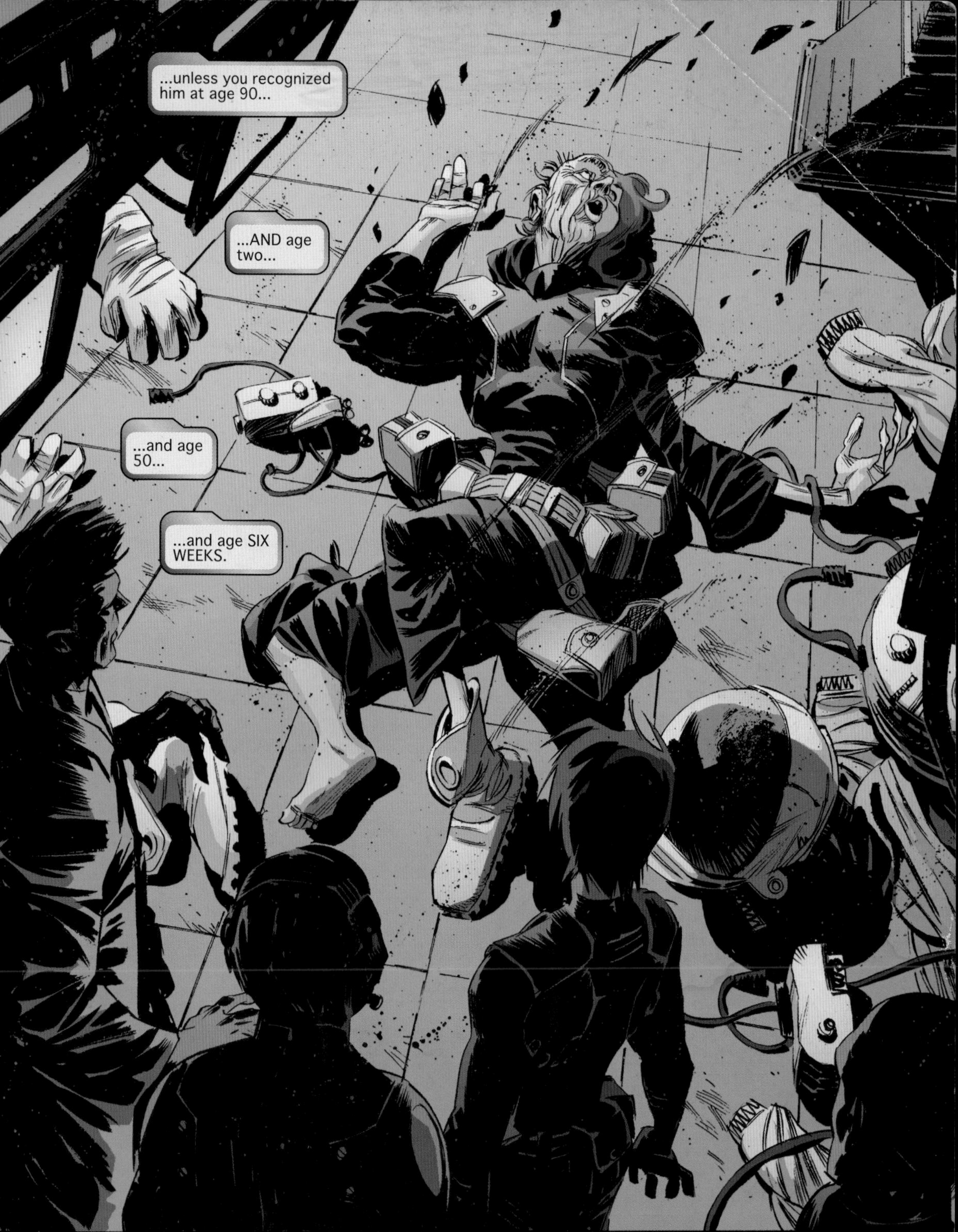
...unless you recognized him at age 90...
...AND age two...
...and age 50...
...and age SIX WEEKS.

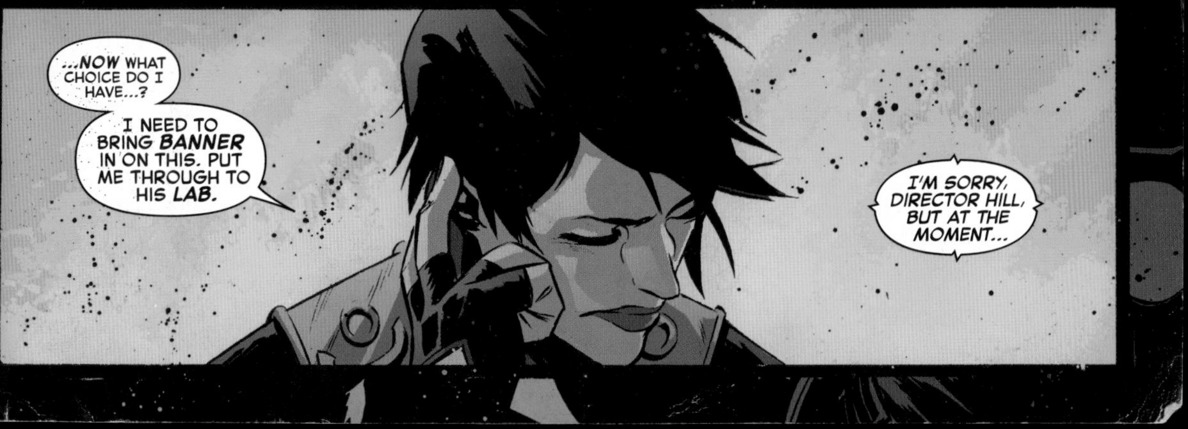
...NOW WHAT CHOICE DO I HAVE...?
I NEED TO BRING BANNER IN ON THIS. PUT ME THROUGH TO HIS LAB.
I'M SORRY, DIRECTOR HILL, BUT AT THE MOMENT...

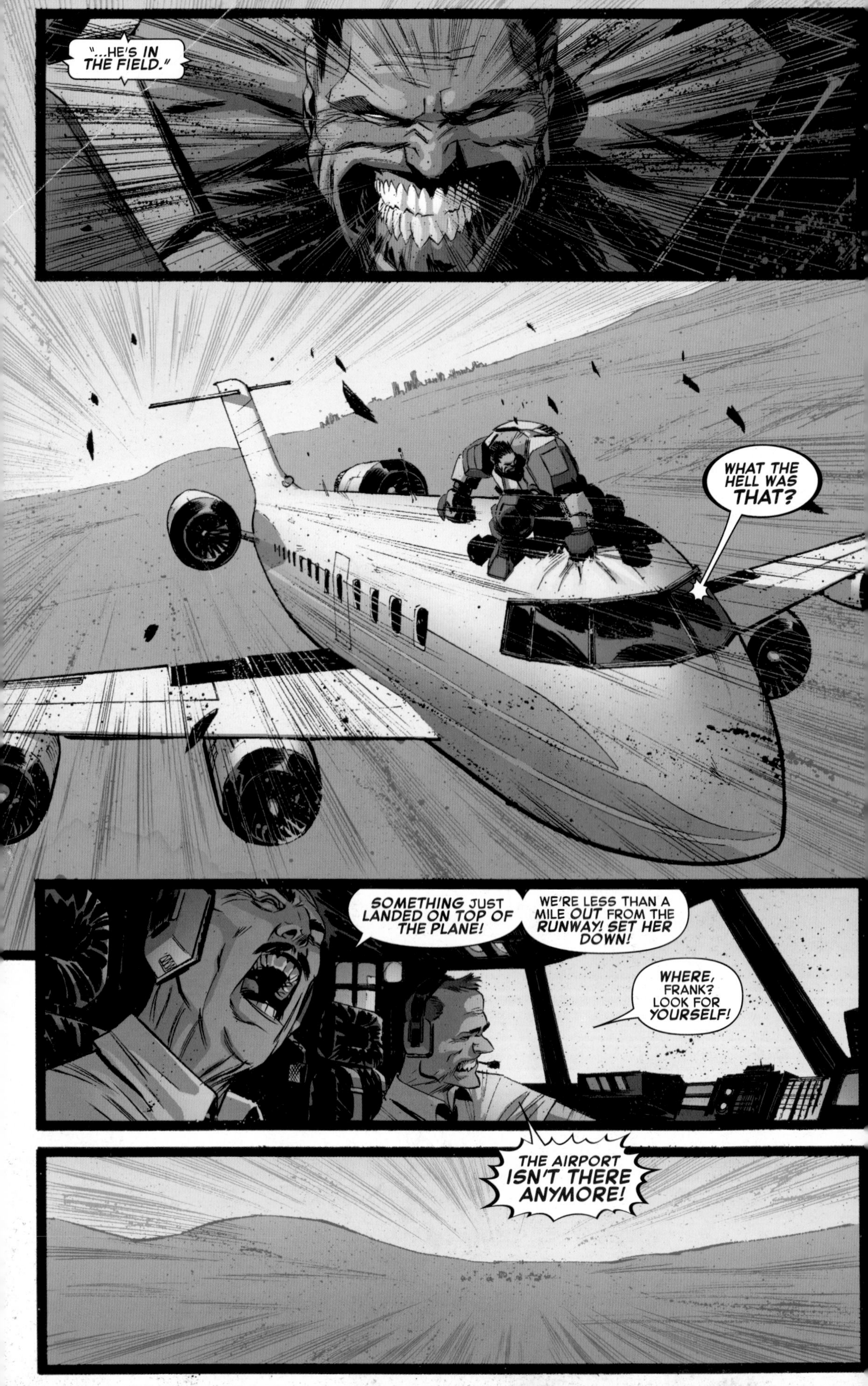
"...HE'S IN THE FIELD."
WHAT THE HELL WAS THAT?
SOMETHING JUST LANDED ON TOP OF THE PLANE!
WE'RE LESS THAN A MILE OUT FROM THE RUNWAY! SET HER DOWN!
WHERE, FRANK? LOOK FOR YOURSELF!
THE AIRPORT ISN'T THERE ANYMORE!

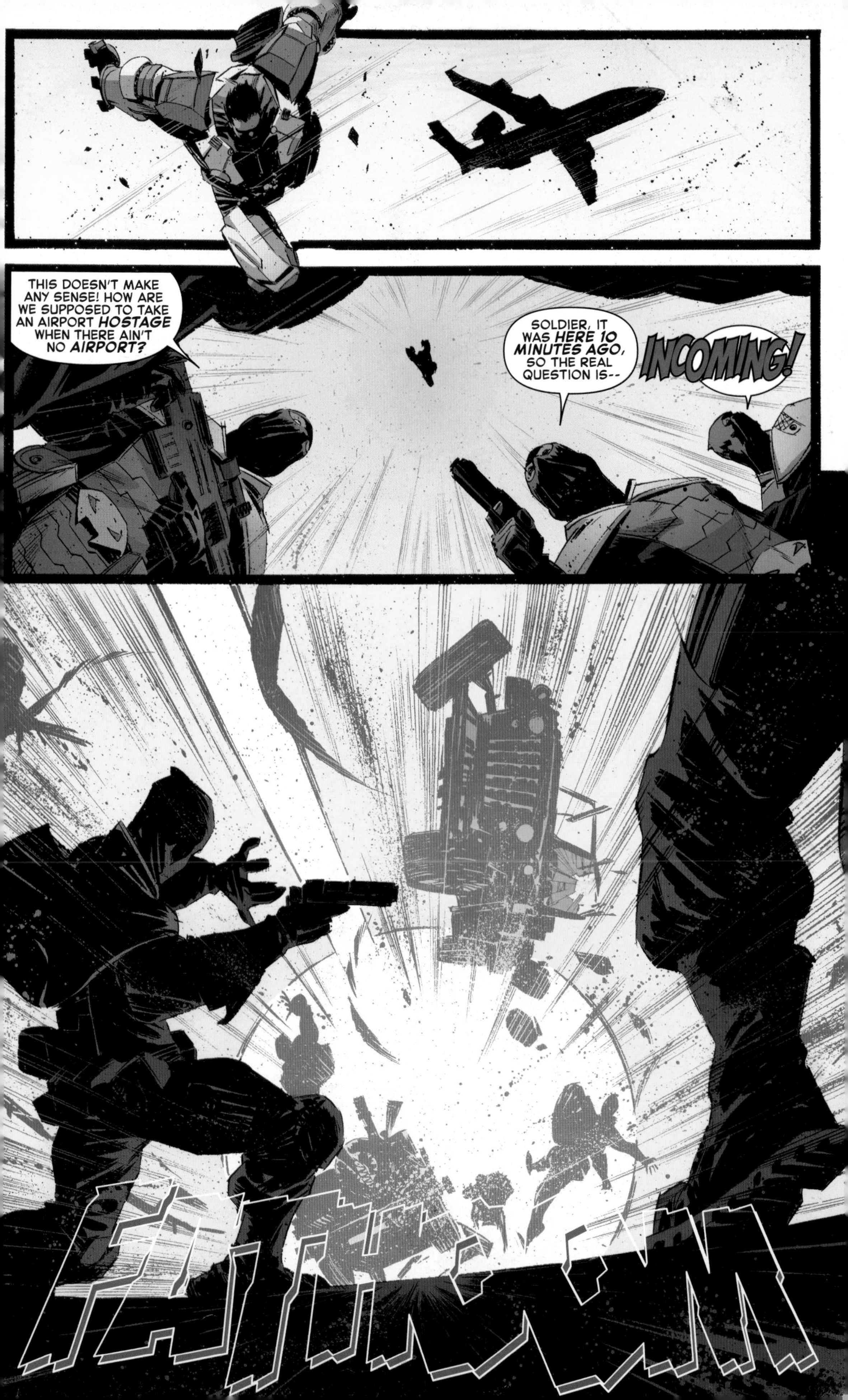
THIS DOESN'T MAKE ANY SENSE! HOW ARE WE SUPPOSED TO TAKE AN AIRPORT HOSTAGE WHEN THERE AIN'T NO AIRPORT?
SOLDIER, IT WAS HERE 10 MINUTES AGO, SO THE REAL QUESTION IS--
INCOMING!

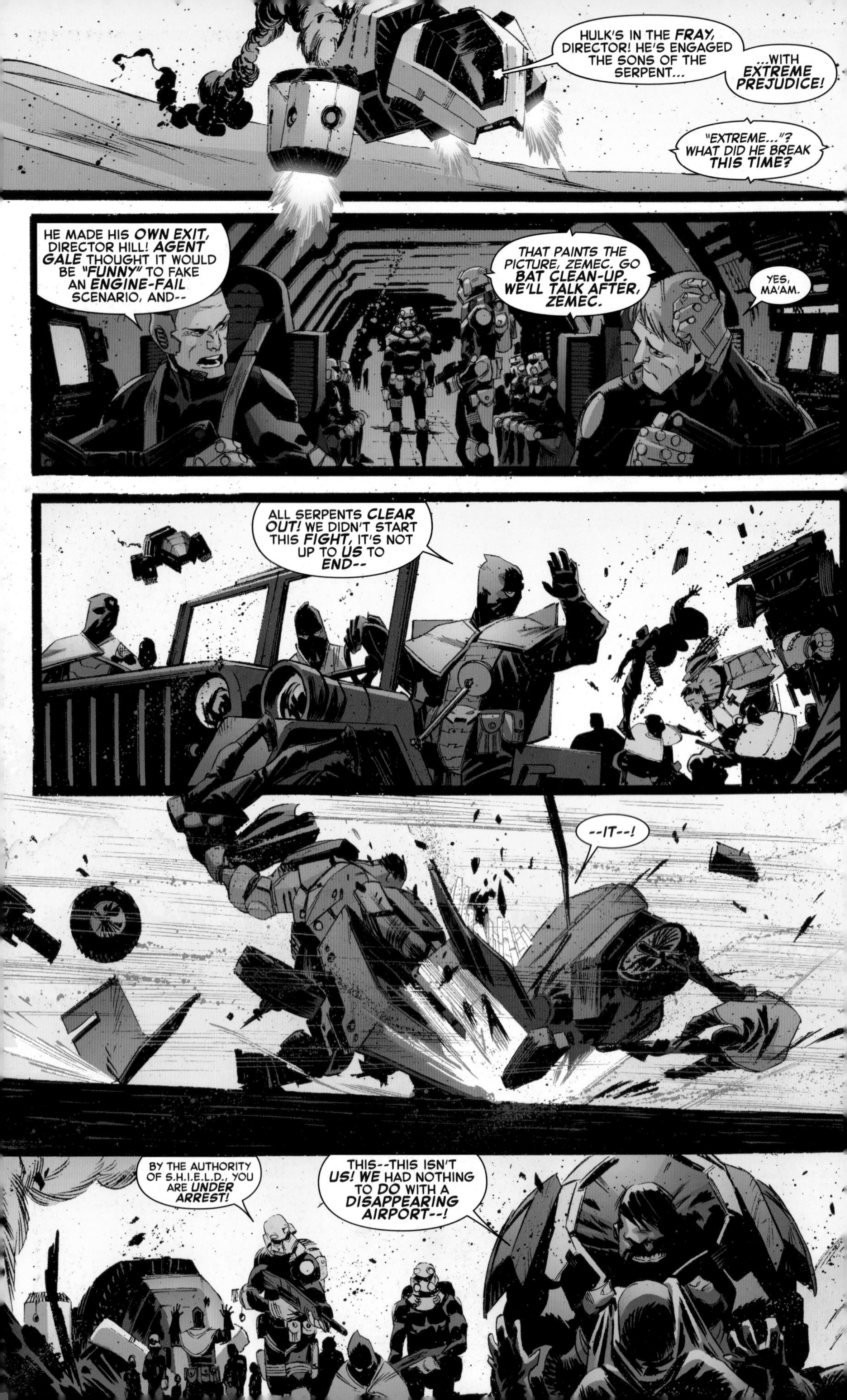

HULK'S IN THE FRAY, DIRECTOR! HE'S ENGAGED THE SONS OF THE SERPENT...
...WITH EXTREME PREJUDICE!
"EXTREME..."? WHAT DID HE BREAK THIS TIME?
HE MADE HIS OWN EXIT, DIRECTOR HILL! AGENT GALE THOUGHT IT WOULD BE "FUNNY" TO FAKE AN ENGINE-FAIL SCENARIO, AND--
THAT PAINTS THE PICTURE, ZEMEC. GO BAT CLEAN-UP. WE'LL TALK AFTER, ZEMEC.
YES, MA'AM.
ALL SERPENTS CLEAR OUT! WE DIDN'T START THIS FIGHT, IT'S NOT UP TO US TO END--
--IT--!
BY THE AUTHORITY OF S.H.I.E.L.D., YOU ARE UNDER ARREST!
THIS--THIS ISN'T US! WE HAD NOTHING TO DO WITH A DISAPPEARING AIRPORT--!

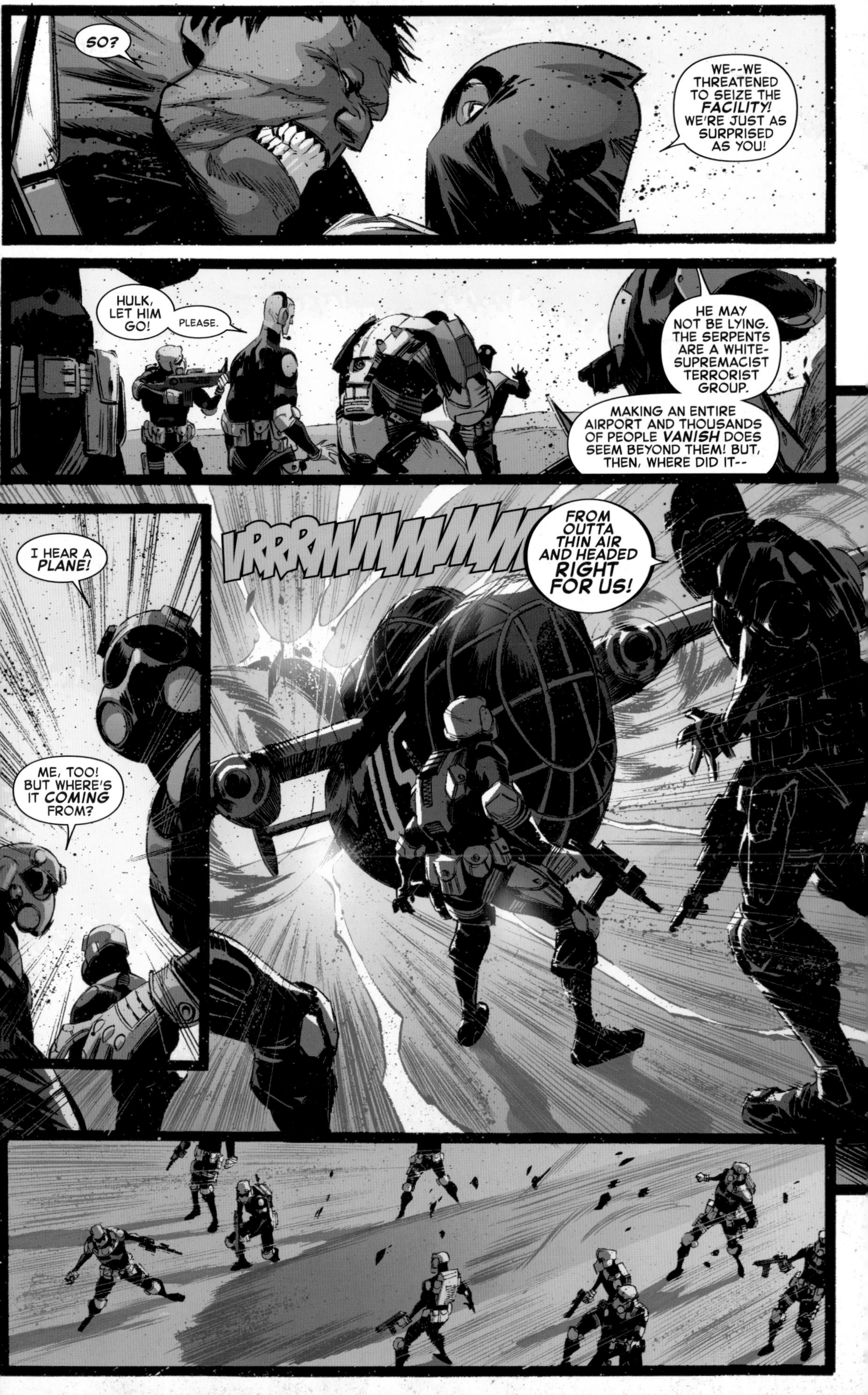
SO?
WE--WE THREATENED TO SEIZE THE FACILITY! WE'RE JUST AS SURPRISED AS YOU!
HULK, LET HIM GO!
PLEASE.
HE MAY NOT BE LYING. THE SERPENTS ARE A WHITE-SUPREMACIST TERRORIST GROUP.
MAKING AN ENTIRE AIRPORT AND THOUSANDS OF PEOPLE VANISH DOES SEEM BEYOND THEM! BUT, THEN, WHERE DID IT--
I HEAR A PLANE!
ME, TOO! BUT WHERE'S IT COMING FROM?
VRRRMMMMMMM
FROM OUTTA THIN AIR AND HEADED RIGHT FOR US!

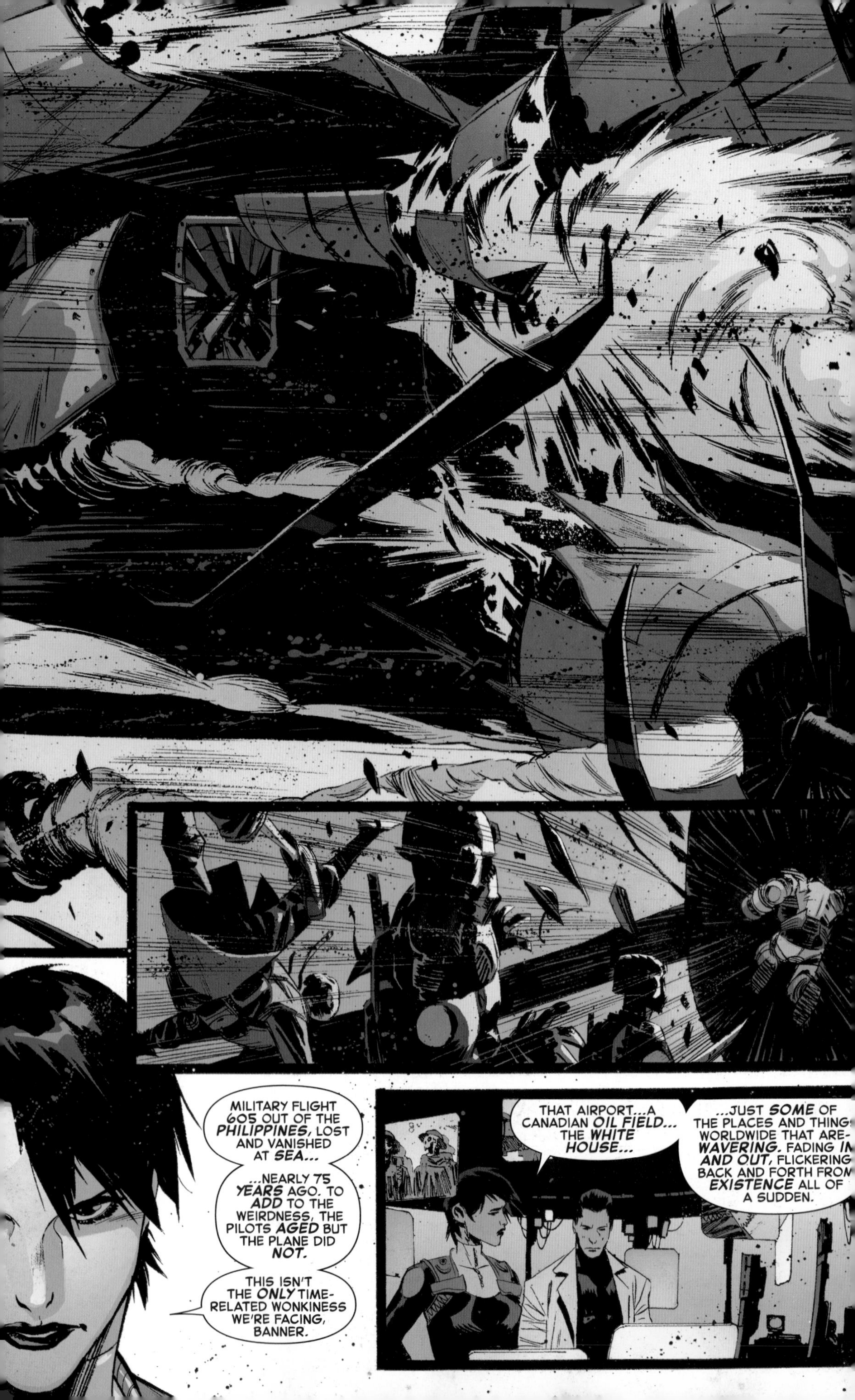
MILITARY FLIGHT 605 OUT OF THE PHILIPPINES, LOST AND VANISHED AT SEA...
...NEARLY 75 YEARS AGO. TO ADD TO THE WEIRDNESS, THE PILOTS AGED BUT THE PLANE DID NOT.
THIS ISN'T THE ONLY TIME-RELATED WONKINESS WE'RE FACING, BANNER.
THAT AIRPORT...A CANADIAN OIL FIELD... THE WHITE HOUSE...
...JUST SOME OF THE PLACES AND THINGS WORLDWIDE THAT ARE WAVERING. FADING IN AND OUT, FLICKERING BACK AND FORTH FROM EXISTENCE ALL OF A SUDDEN.

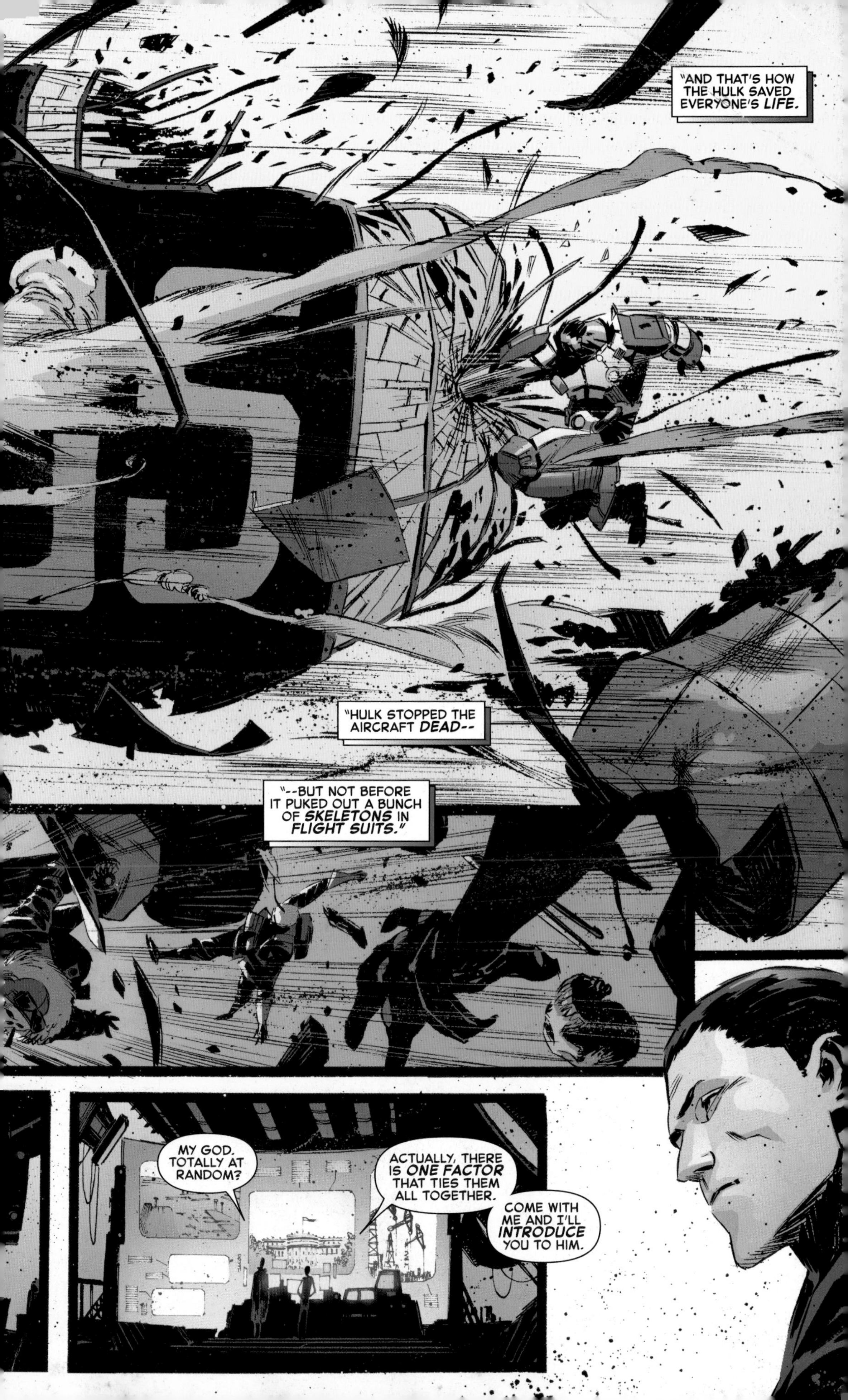
"AND THAT'S HOW THE HULK SAVED EVERYONE'S LIFE.
"HULK STOPPED THE AIRCRAFT DEAD--
"--BUT NOT BEFORE IT PUKED OUT A BUNCH OF SKELETONS IN FLIGHT SUITS."
MY GOD. TOTALLY AT RANDOM?
ACTUALLY, THERE IS ONE FACTOR THAT TIES THEM ALL TOGETHER.
COME WITH ME AND I'LL INTRODUCE YOU TO HIM.

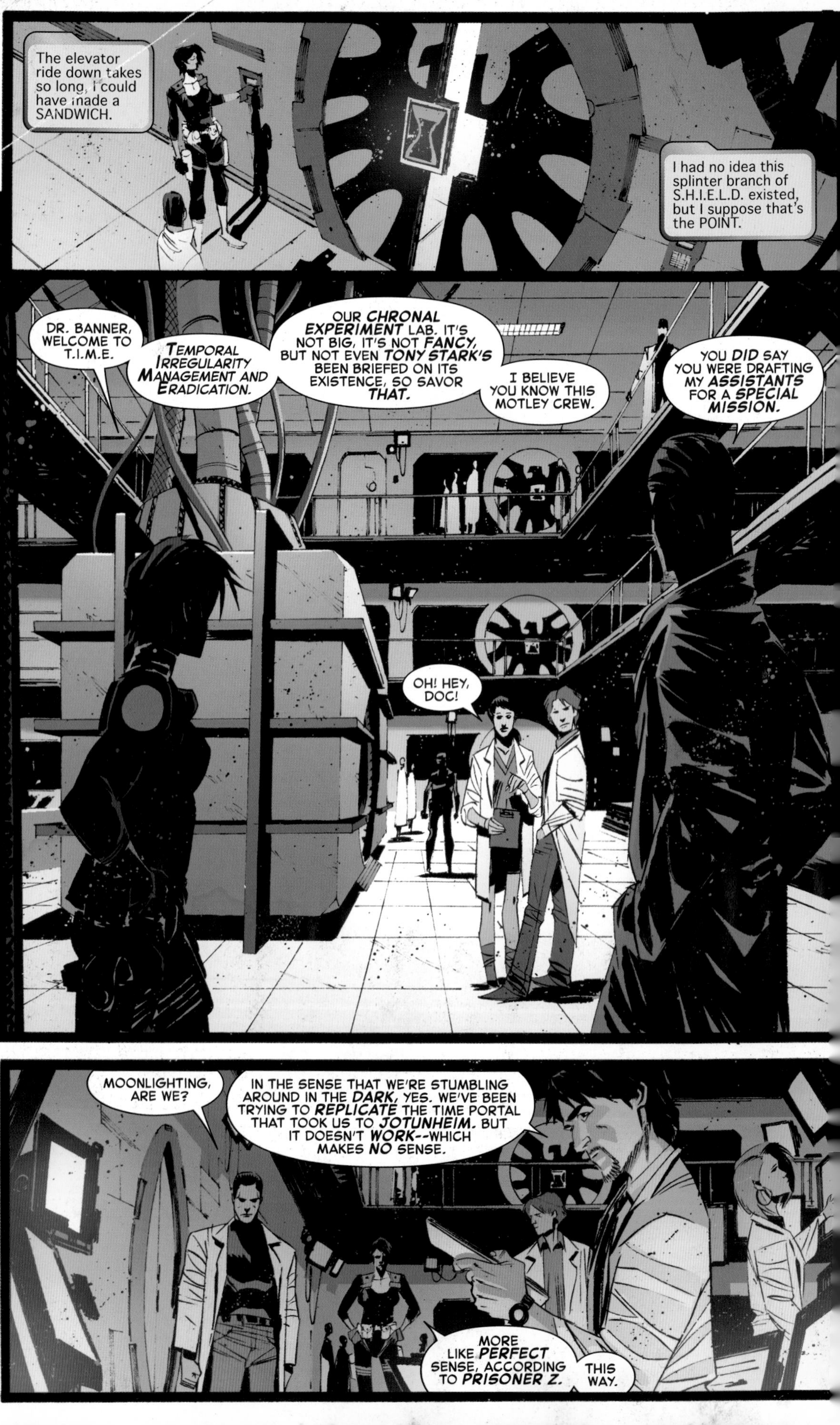

The elevator ride down takes so long, I could have made a SANDWICH.
I had no idea this splinter branch of S.H.I.E.L.D. existed, but I suppose that's the POINT.
DR. BANNER, WELCOME TO T.I.M.E.
TEMPORAL IRREGULARITY MANAGEMENT AND ERADICATION.
OUR CHRONAL EXPERIMENT LAB. IT'S NOT BIG, IT'S NOT FANCY, BUT NOT EVEN TONY STARK'S BEEN BRIEFED ON ITS EXISTENCE, SO SAVOR THAT.
I BELIEVE YOU KNOW THIS MOTLEY CREW.
YOU DID SAY YOU WERE DRAFTING MY ASSISTANTS FOR A SPECIAL MISSION.
OH! HEY, DOC!
MOONLIGHTING, ARE WE?
IN THE SENSE THAT WE'RE STUMBLING AROUND IN THE DARK, YES. WE'VE BEEN TRYING TO REPLICATE THE TIME PORTAL THAT TOOK US TO JOTUNHEIM. BUT IT DOESN'T WORK--WHICH MAKES NO SENSE.
MORE LIKE PERFECT SENSE, ACCORDING TO PRISONER Z.
THIS WAY.

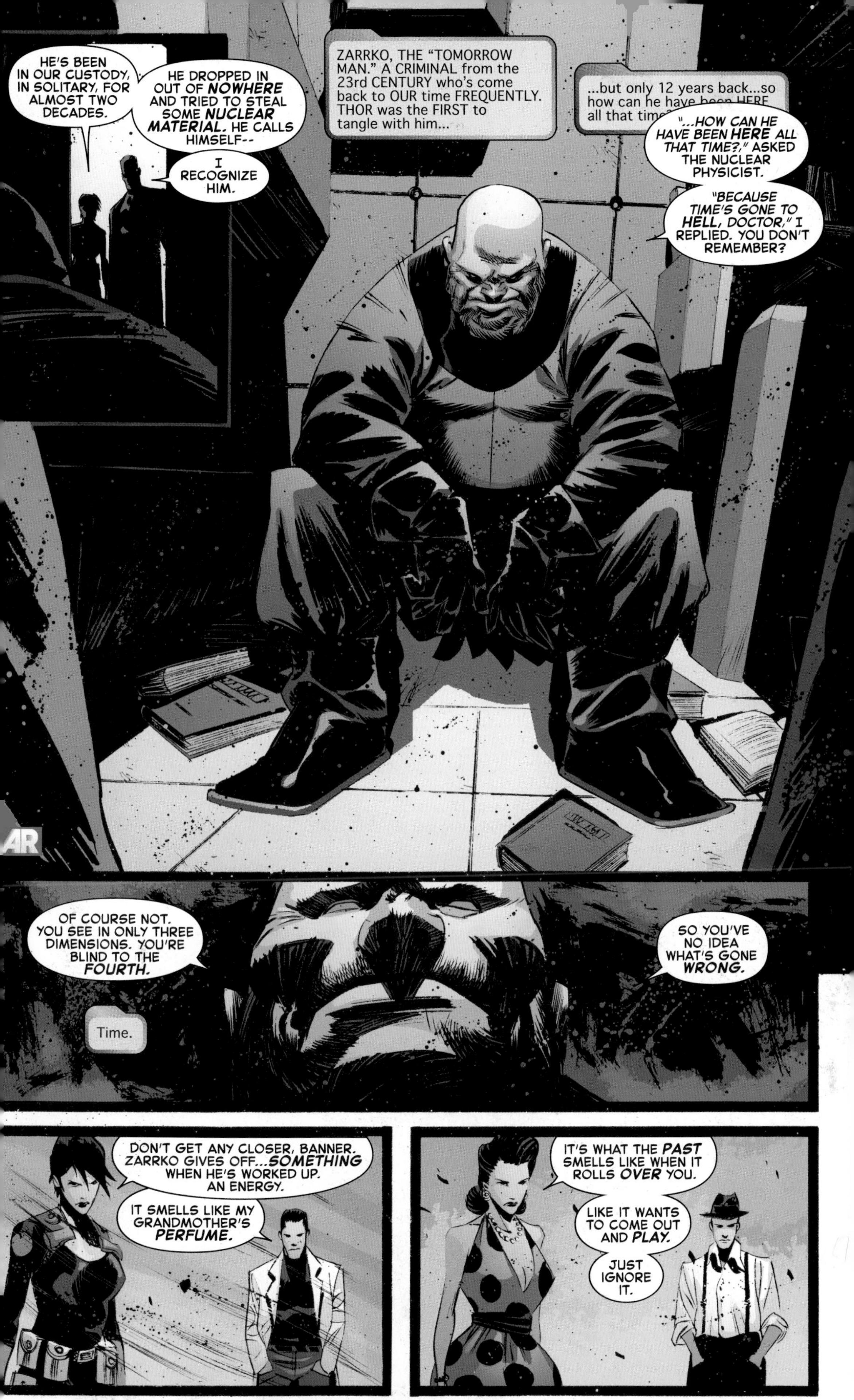
HE'S BEEN IN OUR CUSTODY, IN SOLITARY, FOR ALMOST TWO DECADES.
HE DROPPED IN OUT OF NOWHERE AND TRIED TO STEAL SOME NUCLEAR MATERIAL. HE CALLS HIMSELF--
I RECOGNIZE HIM.
ZARRKO, THE "TOMORROW MAN." A CRIMINAL from the 23rd CENTURY who's come back to OUR time FREQUENTLY. THOR was the FIRST to tangle with him...
...but only 12 years back...so how can he have been HERE all that tim
"...HOW CAN HE HAVE BEEN HERE ALL THAT TIME?," ASKED THE NUCLEAR PHYSICIST.
"BECAUSE TIME'S GONE TO HELL, DOCTOR," I REPLIED. YOU DON'T REMEMBER?
OF COURSE NOT. YOU SEE IN ONLY THREE DIMENSIONS. YOU'RE BLIND TO THE FOURTH.
Time.
SO YOU'VE NO IDEA WHAT'S GONE WRONG.
DON'T GET ANY CLOSER, BANNER. ZARRKO GIVES OFF...SOMETHING WHEN HE'S WORKED UP. AN ENERGY.
IT SMELLS LIKE MY GRANDMOTHER'S PERFUME.
IT'S WHAT THE PAST SMELLS LIKE WHEN IT ROLLS OVER YOU.
LIKE IT WANTS TO COME OUT AND PLAY.
JUST IGNORE IT.

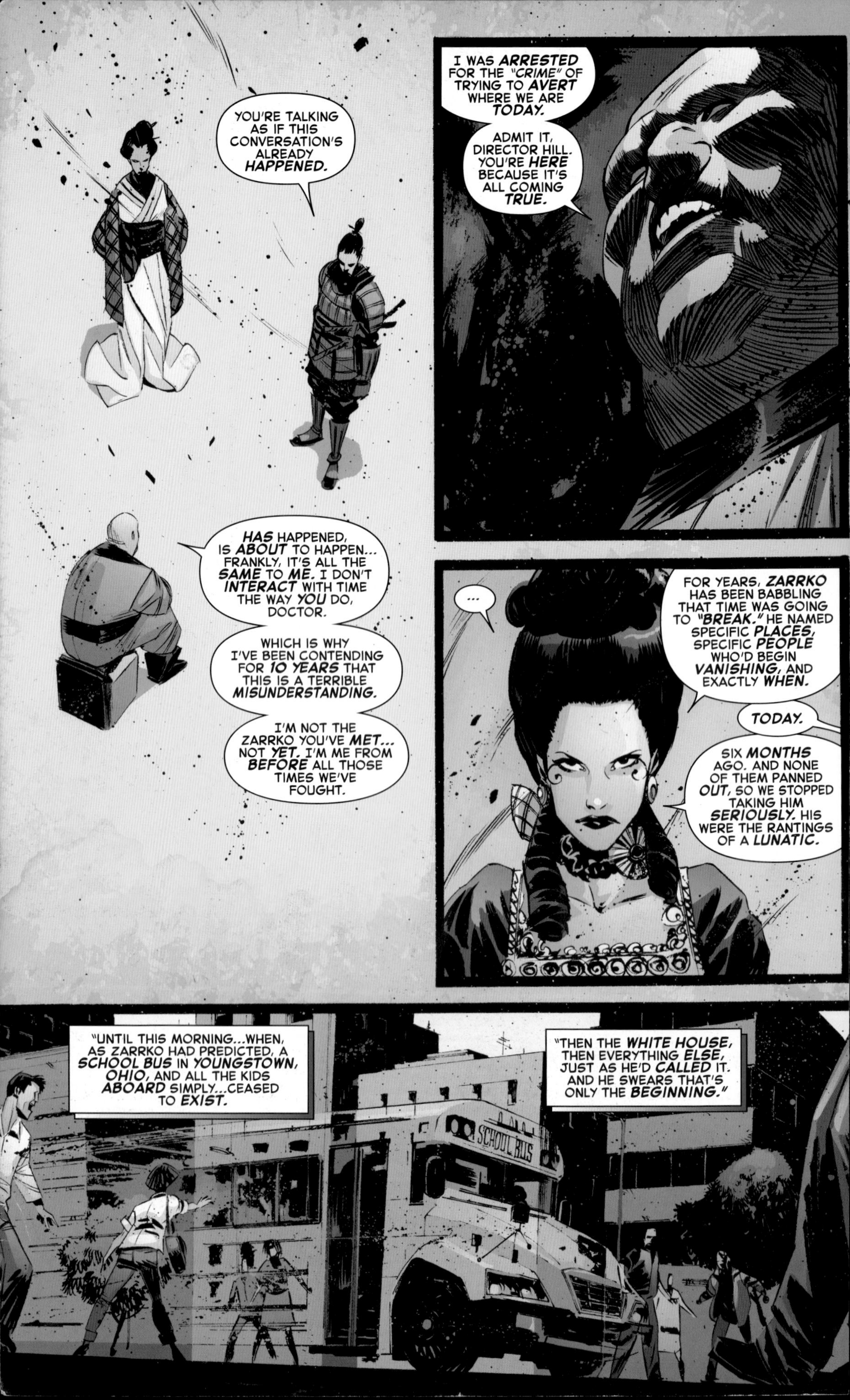
YOU'RE TALKING AS IF THIS CONVERSATION'S ALREADY HAPPENED.
I WAS ARRESTED FOR THE "CRIME" OF TRYING TO AVERT WHERE WE ARE TODAY.
ADMIT IT, DIRECTOR HILL. YOU'RE HERE BECAUSE IT'S ALL COMING TRUE.
HAS HAPPENED, IS ABOUT TO HAPPEN... FRANKLY, IT'S ALL THE SAME TO ME. I DON'T INTERACT WITH TIME THE WAY YOU DO, DOCTOR.
WHICH IS WHY I'VE BEEN CONTENDING FOR 10 YEARS THAT THIS IS A TERRIBLE MISUNDERSTANDING.
I'M NOT THE ZARRKO YOU'VE MET... NOT YET. I'M ME FROM BEFORE ALL THOSE TIMES WE'VE FOUGHT.
...
FOR YEARS, ZARRKO HAS BEEN BABBLING THAT TIME WAS GOING TO "BREAK." HE NAMED SPECIFIC PLACES, SPECIFIC PEOPLE WHO'D BEGIN VANISHING, AND EXACTLY WHEN.
TODAY.
SIX MONTHS AGO. AND NONE OF THEM PANNED OUT, SO WE STOPPED TAKING HIM SERIOUSLY. HIS WERE THE RANTINGS OF A LUNATIC.
"UNTIL THIS MORNING...WHEN, AS ZARRKO HAD PREDICTED, A SCHOOL BUS IN YOUNGSTOWN, OHIO, AND ALL THE KIDS ABOARD SIMPLY...CEASED TO EXIST.
"THEN THE WHITE HOUSE, THEN EVERYTHING ELSE, JUST AS HE'D CALLED IT. AND HE SWEARS THAT'S ONLY THE BEGINNING."
SCHOOL BUS

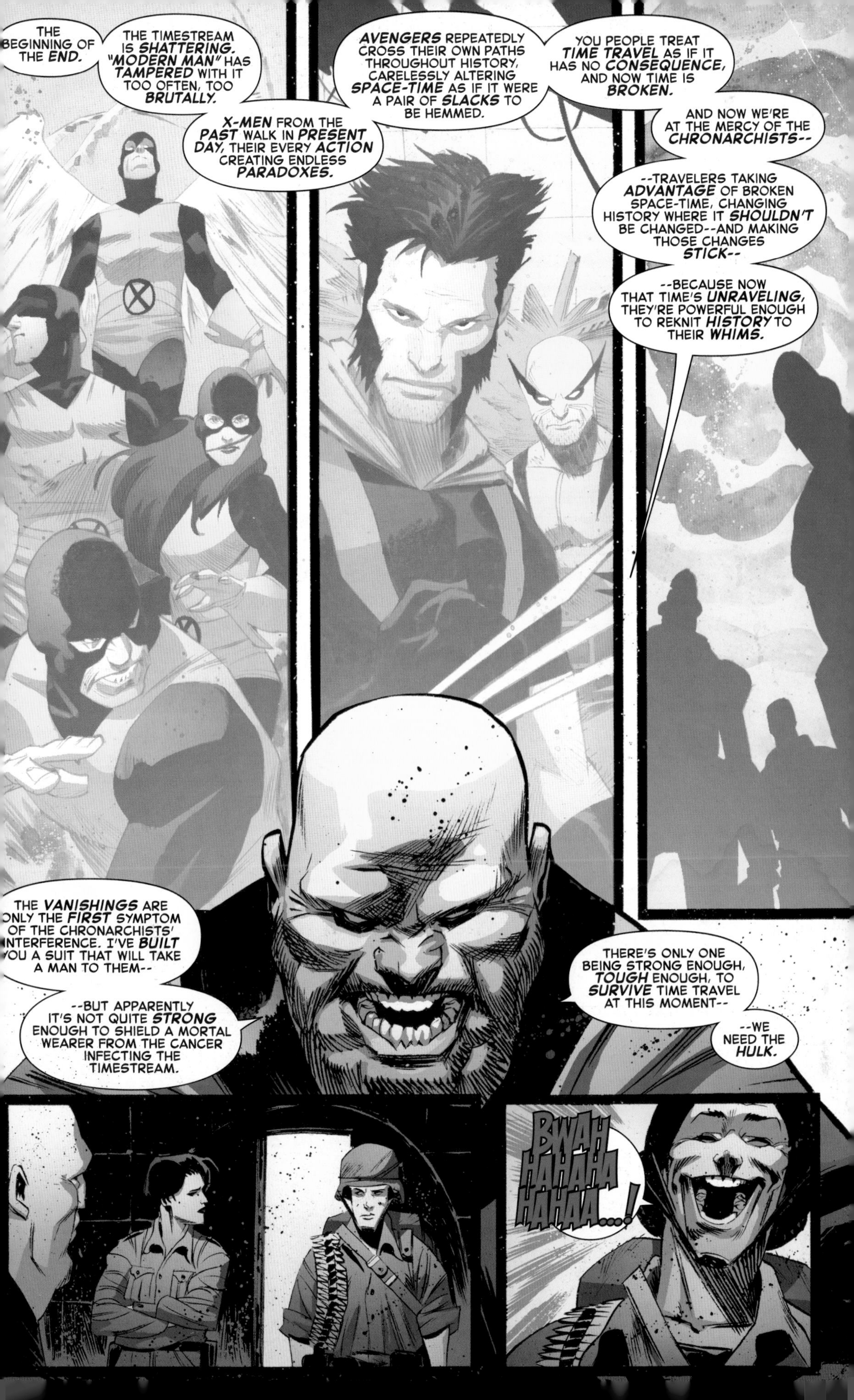
THE BEGINNING OF THE END.
THE TIMESTREAM IS SHATTERING. "MODERN MAN" HAS TAMPERED WITH IT TOO OFTEN, TOO BRUTALLY.
X-MEN FROM THE PAST WALK IN PRESENT DAY, THEIR EVERY ACTION CREATING ENDLESS PARADOXES.
AVENGERS REPEATEDLY CROSS THEIR OWN PATHS THROUGHOUT HISTORY, CARELESSLY ALTERING SPACE-TIME AS IF IT WERE A PAIR OF SLACKS TO BE HEMMED.
YOU PEOPLE TREAT TIME TRAVEL AS IF IT HAS NO CONSEQUENCE, AND NOW TIME IS BROKEN.
AND NOW WE'RE AT THE MERCY OF THE CHRONARCHISTS--
--TRAVELERS TAKING ADVANTAGE OF BROKEN SPACE-TIME, CHANGING HISTORY WHERE IT SHOULDN'T BE CHANGED--AND MAKING THOSE CHANGES STICK--
--BECAUSE NOW THAT TIME'S UNRAVELING, THEY'RE POWERFUL ENOUGH TO REKNIT HISTORY TO THEIR WHIMS.
THE VANISHINGS ARE ONLY THE FIRST SYMPTOM OF THE CHRONARCHISTS' INTERFERENCE. I'VE BUILT YOU A SUIT THAT WILL TAKE A MAN TO THEM--
--BUT APPARENTLY IT'S NOT QUITE STRONG ENOUGH TO SHIELD A MORTAL WEARER FROM THE CANCER INFECTING THE TIMESTREAM.
THERE'S ONLY ONE BEING STRONG ENOUGH, TOUGH ENOUGH, TO SURVIVE TIME TRAVEL AT THIS MOMENT--
--WE NEED THE HULK.
BWAH HAHAHA HAHAA...!

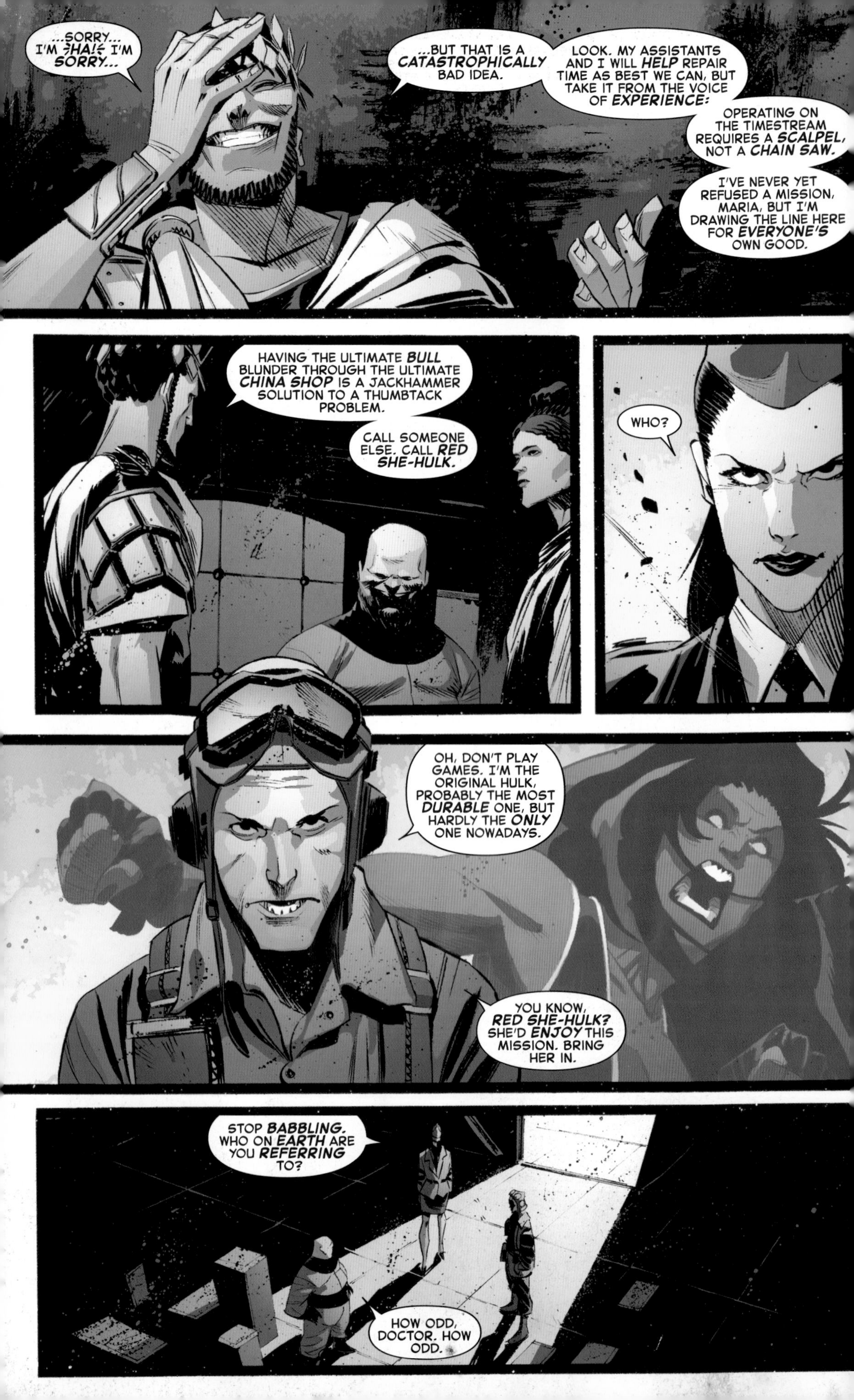
...SORRY... I'M ≷HA!≶ I'M SORRY...
...BUT THAT IS A CATASTROPHICALLY BAD IDEA.
LOOK. MY ASSISTANTS AND I WILL HELP REPAIR TIME AS BEST WE CAN, BUT TAKE IT FROM THE VOICE OF EXPERIENCE:
OPERATING ON THE TIMESTREAM REQUIRES A SCALPEL, NOT A CHAIN SAW.
I'VE NEVER YET REFUSED A MISSION, MARIA, BUT I'M DRAWING THE LINE HERE FOR EVERYONE'S OWN GOOD.
HAVING THE ULTIMATE BULL BLUNDER THROUGH THE ULTIMATE CHINA SHOP IS A JACKHAMMER SOLUTION TO A THUMBTACK PROBLEM.
CALL SOMEONE ELSE. CALL RED SHE-HULK.
WHO?
OH, DON'T PLAY GAMES. I'M THE ORIGINAL HULK, PROBABLY THE MOST DURABLE ONE, BUT HARDLY THE ONLY ONE NOWADAYS.
YOU KNOW, RED SHE-HULK? SHE'D ENJOY THIS MISSION. BRING HER IN.
STOP BABBLING. WHO ON EARTH ARE YOU REFERRING TO?
HOW ODD, DOCTOR. HOW ODD.

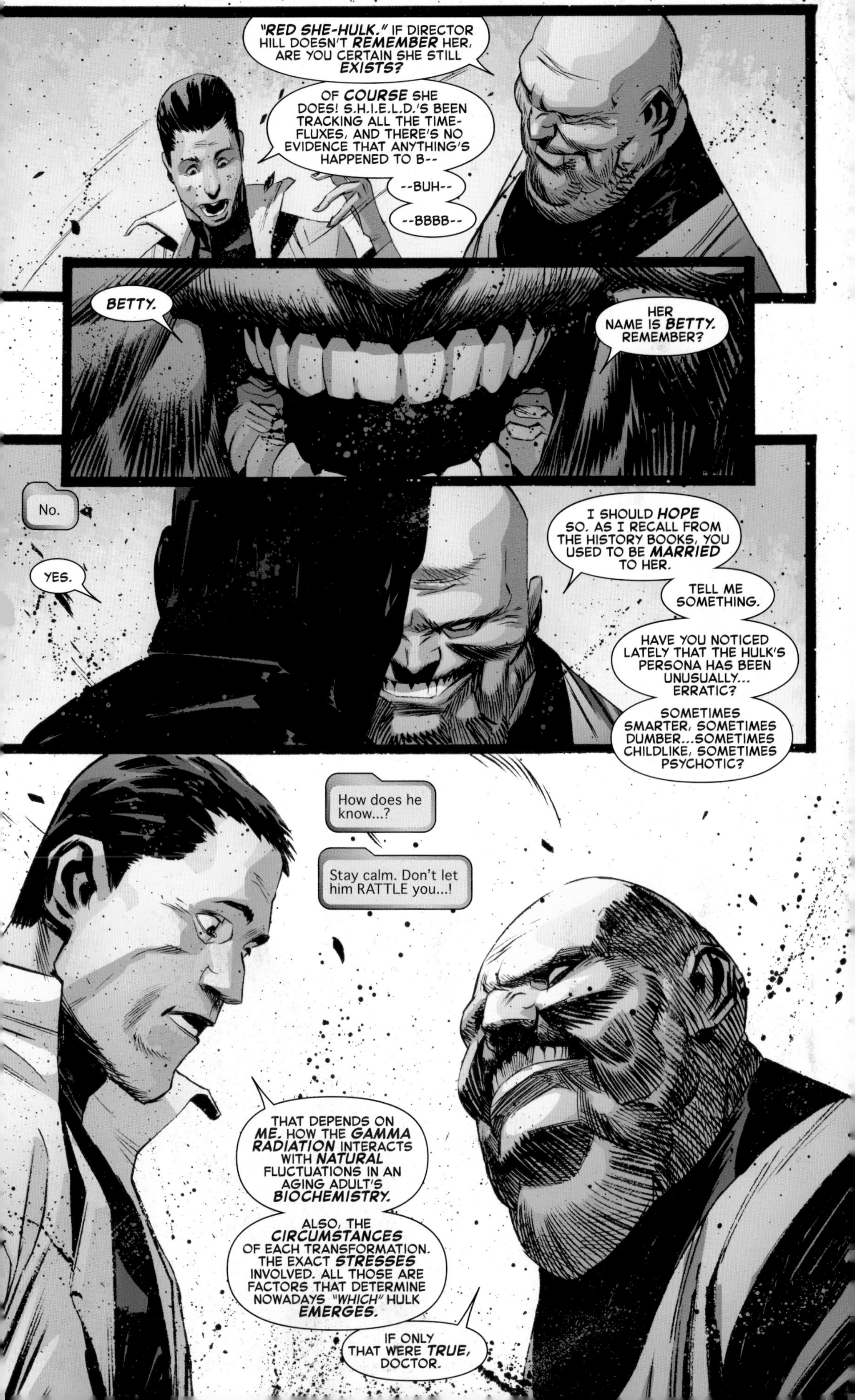
"RED SHE-HULK." IF DIRECTOR HILL DOESN'T REMEMBER HER, ARE YOU CERTAIN SHE STILL EXISTS?
OF COURSE SHE DOES! S.H.I.E.L.D.'S BEEN TRACKING ALL THE TIME-FLUXES, AND THERE'S NO EVIDENCE THAT ANYTHING'S HAPPENED TO B--
--BUH--
--BBBB--
BETTY.
HER NAME IS BETTY. REMEMBER?
No.
YES.
I SHOULD HOPE SO. AS I RECALL FROM THE HISTORY BOOKS, YOU USED TO BE MARRIED TO HER.
TELL ME SOMETHING.
HAVE YOU NOTICED LATELY THAT THE HULK'S PERSONA HAS BEEN UNUSUALLY... ERRATIC?
SOMETIMES SMARTER, SOMETIMES DUMBER...SOMETIMES CHILDLIKE, SOMETIMES PSYCHOTIC?
How does he know...?
Stay calm. Don't let him RATTLE you...!
THAT DEPENDS ON ME. HOW THE GAMMA RADIATION INTERACTS WITH NATURAL FLUCTUATIONS IN AN AGING ADULT'S BIOCHEMISTRY.
ALSO, THE CIRCUMSTANCES OF EACH TRANSFORMATION. THE EXACT STRESSES INVOLVED. ALL THOSE ARE FACTORS THAT DETERMINE NOWADAYS "WHICH" HULK EMERGES.
IF ONLY THAT WERE TRUE, DOCTOR.

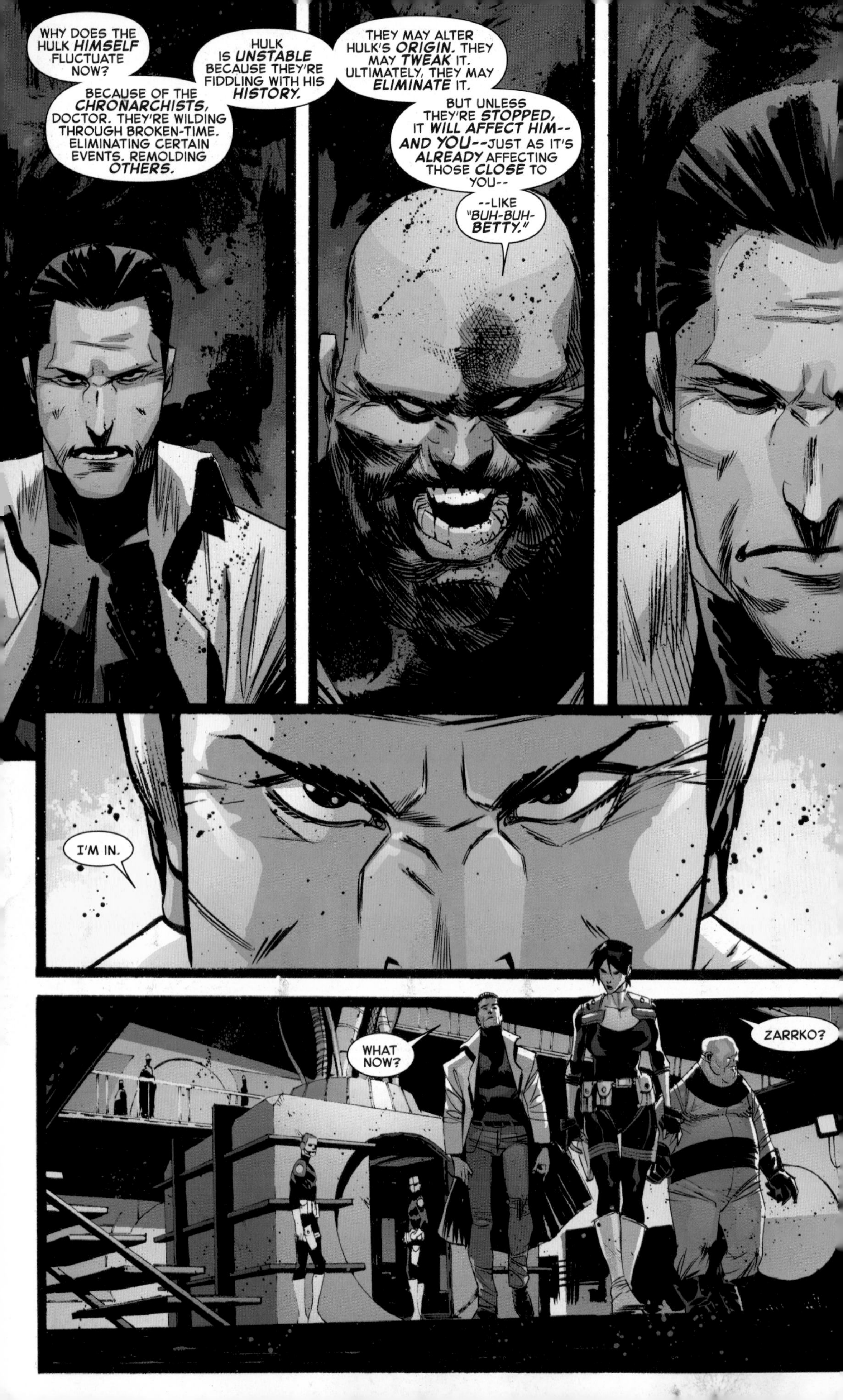
WHY DOES THE HULK HIMSELF FLUCTUATE NOW?
BECAUSE OF THE CHRONARCHISTS, DOCTOR. THEY'RE WILDING THROUGH BROKEN-TIME. ELIMINATING CERTAIN EVENTS. REMOLDING OTHERS.
HULK IS UNSTABLE BECAUSE THEY'RE FIDDLING WITH HIS HISTORY.
THEY MAY ALTER HULK'S ORIGIN. THEY MAY TWEAK IT. ULTIMATELY, THEY MAY ELIMINATE IT.
BUT UNLESS THEY'RE STOPPED, IT WILL AFFECT HIM-- AND YOU--JUST AS IT'S ALREADY AFFECTING THOSE CLOSE TO YOU--
--LIKE "BUH-BUH-BETTY."
I'M IN.
WHAT NOW?
ZARRKO?

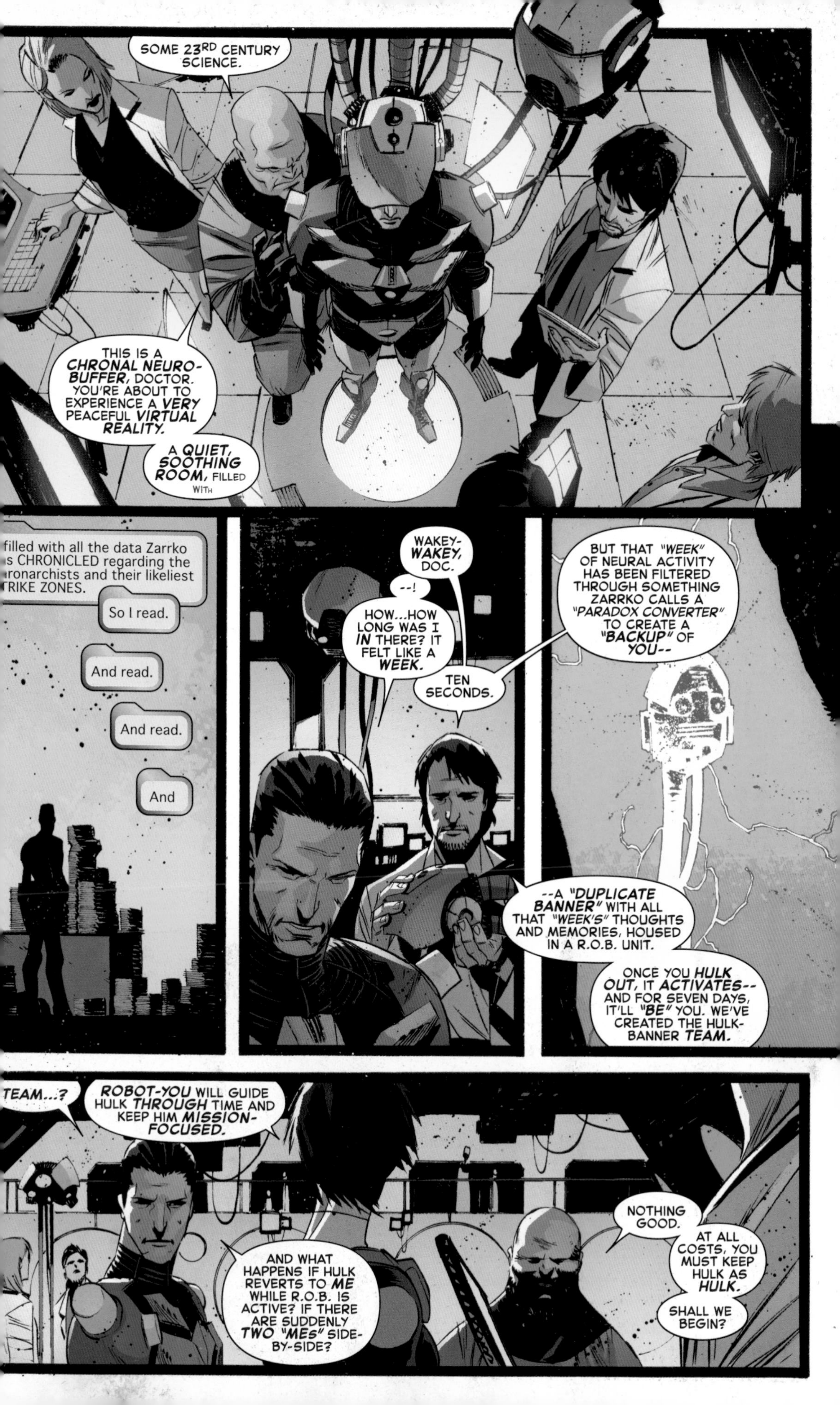

SOME 23RD CENTURY SCIENCE.
THIS IS A CHRONAL NEURO-BUFFER, DOCTOR. YOU'RE ABOUT TO EXPERIENCE A VERY PEACEFUL VIRTUAL REALITY.
A QUIET, SOOTHING ROOM, FILLED WITH
filled with all the data Zarrko
s CHRONICLED regarding the
ironarchists and their likeliest
TRIKE ZONES.
So I read.
And read.
And read.
And
WAKEY-WAKEY, DOC.
--!
HOW...HOW LONG WAS I IN THERE? IT FELT LIKE A WEEK.
TEN SECONDS.
BUT THAT "WEEK" OF NEURAL ACTIVITY HAS BEEN FILTERED THROUGH SOMETHING ZARRKO CALLS A "PARADOX CONVERTER" TO CREATE A "BACKUP" OF YOU--
--A "DUPLICATE BANNER" WITH ALL THAT "WEEK'S" THOUGHTS AND MEMORIES, HOUSED IN A R.O.B. UNIT.
ONCE YOU HULK OUT, IT ACTIVATES--AND FOR SEVEN DAYS, IT'LL "BE" YOU. WE'VE CREATED THE HULK-BANNER TEAM.
TEAM...?
ROBOT-YOU WILL GUIDE HULK THROUGH TIME AND KEEP HIM MISSION-FOCUSED.
AND WHAT HAPPENS IF HULK REVERTS TO ME WHILE R.O.B. IS ACTIVE? IF THERE ARE SUDDENLY TWO "MEs" SIDE-BY-SIDE?
NOTHING GOOD.
AT ALL COSTS, YOU MUST KEEP HULK AS HULK.
SHALL WE BEGIN?

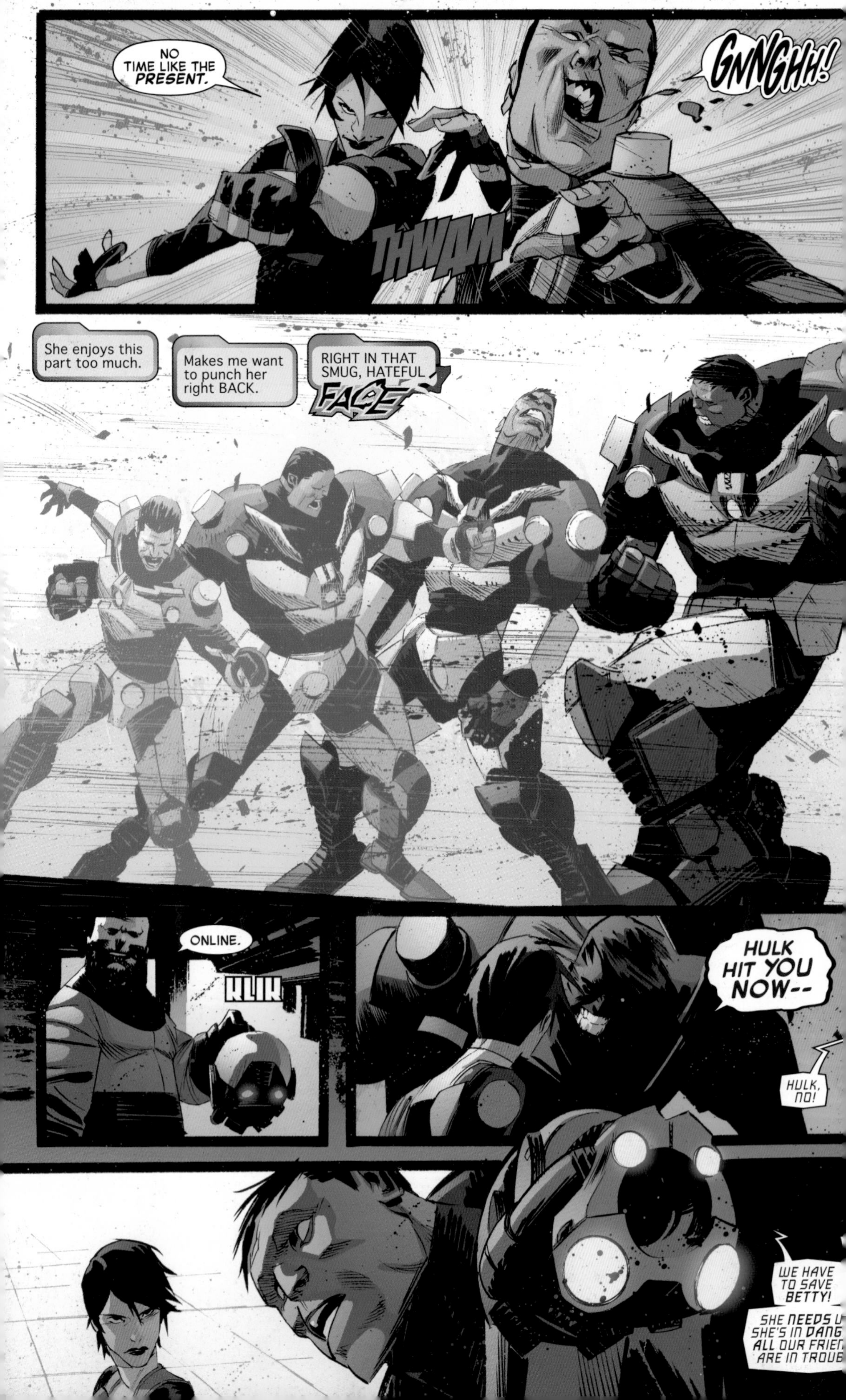

NO TIME LIKE THE PRESENT.
GNNGHH!
THWAM
She enjoys this part too much.
Makes me want to punch her right BACK.
RIGHT IN THAT SMUG, HATEFUL FACE
ONLINE.
KLIK
HULK HIT YOU NOW--
HULK, NO!
WE HAVE TO SAVE BETTY!

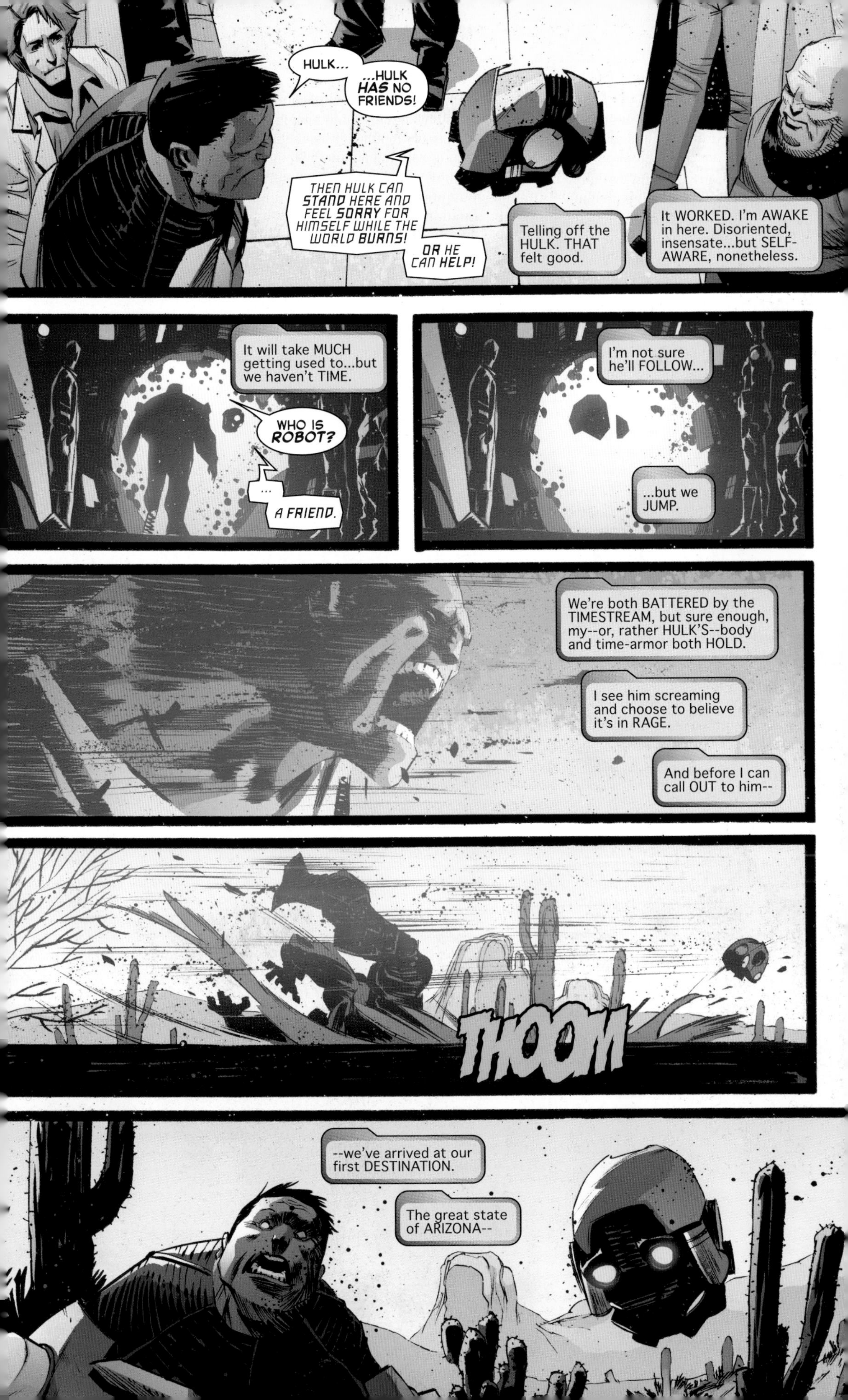
HULK...
...HULK HAS NO FRIENDS!
THEN HULK CAN STAND HERE AND FEEL SORRY FOR HIMSELF WHILE THE WORLD BURNS!
OR HE CAN HELP!
It WORKED. I'm AWAKE in here. Disoriented, insensate...but SELF-AWARE, nonetheless.
Telling off the HULK. THAT felt good.
It will take MUCH getting used to...but we haven't TIME.
WHO IS ROBOT?
...
A FRIEND.
I'm not sure he'll FOLLOW...
...but we JUMP.
We're both BATTERED by the TIMESTREAM, but sure enough, my--or, rather HULK'S--body and time-armor both HOLD.
I see him screaming and choose to believe it's in RAGE.
And before I can call OUT to him--
THOOM
--we've arrived at our first DESTINATION.
The great state of ARIZONA--

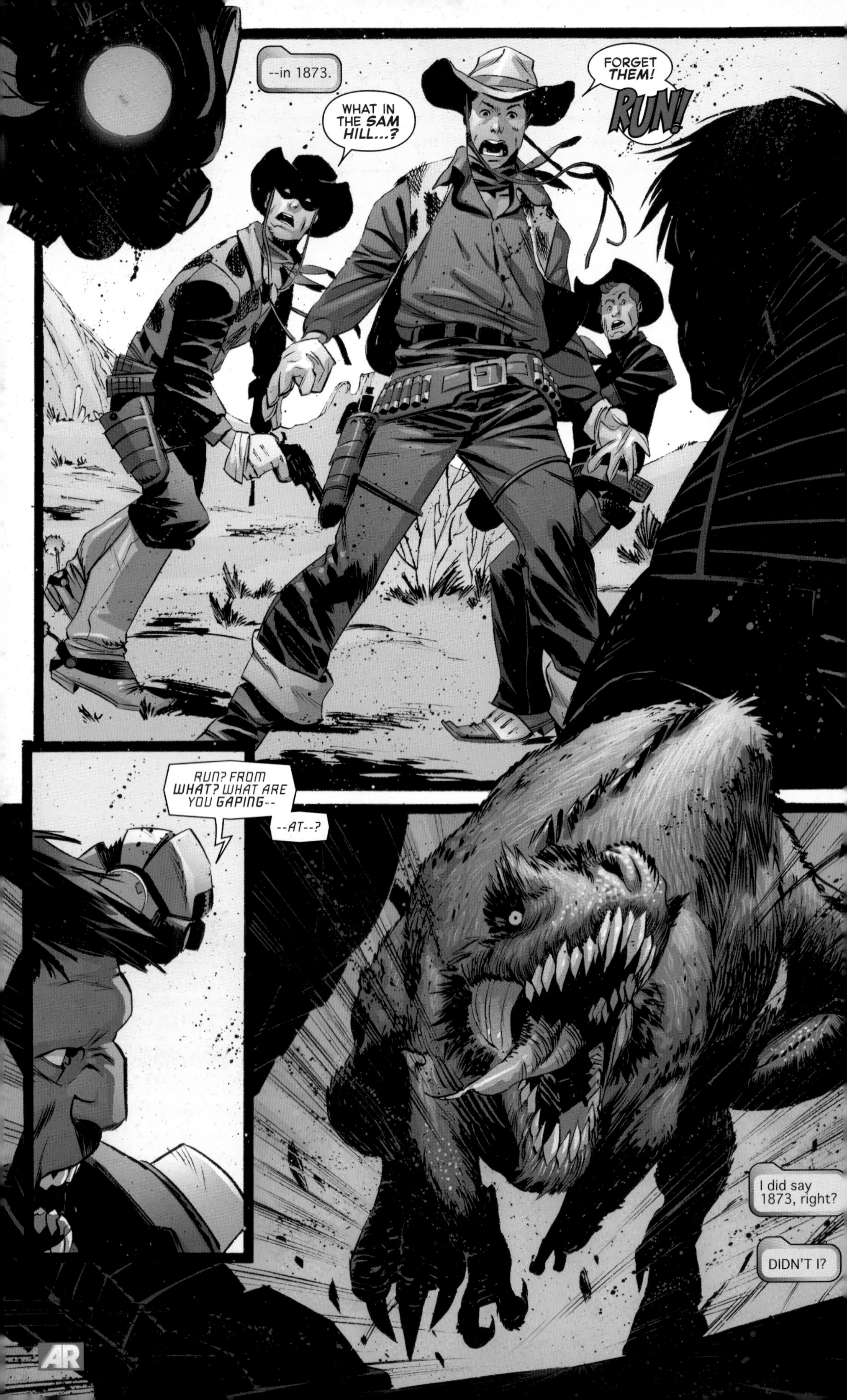
--in 1873.
WHAT IN THE SAM HILL...?
FORGET THEM!
RUN!
RUN? FROM WHAT? WHAT ARE YOU GAPING--
--AT--?
I did say 1873, right?
DIDN'T I?

INDESTRUCTIBLE HULK

Variant Cover Gallery

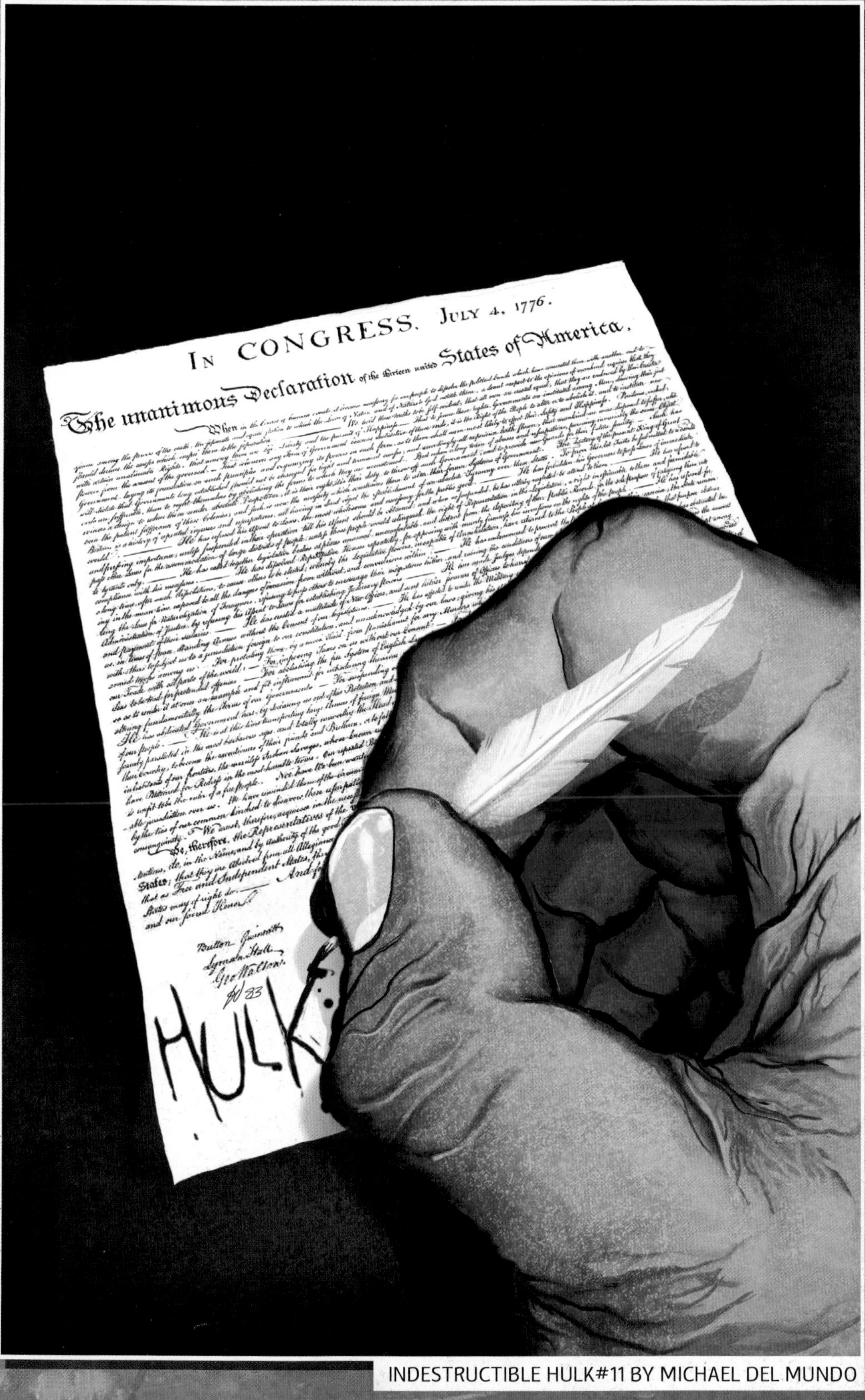

IN CONGRESS, JULY 4, 1776.
The unanimous Declaration of the thirteen united States of America,
HULK

INDESTRUCTIBLE HULK#11 BY MICHAEL DEL MUNDO

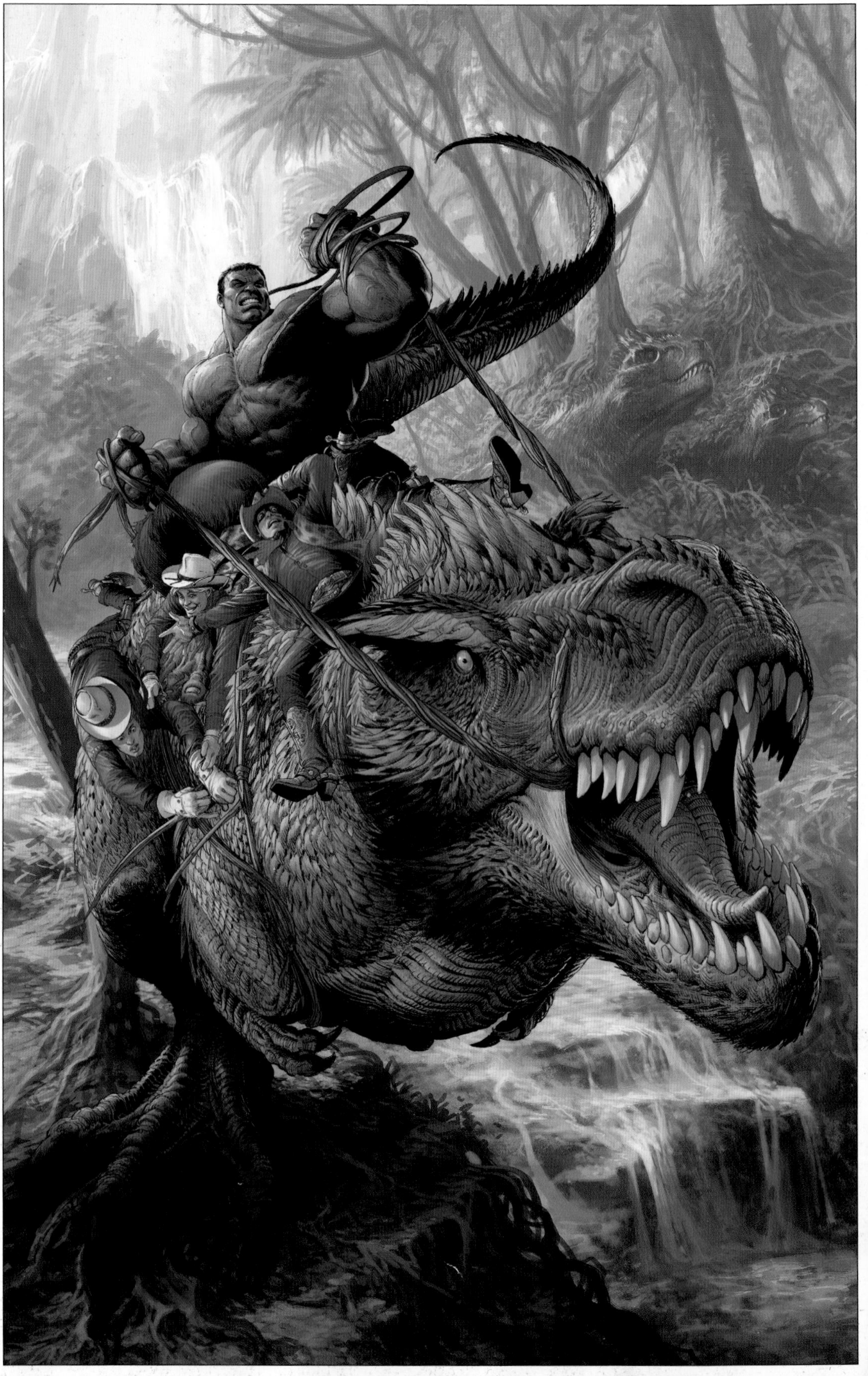

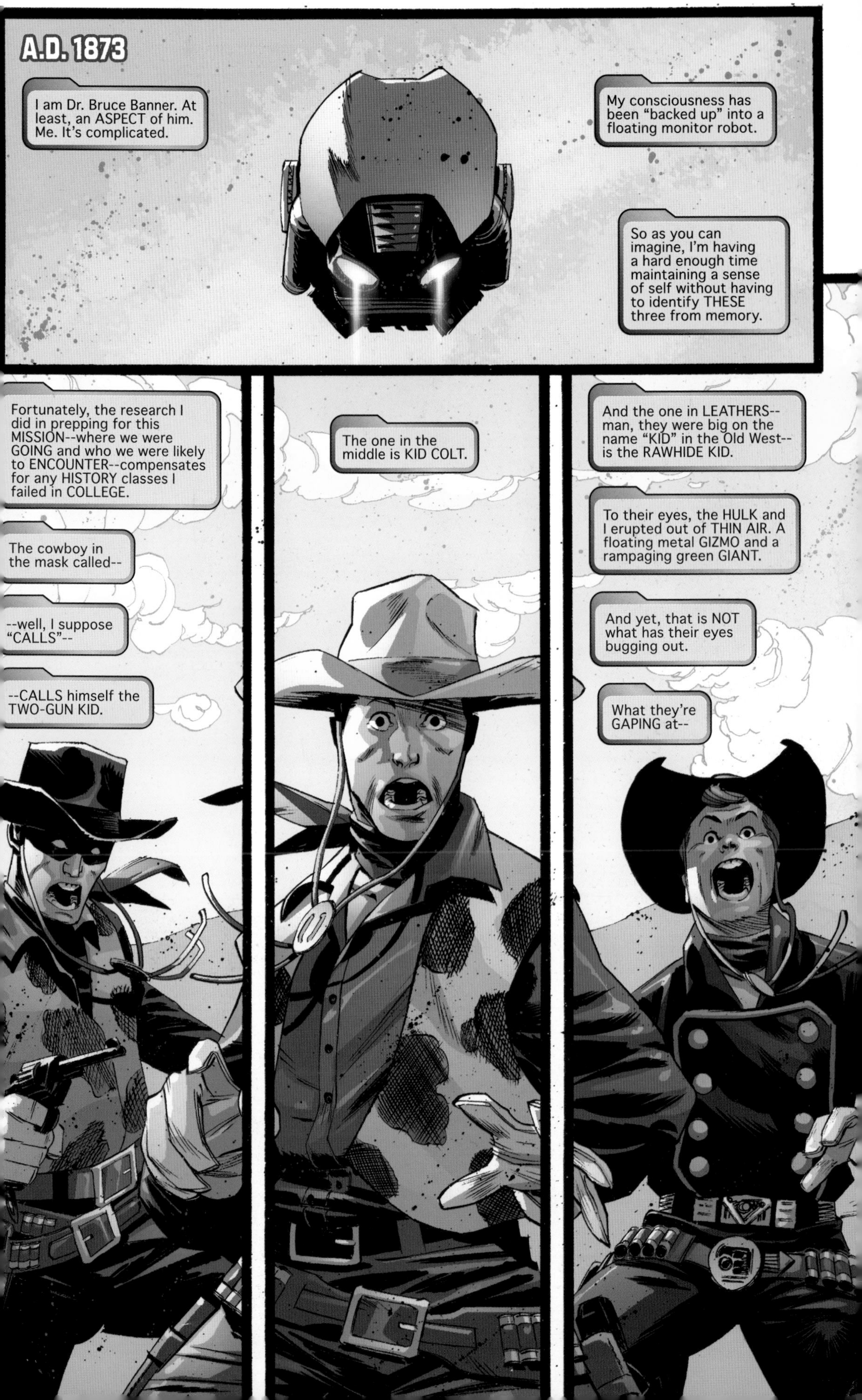
A.D. 1873
I am Dr. Bruce Banner. At least, an ASPECT of him. Me. It's complicated.
My consciousness has been "backed up" into a floating monitor robot.
So as you can imagine, I'm having a hard enough time maintaining a sense of self without having to identify THESE three from memory.
Fortunately, the research I did in prepping for this MISSION--where we were GOING and who we were likely to ENCOUNTER--compensates for any HISTORY classes I failed in COLLEGE.
The cowboy in the mask called--
--well, I suppose "CALLS"--
--CALLS himself the TWO-GUN KID.
The one in the middle is KID COLT.
And the one in LEATHERS--man, they were big on the name "KID" in the Old West--is the RAWHIDE KID.
To their eyes, the HULK and I erupted out of THIN AIR. A floating metal GIZMO and a rampaging green GIANT.
And yet, that is NOT what has their eyes bugging out.
What they're GAPING at--

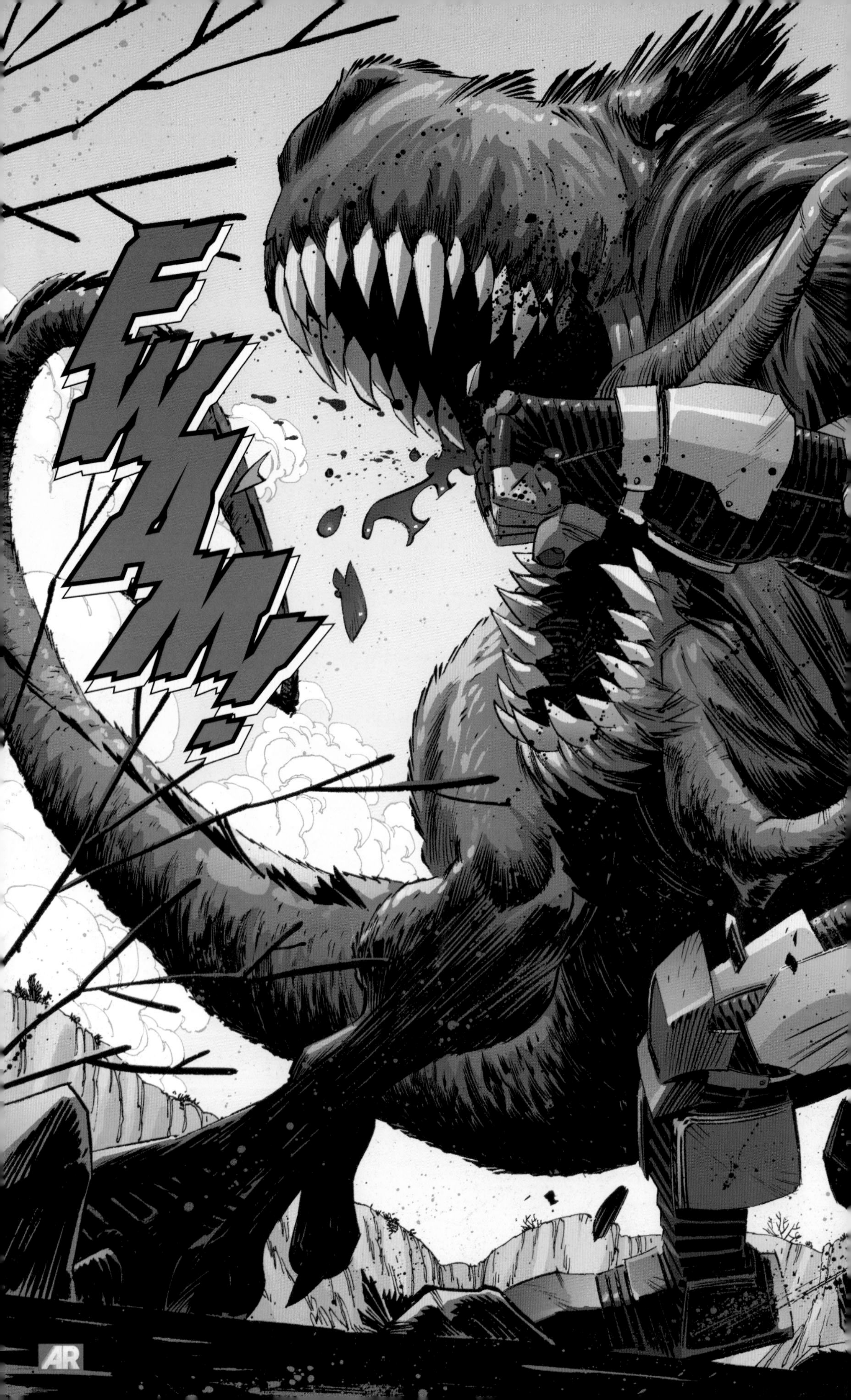
FWAM!

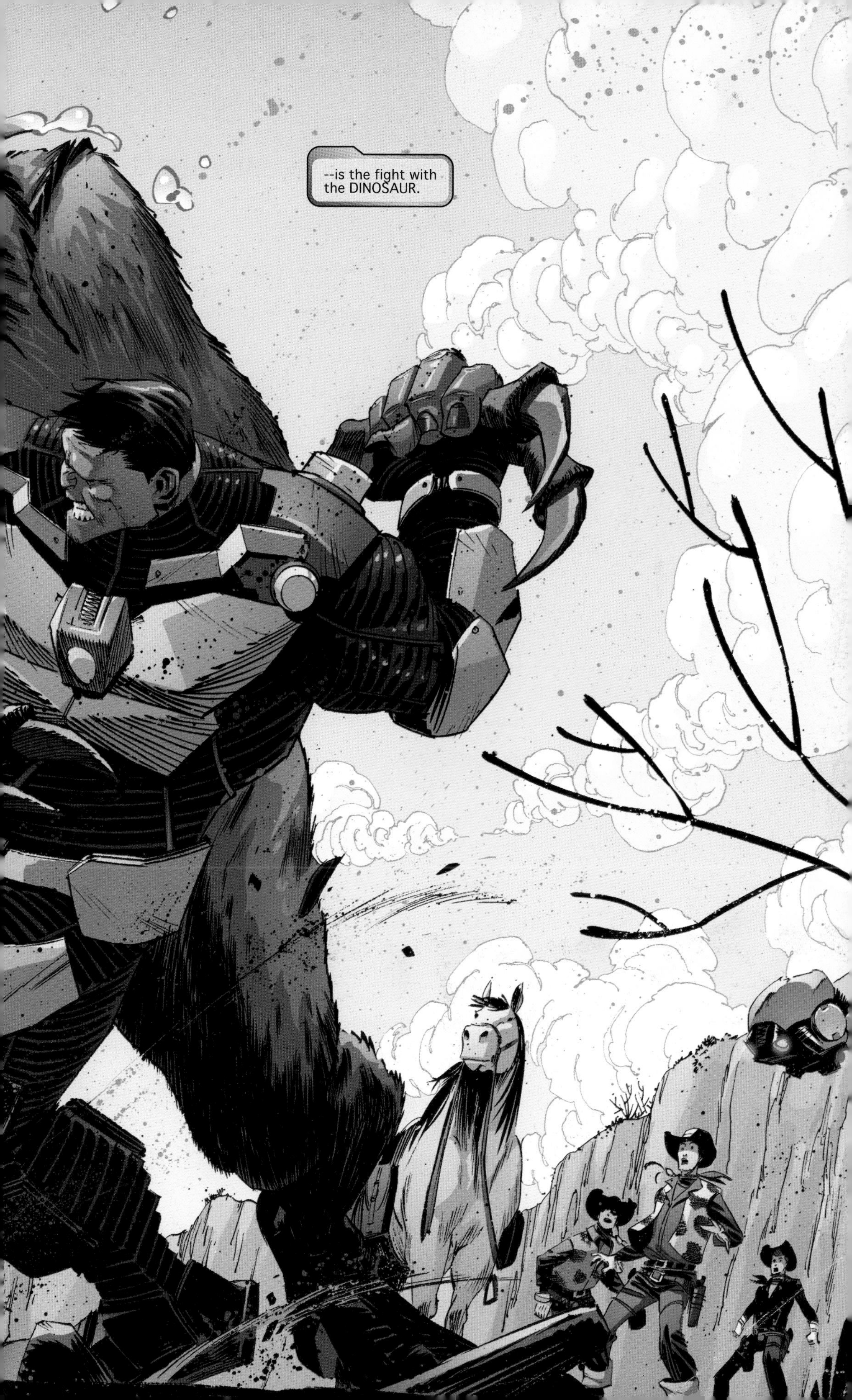
--is the fight with the DINOSAUR.

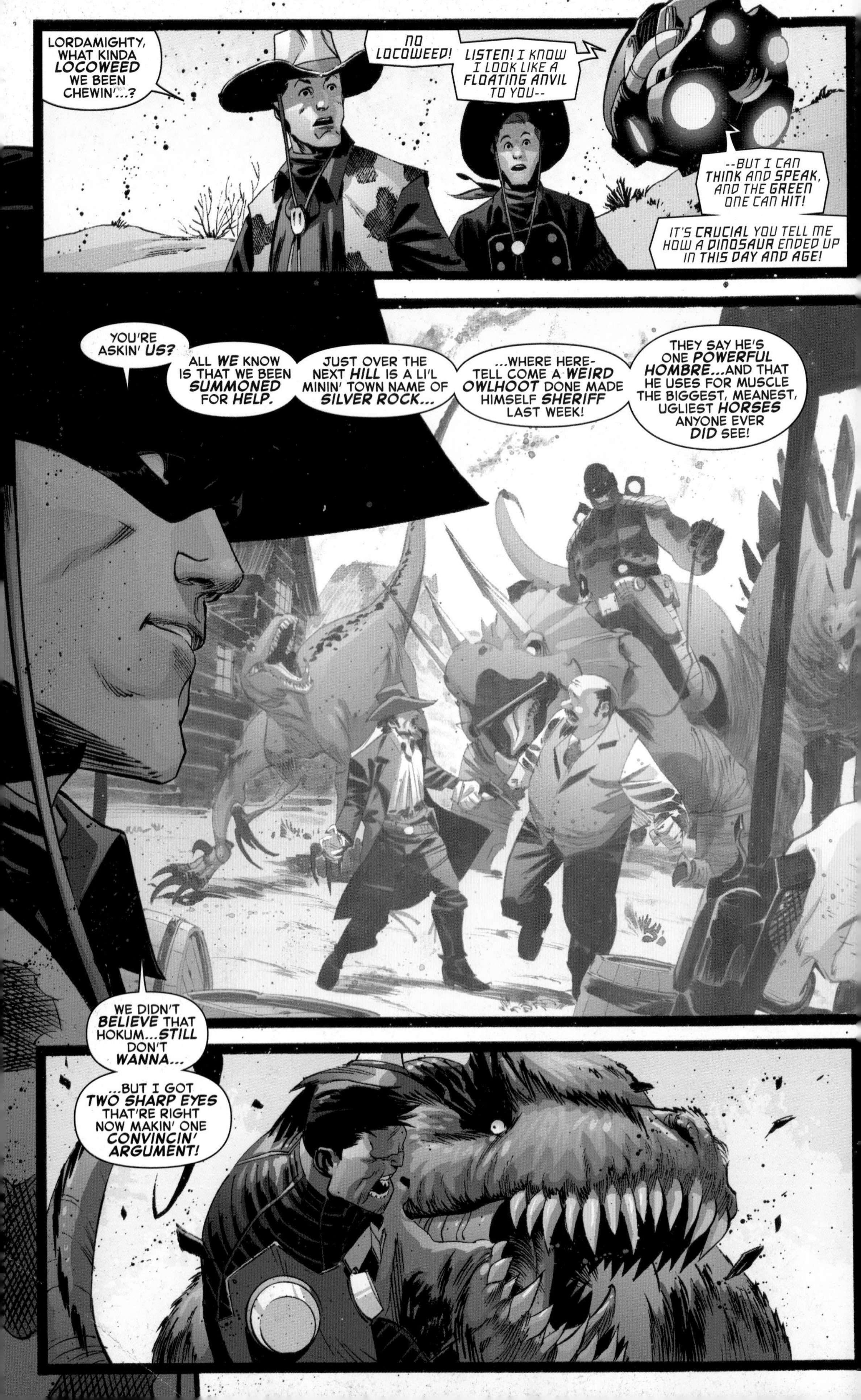
LORDAMIGHTY, WHAT KINDA LOCOWEED WE BEEN CHEWIN'...?
NO LOCOWEED!
LISTEN! I KNOW I LOOK LIKE A FLOATING ANVIL TO YOU--
--BUT I CAN THINK AND SPEAK, AND THE GREEN ONE CAN HIT!
IT'S CRUCIAL YOU TELL ME HOW A DINOSAUR ENDED UP IN THIS DAY AND AGE!
YOU'RE ASKIN' US?
ALL WE KNOW IS THAT WE BEEN SUMMONED FOR HELP.
JUST OVER THE NEXT HILL IS A LI'L MININ' TOWN NAME OF SILVER ROCK...
...WHERE HERE-TELL COME A WEIRD OWLHOOT DONE MADE HIMSELF SHERIFF LAST WEEK!
THEY SAY HE'S ONE POWERFUL HOMBRE...AND THAT HE USES FOR MUSCLE THE BIGGEST, MEANEST, UGLIEST HORSES ANYONE EVER DID SEE!
WE DIDN'T BELIEVE THAT HOKUM...STILL DON'T WANNA...
...BUT I GOT TWO SHARP EYES THAT'RE RIGHT NOW MAKIN' ONE CONVINCIN' ARGUMENT!

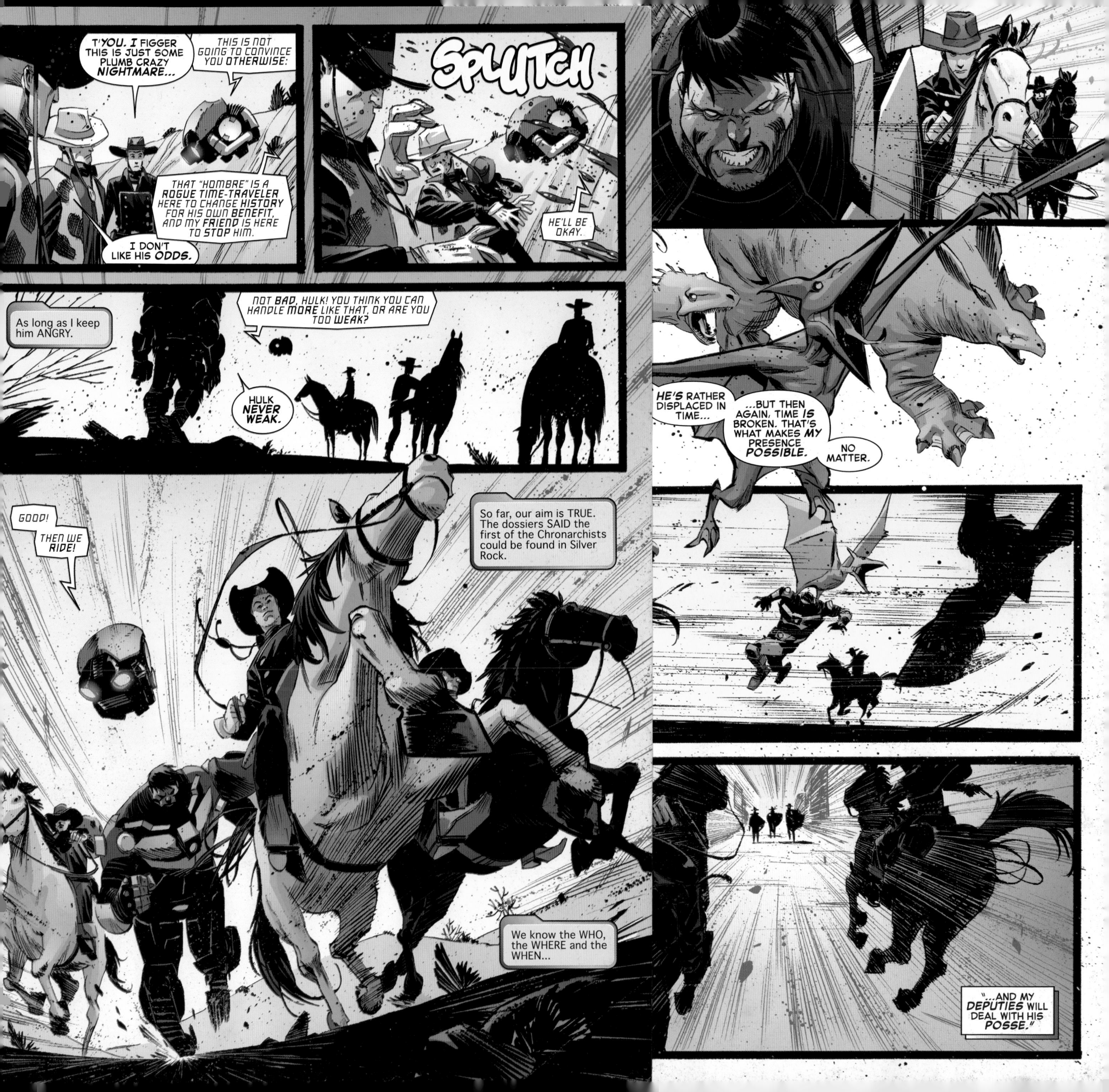

T'YOU. I FIGGER THIS IS JUST SOME PLUMB CRAZY NIGHTMARE...
THIS IS NOT GOING TO CONVINCE YOU OTHERWISE:
THAT "HOMBRE" IS A ROGUE TIME-TRAVELER HERE TO CHANGE HISTORY FOR HIS OWN BENEFIT, AND MY FRIEND IS HERE TO STOP HIM.
I DON'T LIKE HIS ODDS.
SPLUTCH
HE'LL BE OKAY.
As long as I keep him ANGRY.
NOT BAD, HULK! YOU THINK YOU CAN HANDLE MORE LIKE THAT, OR ARE YOU TOO WEAK?
HULK NEVER WEAK.
GOOD!
THEN WE RIDE!
So far, our aim is TRUE. The dossiers SAID the first of the Chronarchists could be found in Silver Rock.
We know the WHO, the WHERE and the WHEN...
HE'S RATHER DISPLACED IN TIME...
...BUT THEN AGAIN, TIME IS BROKEN. THAT'S WHAT MAKES MY PRESENCE POSSIBLE.
NO MATTER.
"...AND MY DEPUTIES WILL DEAL WITH HIS POSSE."

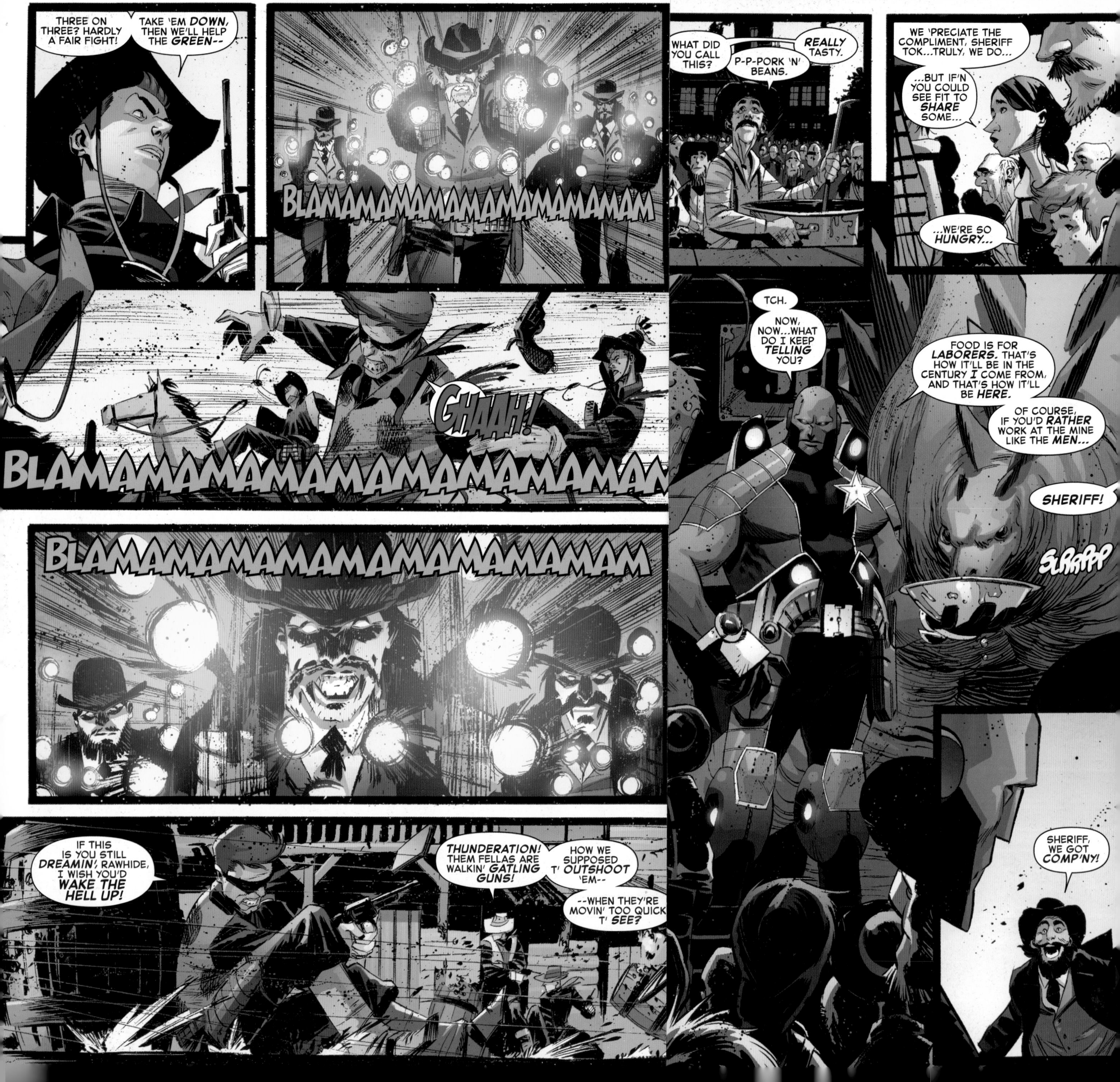
THREE ON THREE? HARDLY A FAIR FIGHT!
TAKE 'EM DOWN, THEN WE'LL HELP THE GREEN--
BLAMAMAMAMAMAMAMAMAMAMAM
GHAAH!
BLAMAMAMAMAMAMAMAMAMAMAMAM
BLAMAMAMAMAMAMAMAMAMAMAM
IF THIS IS YOU STILL DREAMIN', RAWHIDE, I WISH YOU'D WAKE THE HELL UP!
THUNDERATION! THEM FELLAS ARE WALKIN' GATLING GUNS!
HOW WE SUPPOSED T' OUTSHOOT 'EM--
--WHEN THEY'RE MOVIN' TOO QUICK T' SEE?
WHAT DID YOU CALL THIS?
REALLY TASTY.
P-P-PORK 'N' BEANS.
WE 'PRECIATE THE COMPLIMENT, SHERIFF TOK...TRULY, WE DO...
...BUT IF'N YOU COULD SEE FIT TO SHARE SOME...
...WE'RE SO HUNGRY...
TCH.
NOW, NOW...WHAT DO I KEEP TELLING YOU?
FOOD IS FOR LABORERS. THAT'S HOW IT'LL BE IN THE CENTURY I COME FROM, AND THAT'S HOW IT'LL BE HERE.
OF COURSE, IF YOU'D RATHER WORK AT THE MINE LIKE THE MEN...
SHERIFF!
SLRRPP
SHERIFF, WE GOT COMP'NY!

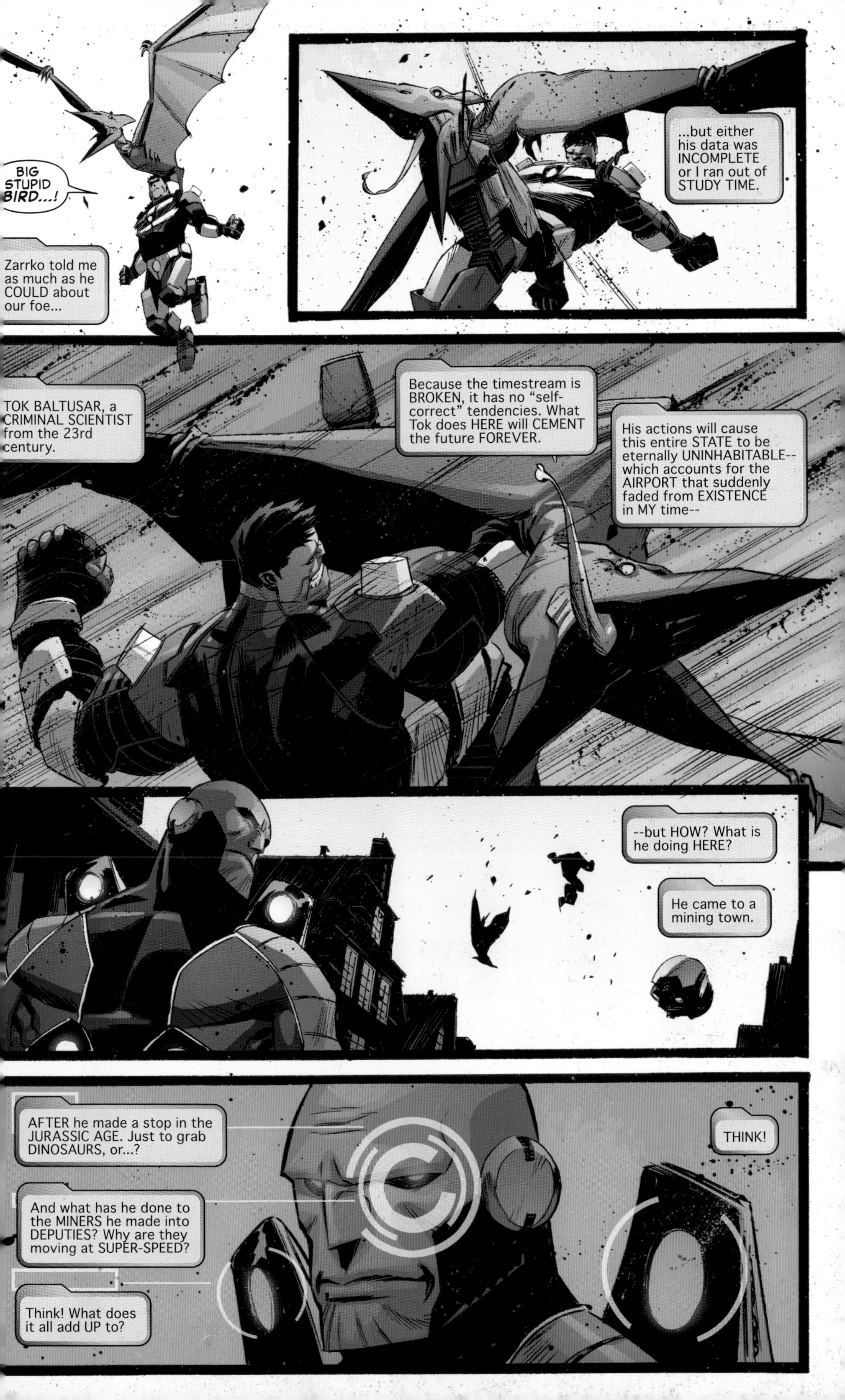

BIG STUPID BIRD...!
Zarrko told me as much as he COULD about our foe...
...but either his data was INCOMPLETE or I ran out of STUDY TIME.
TOK BALTUSAR, a CRIMINAL SCIENTIST from the 23rd century.
Because the timestream is BROKEN, it has no "self-correct" tendencies. What Tok does HERE will CEMENT the future FOREVER.
His actions will cause this entire STATE to be eternally UNINHABITABLE--which accounts for the AIRPORT that suddenly faded from EXISTENCE in MY time--
--but HOW? What is he doing HERE?
He came to a mining town.
AFTER he made a stop in the JURASSIC AGE. Just to grab DINOSAURS, or...?
And what has he done to the MINERS he made into DEPUTIES? Why are they moving at SUPER-SPEED?
Think! What does it all add UP to?
THINK!

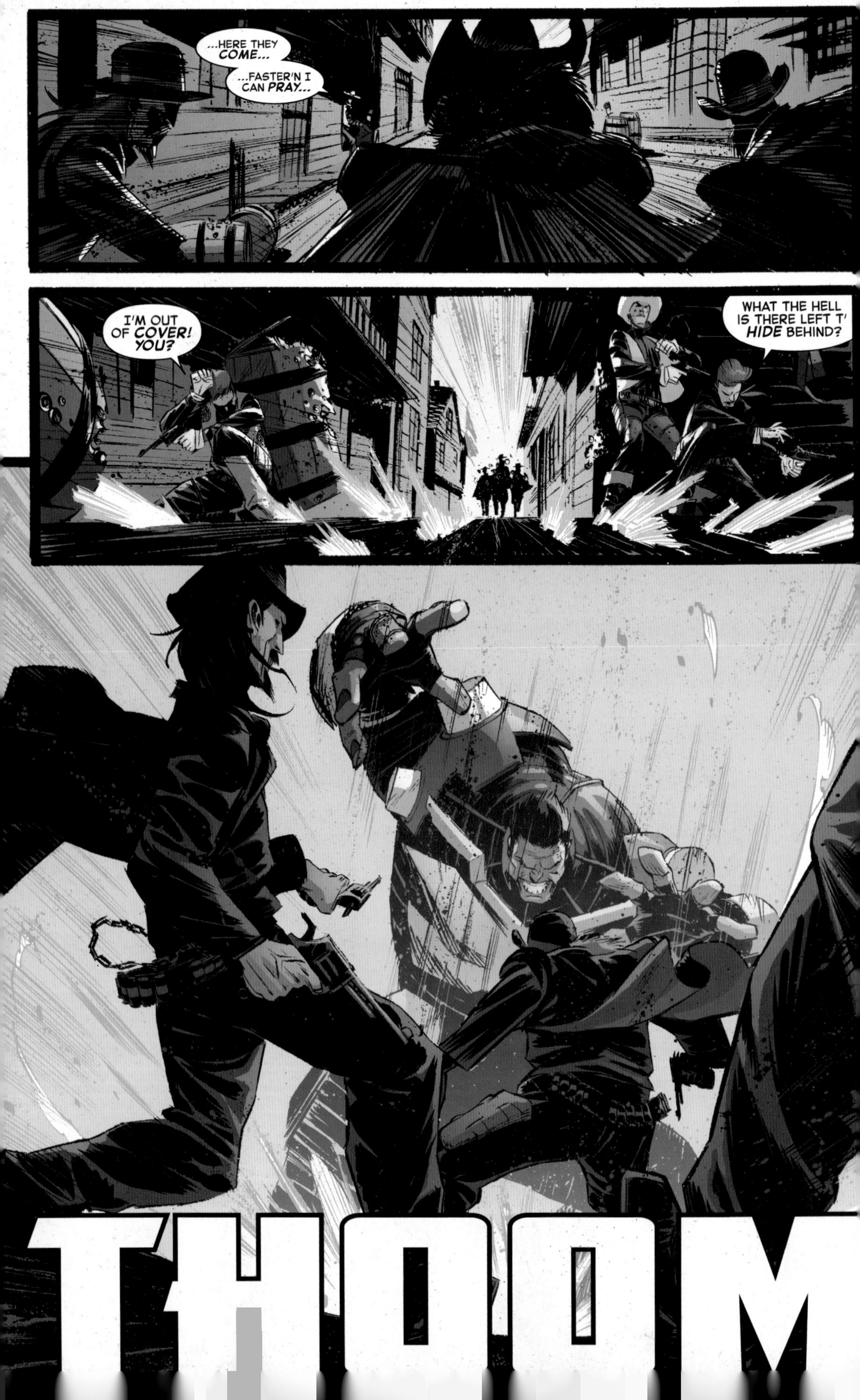
...HERE THEY COME...
...FASTER'N I CAN PRAY...
I'M OUT OF COVER! YOU?
WHAT THE HELL IS THERE LEFT T' HIDE BEHIND?
THOOM

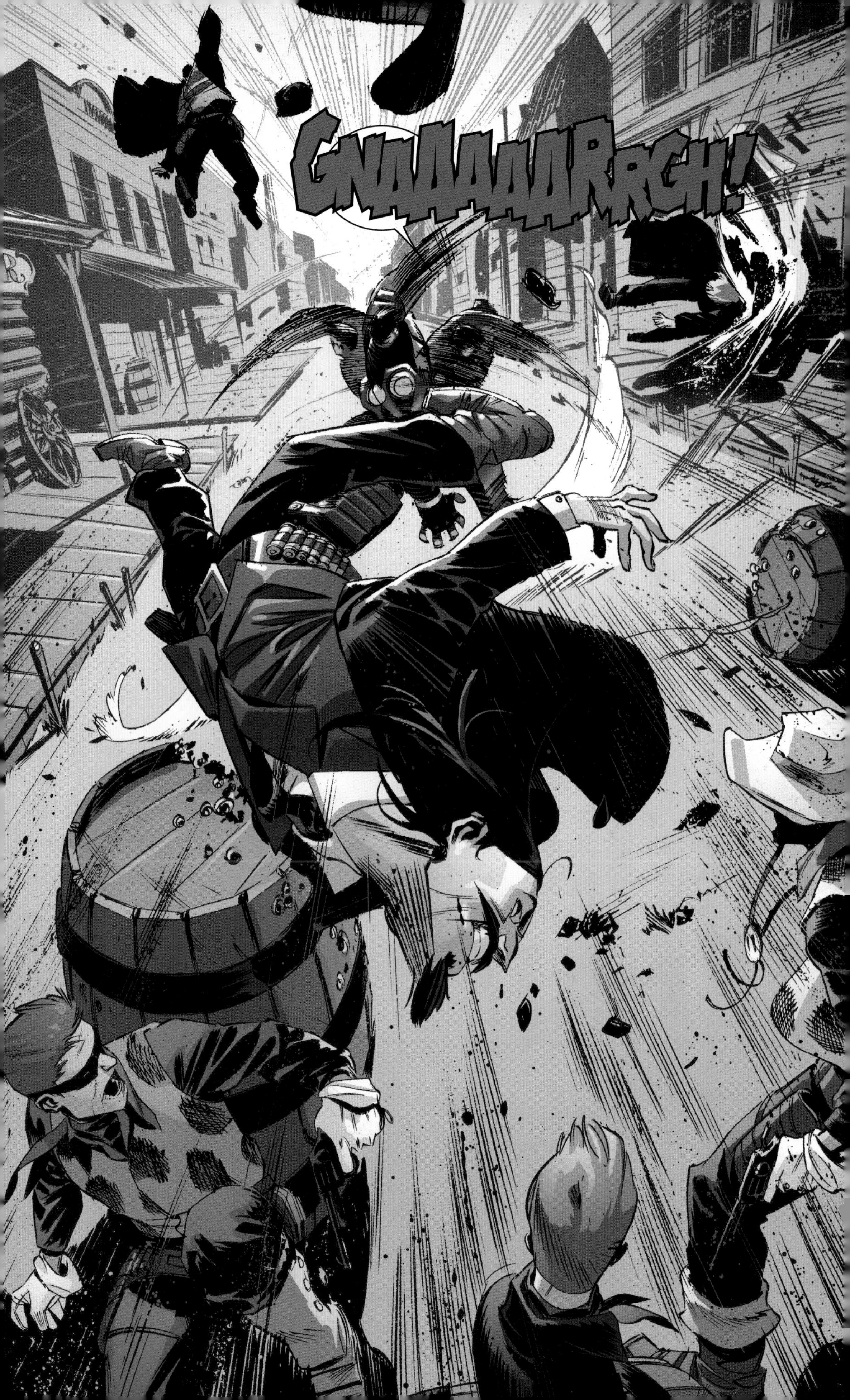
GNAAAAAARRRGH!

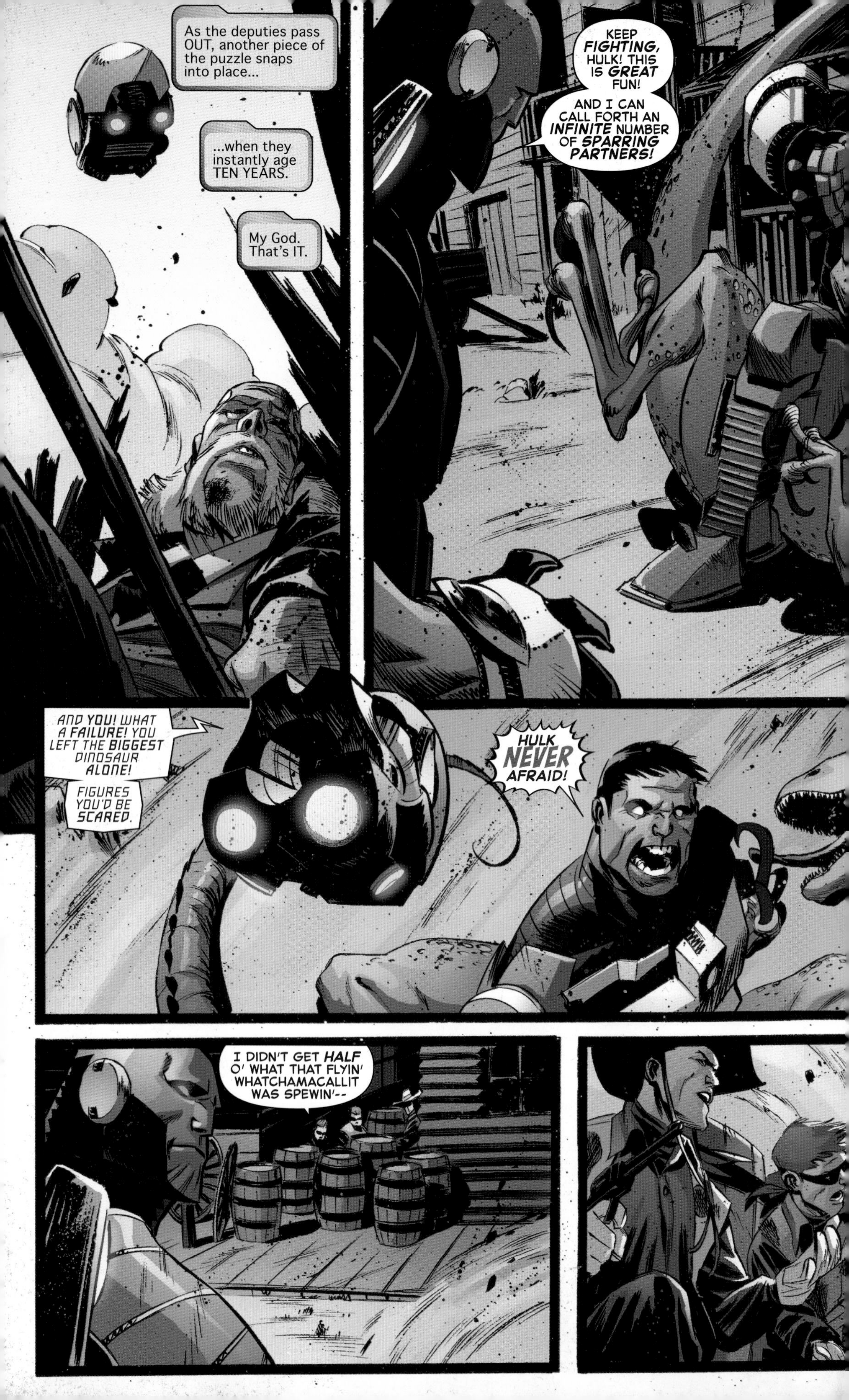
As the deputies pass OUT, another piece of the puzzle snaps into place...
...when they instantly age TEN YEARS.
My God. That's IT.
KEEP FIGHTING, HULK! THIS IS GREAT FUN!
AND I CAN CALL FORTH AN INFINITE NUMBER OF SPARRING PARTNERS!
AND YOU! WHAT A FAILURE! YOU LEFT THE BIGGEST DINOSAUR ALONE!
FIGURES YOU'D BE SCARED.
HULK NEVER AFRAID!
I DIDN'T GET HALF O' WHAT THAT FLYIN' WHATCHAMACALLIT WAS SPEWIN'--

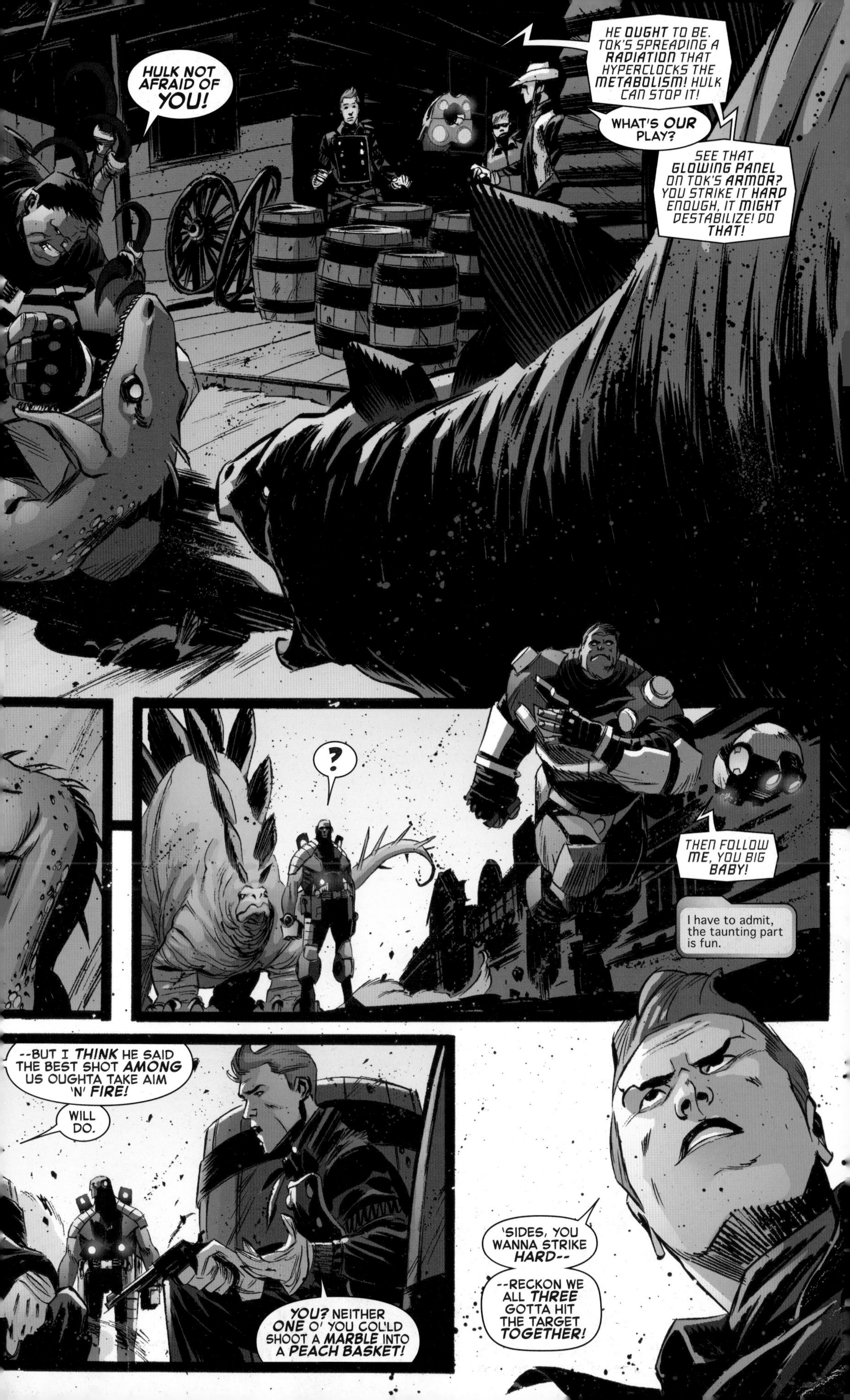
HULK NOT AFRAID OF YOU!
HE OUGHT TO BE. TOK'S SPREADING A RADIATION THAT HYPERCLOCKS THE METABOLISM! HULK CAN STOP IT!
WHAT'S OUR PLAY?
SEE THAT GLOWING PANEL ON TOK'S ARMOR? YOU STRIKE IT HARD ENOUGH, IT MIGHT DESTABILIZE! DO THAT!
?
THEN FOLLOW ME, YOU BIG BABY!
I have to admit, the taunting part is fun.
--BUT I THINK HE SAID THE BEST SHOT AMONG US OUGHTA TAKE AIM 'N' FIRE!
WILL DO.
YOU? NEITHER ONE O' YOU CO'LD SHOOT A MARBLE INTO A PEACH BASKET!
'SIDES, YOU WANNA STRIKE HARD--
--RECKON WE ALL THREE GOTTA HIT THE TARGET TOGETHER!

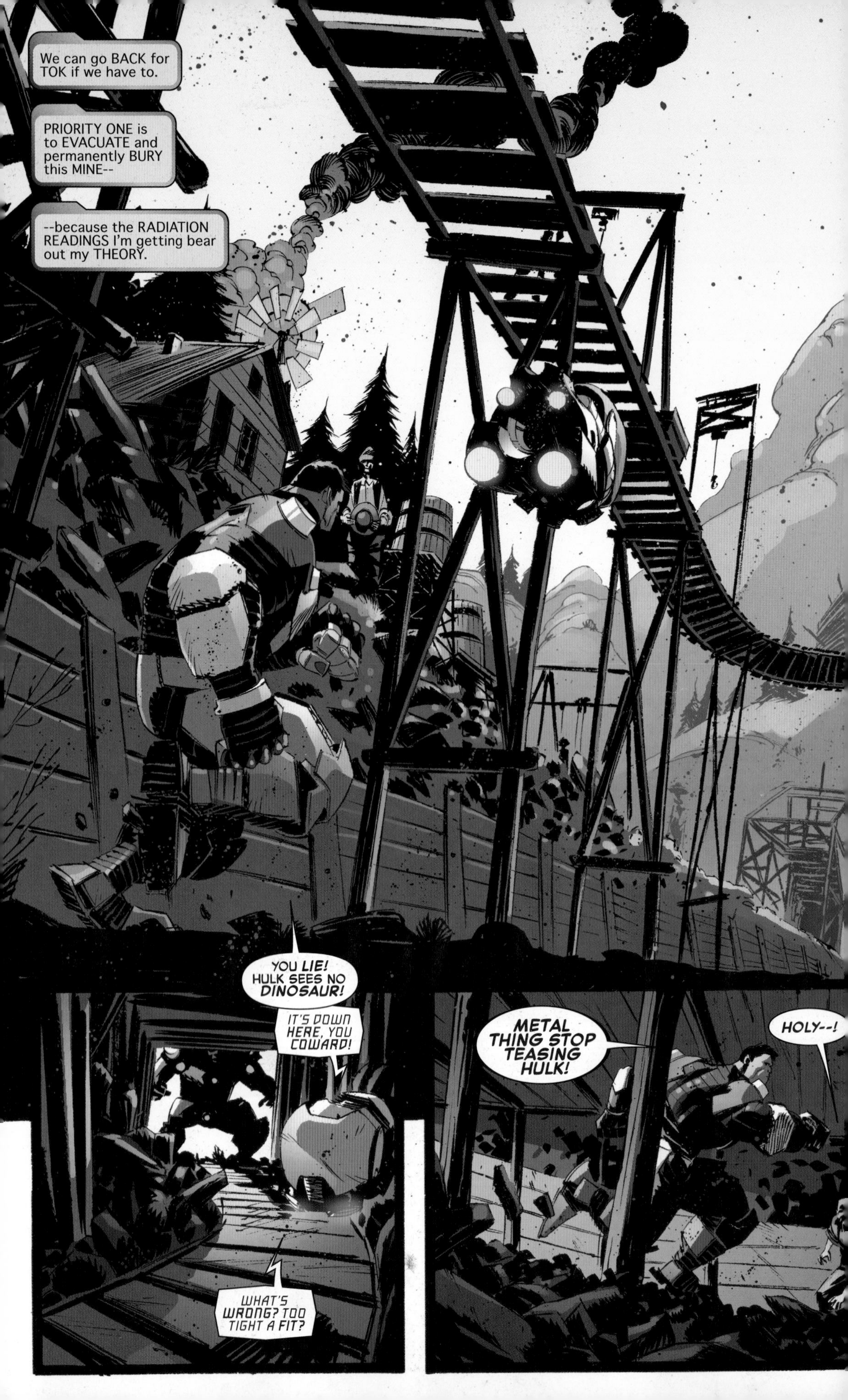
We can go BACK for TOK if we have to.
PRIORITY ONE is to EVACUATE and permanently BURY this MINE--
--because the RADIATION READINGS I'm getting bear out my THEORY.
YOU LIE! HULK SEES NO DINOSAUR!
IT'S DOWN HERE, YOU COWARD!
WHAT'S WRONG? TOO TIGHT A FIT?
METAL THING STOP TEASING HULK!
HOLY--!

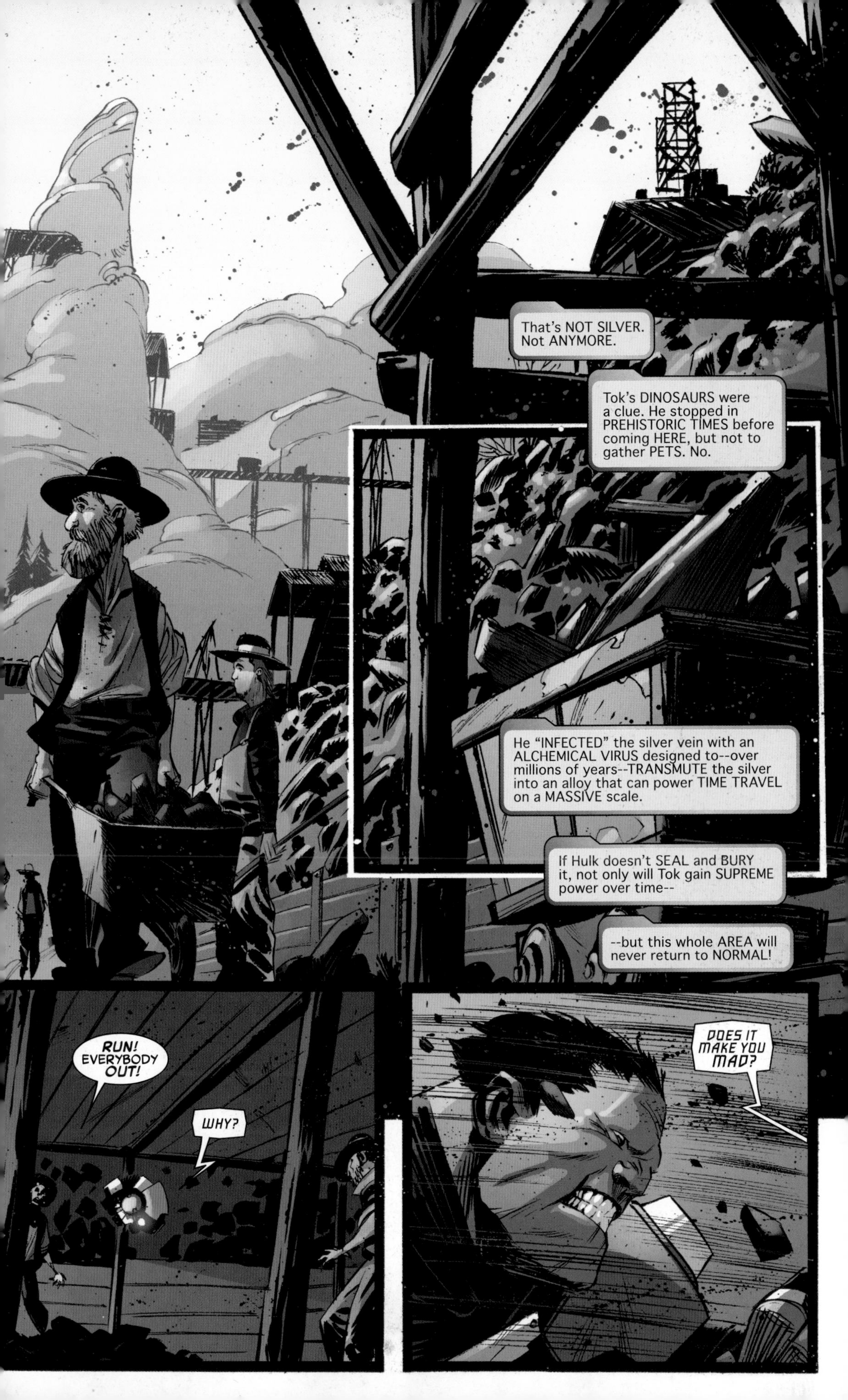

That's NOT SILVER. Not ANYMORE.
Tok's DINOSAURS were a clue. He stopped in PREHISTORIC TIMES before coming HERE, but not to gather PETS. No.
He "INFECTED" the silver vein with an ALCHEMICAL VIRUS designed to--over millions of years--TRANSMUTE the silver into an alloy that can power TIME TRAVEL on a MASSIVE scale.
If Hulk doesn't SEAL and BURY it, not only will Tok gain SUPREME power over time--
--but this whole AREA will never return to NORMAL!
RUN! EVERYBODY OUT!
WHY?
DOES IT MAKE YOU MAD?

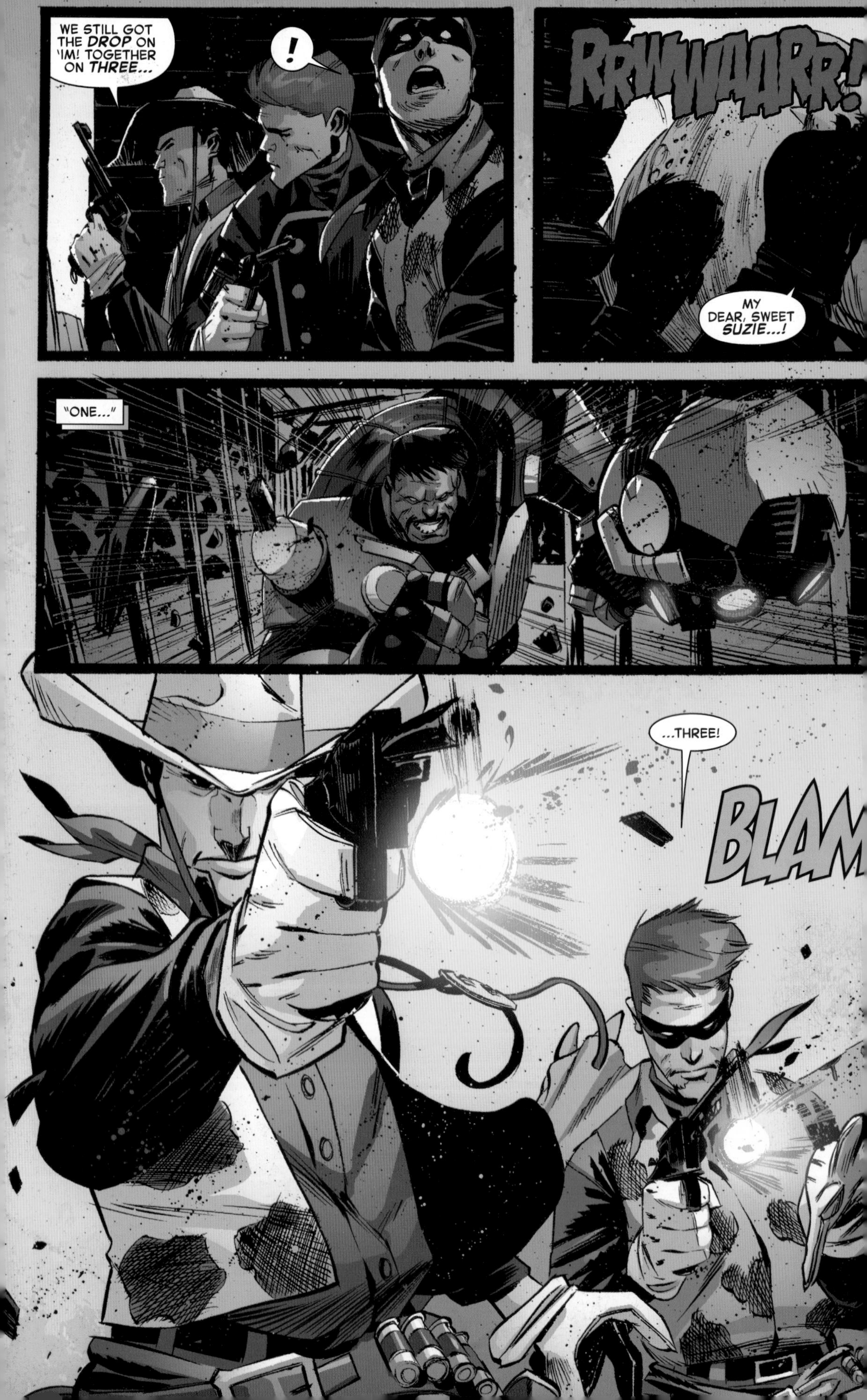
WE STILL GOT THE DROP ON 'IM! TOGETHER ON THREE...
!
RRWWAARR!
MY DEAR, SWEET SUZIE...!
"ONE..."
...THREE!
BLAM

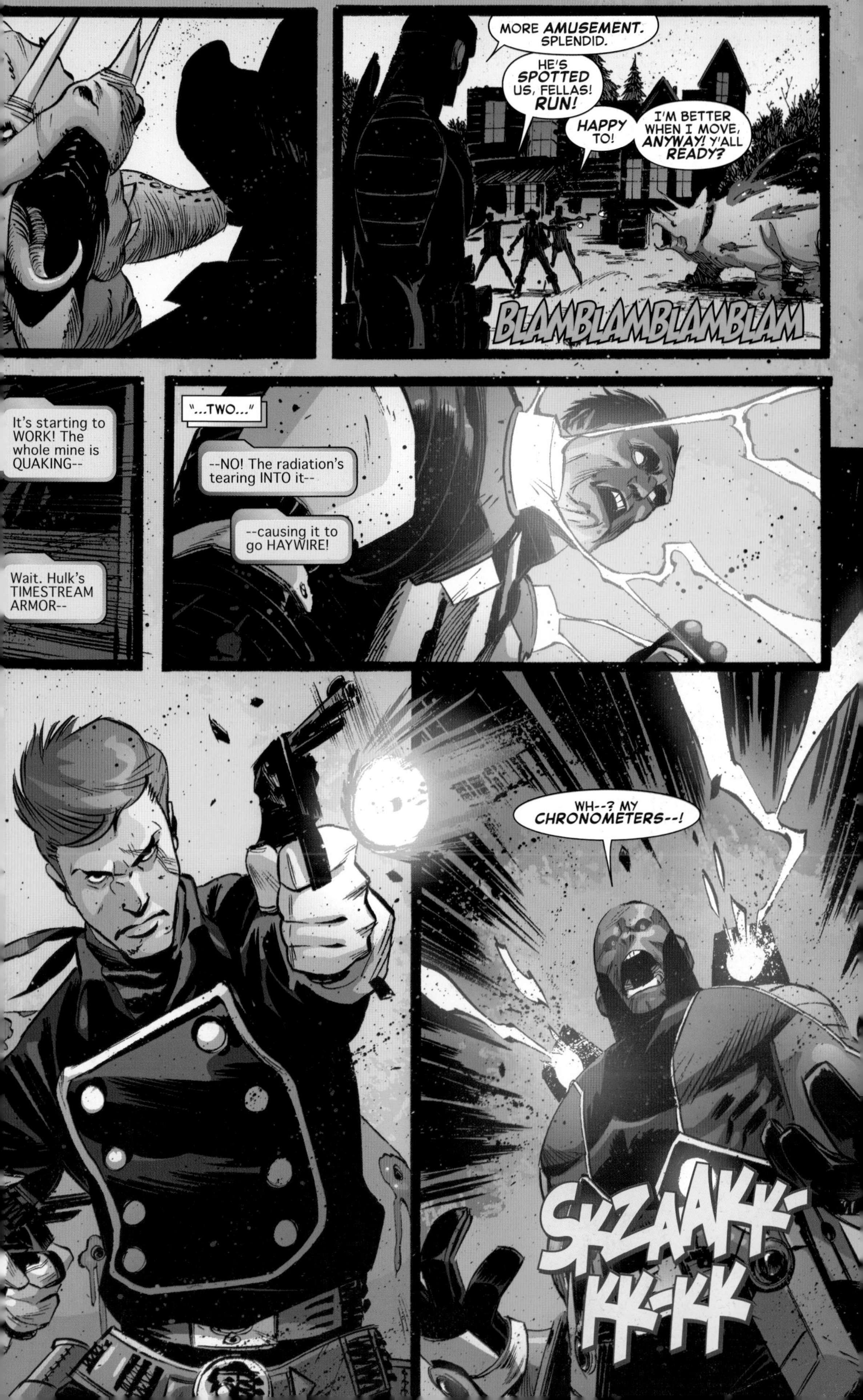
MORE AMUSEMENT. SPLENDID.
HE'S SPOTTED US, FELLAS! RUN!
HAPPY TO!
I'M BETTER WHEN I MOVE, ANYWAY! Y'ALL READY?
BLAMBLAMBLAMBLAM
It's starting to WORK! The whole mine is QUAKING--
Wait. Hulk's TIMESTREAM ARMOR--
"...TWO..."
--NO! The radiation's tearing INTO it--
--causing it to go HAYWIRE!
WH--? MY CHRONOMETERS--!
SKZAKK-KK-KK

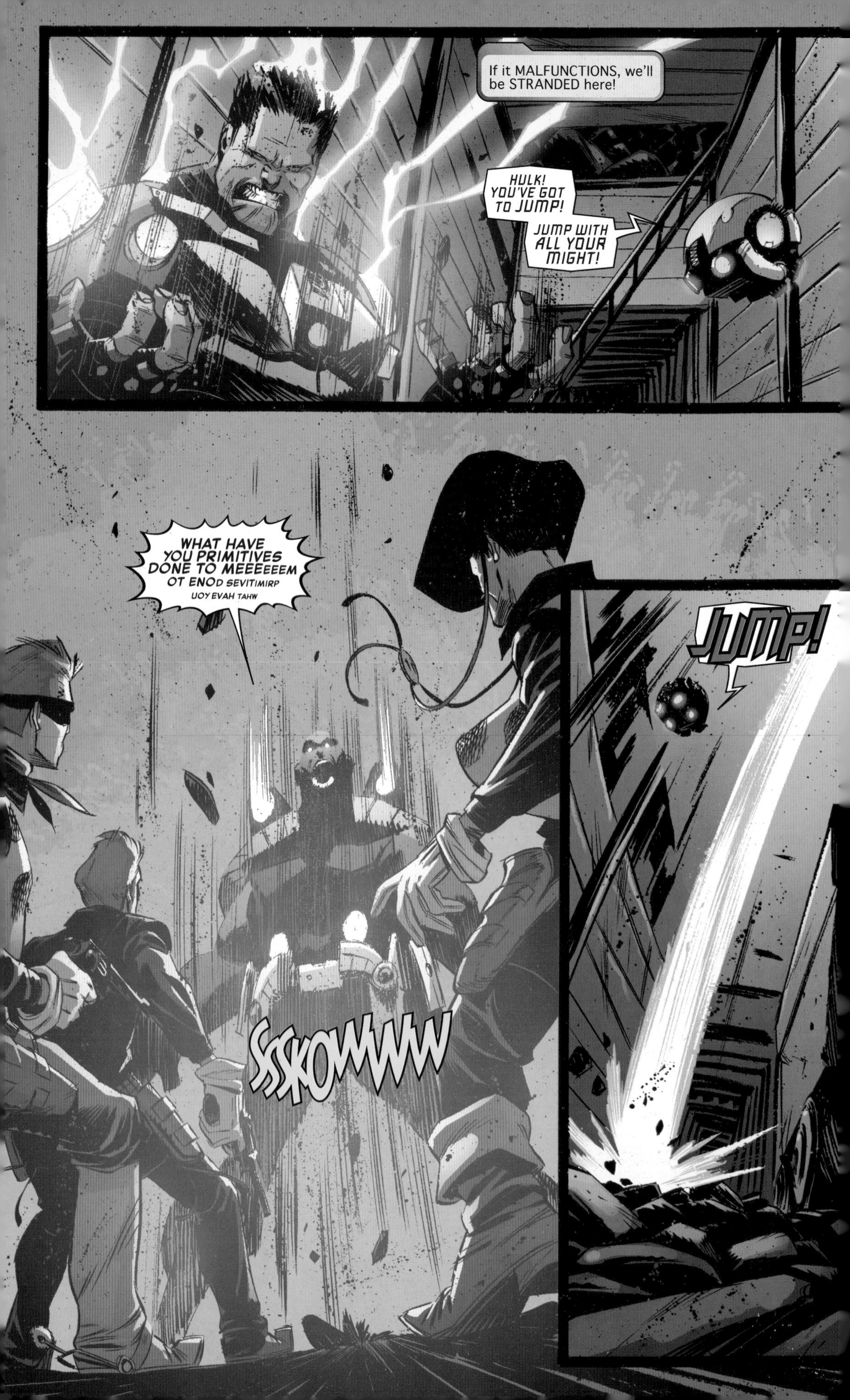
If it MALFUNCTIONS, we'll be STRANDED here!
HULK! YOU'VE GOT TO JUMP!
JUMP WITH ALL YOUR MIGHT!
WHAT HAVE YOU PRIMITIVES DONE TO MEEEEEEEM OT ENOD SEVITIMIRP UOY EVAH TAHW
JUMP!
SSSKOWWWW

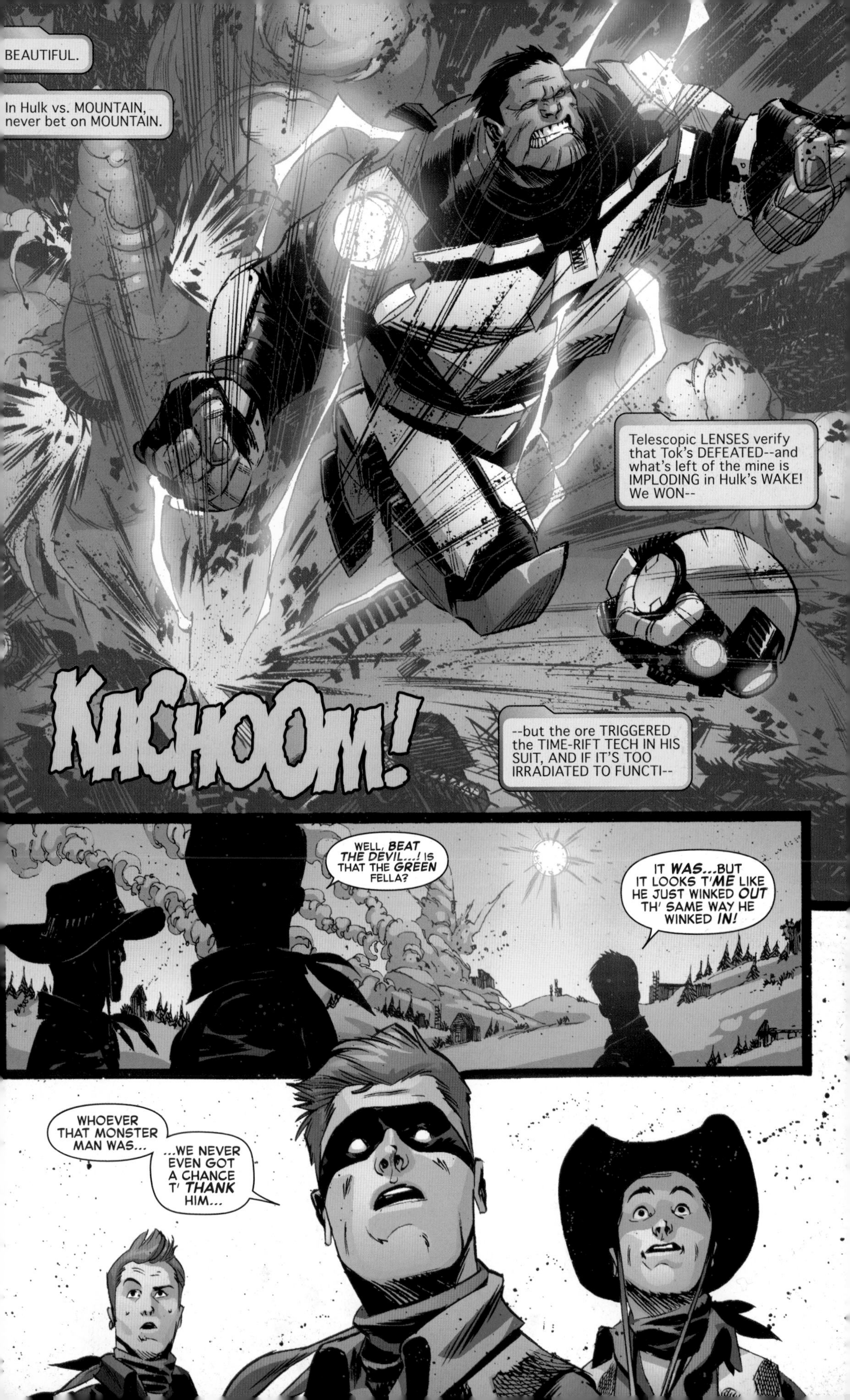

BEAUTIFUL.
In Hulk vs. MOUNTAIN, never bet on MOUNTAIN.
Telescopic LENSES verify that Tok's DEFEATED--and what's left of the mine is IMPLODING in Hulk's WAKE! We WON--
KACHOOM!
--but the ore TRIGGERED the TIME-RIFT TECH IN HIS SUIT, AND IF IT'S TOO IRRADIATED TO FUNCTI--
WELL, BEAT THE DEVIL...! IS THAT THE GREEN FELLA?
IT WAS...BUT IT LOOKS T'ME LIKE HE JUST WINKED OUT TH' SAME WAY HE WINKED IN!
WHOEVER THAT MONSTER MAN WAS...
...WE NEVER EVEN GOT A CHANCE T' THANK HIM...

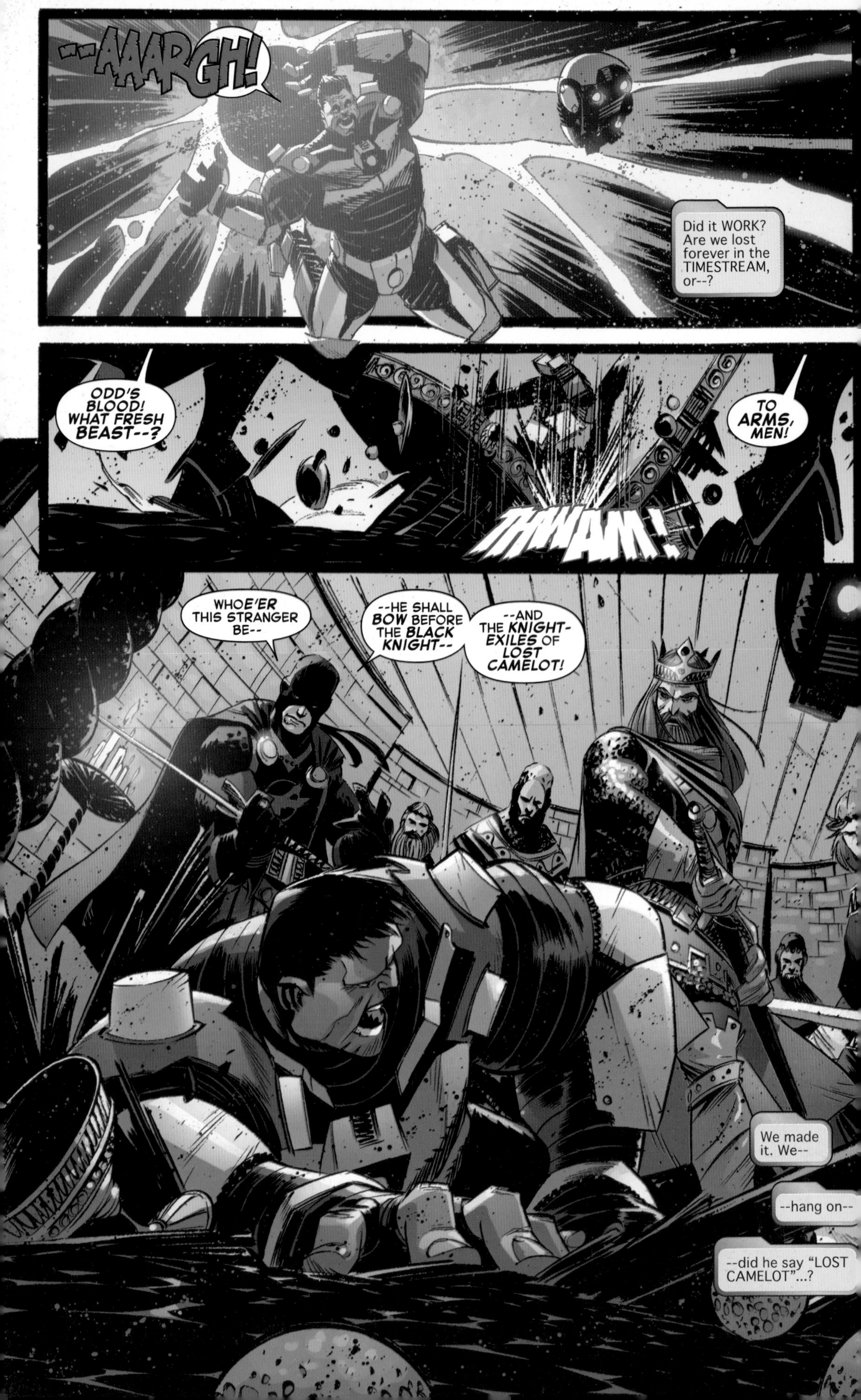
--AAARGH!
Did it WORK? Are we lost forever in the TIMESTREAM, or--?
ODD'S BLOOD! WHAT FRESH BEAST--?
TO ARMS, MEN!
THWAM!
WHOE'ER THIS STRANGER BE--
--HE SHALL BOW BEFORE THE BLACK KNIGHT--
--AND THE KNIGHT-EXILES OF LOST CAMELOT!
We made it. We--
--hang on--
--did he say "LOST CAMELOT"...?

INDESTRUCTIBLE HULK Variant Cover Gallery

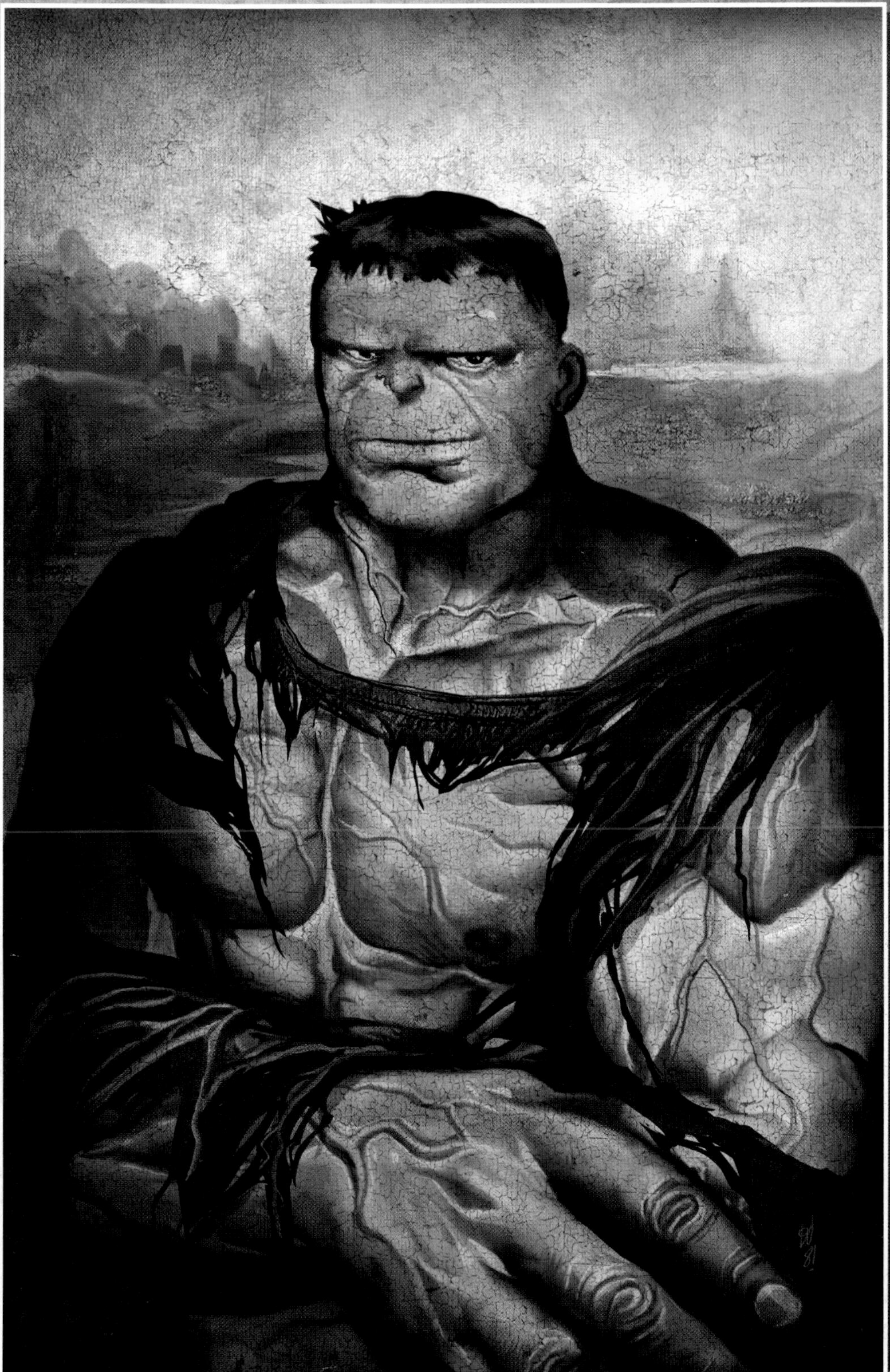

INDESTRUCTIBLE HULK#11 BY MICHAEL DEL MUNDO

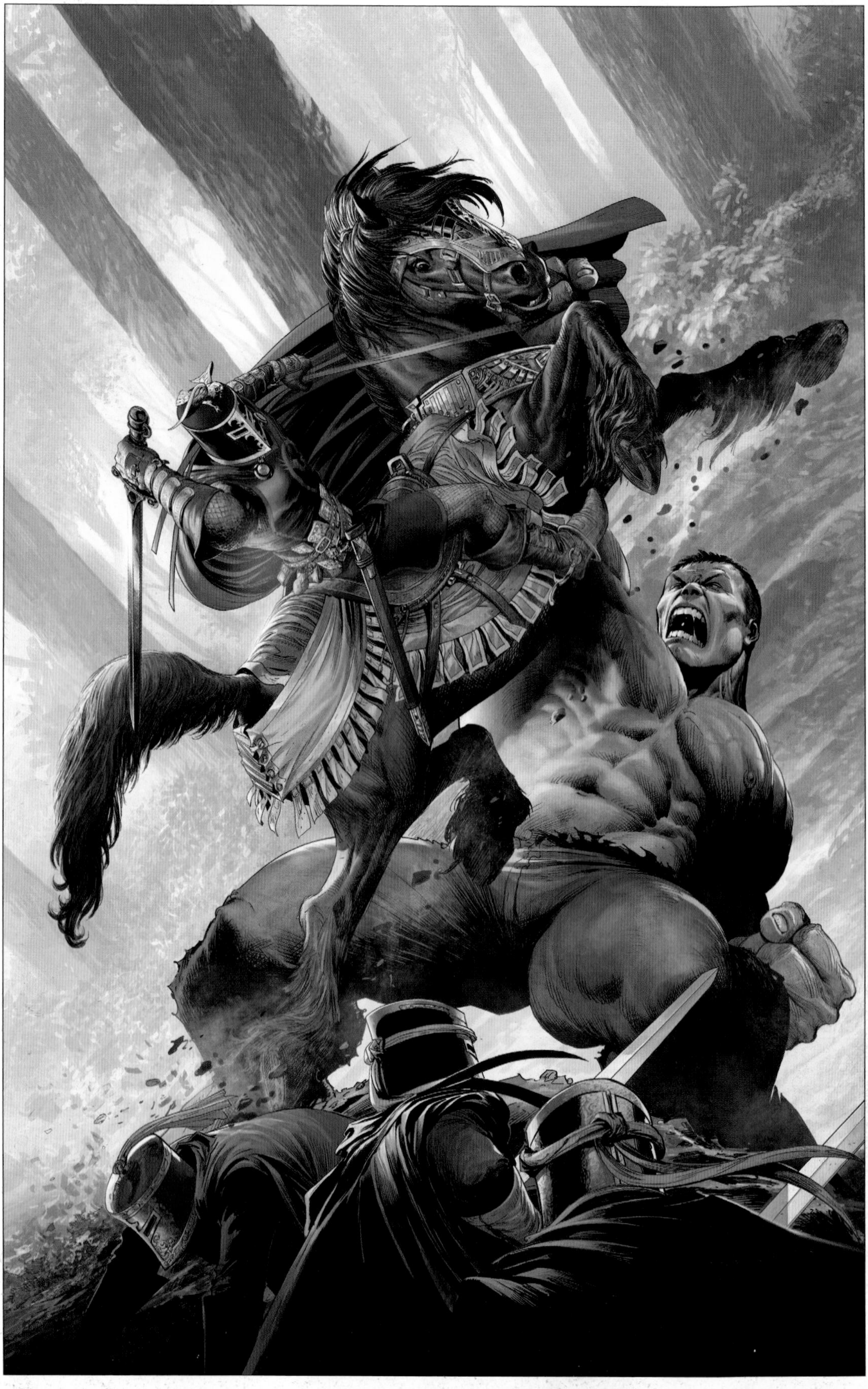

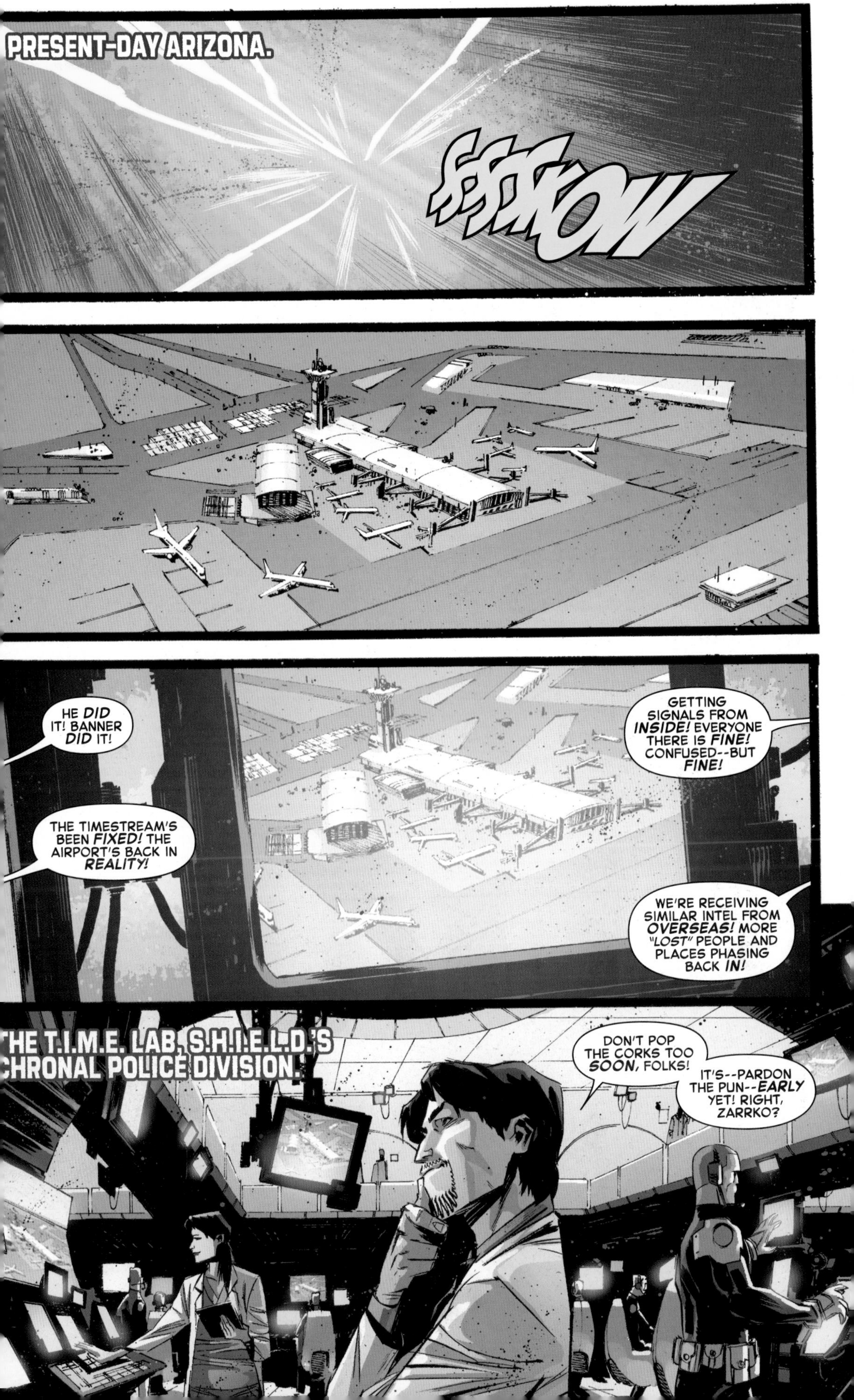
PRESENT-DAY ARIZONA.
FSSSKOW
HE DID IT! BANNER DID IT!
THE TIMESTREAM'S BEEN FIXED! THE AIRPORT'S BACK IN REALITY!
GETTING SIGNALS FROM INSIDE! EVERYONE THERE IS FINE! CONFUSED--BUT FINE!
WE'RE RECEIVING SIMILAR INTEL FROM OVERSEAS! MORE "LOST" PEOPLE AND PLACES PHASING BACK IN!
THE T.I.M.E. LAB, S.H.I.E.L.D.'S CHRONAL POLICE DIVISION.
DON'T POP THE CORKS TOO SOON, FOLKS!
IT'S--PARDON THE PUN--EARLY YET! RIGHT, ZARRKO?

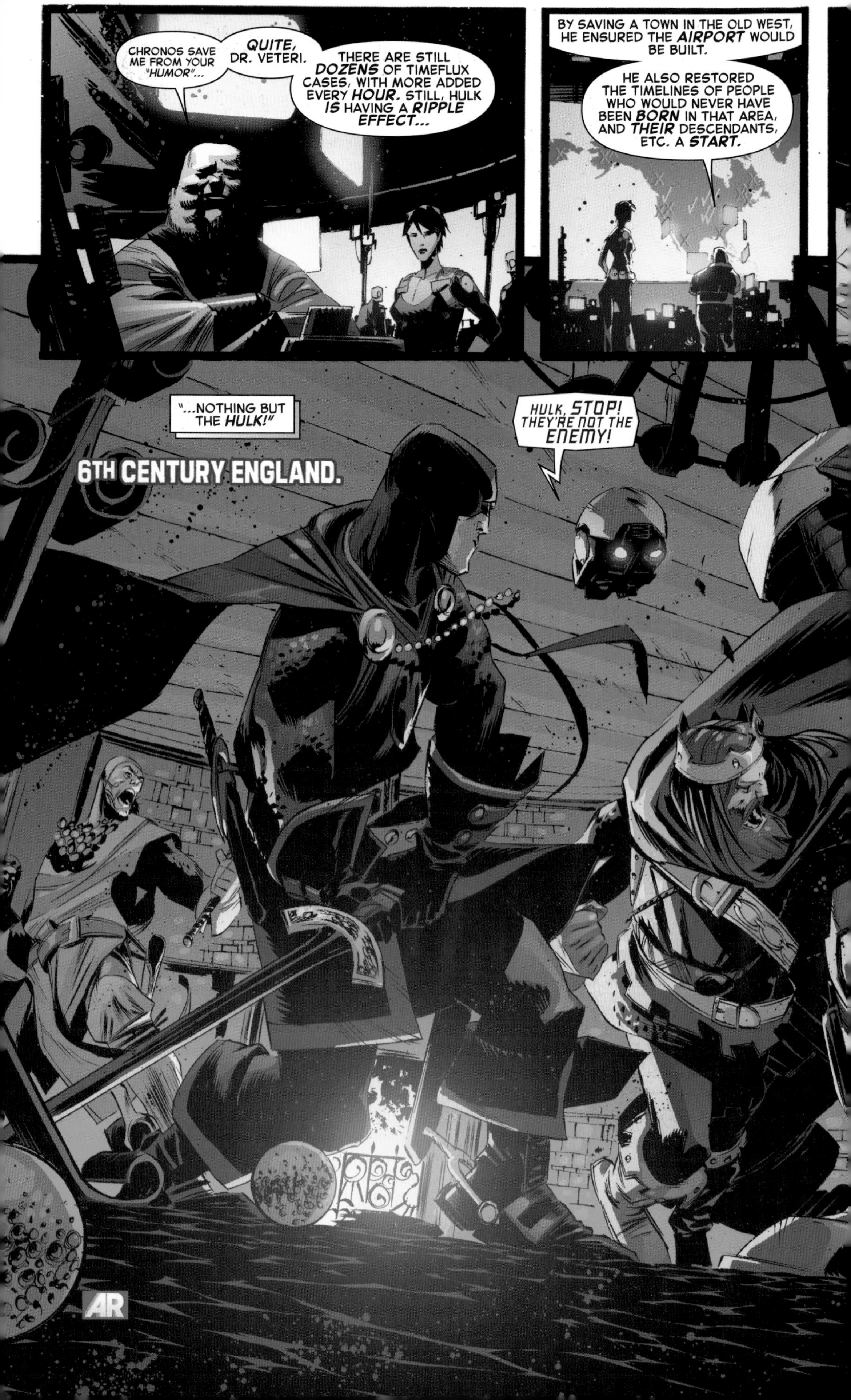
CHRONOS SAVE ME FROM YOUR "HUMOR"...
QUITE, DR. VETERI.
THERE ARE STILL DOZENS OF TIMEFLUX CASES, WITH MORE ADDED EVERY HOUR. STILL, HULK IS HAVING A RIPPLE EFFECT...
BY SAVING A TOWN IN THE OLD WEST, HE ENSURED THE AIRPORT WOULD BE BUILT.
HE ALSO RESTORED THE TIMELINES OF PEOPLE WHO WOULD NEVER HAVE BEEN BORN IN THAT AREA, AND THEIR DESCENDANTS, ETC. A START.
"...NOTHING BUT THE HULK!"
6TH CENTURY ENGLAND.
HULK, STOP! THEY'RE NOT THE ENEMY!
AR

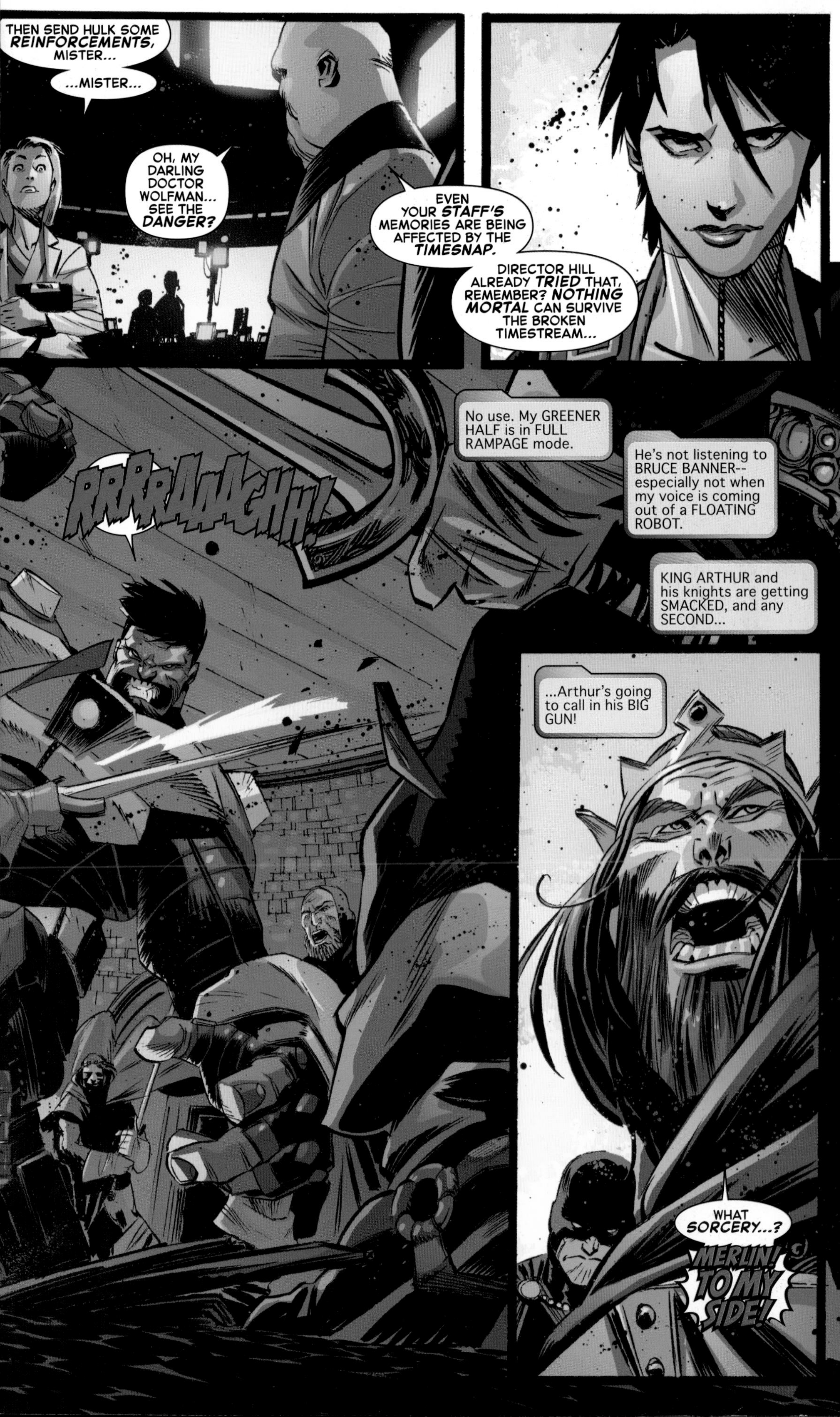
THEN SEND HULK SOME REINFORCEMENTS, MISTER...
...MISTER...
OH, MY DARLING DOCTOR WOLFMAN... SEE THE DANGER?
EVEN YOUR STAFF'S MEMORIES ARE BEING AFFECTED BY THE TIMESNAP.
DIRECTOR HILL ALREADY TRIED THAT, REMEMBER? NOTHING MORTAL CAN SURVIVE THE BROKEN TIMESTREAM...
No use. My GREENER HALF is in FULL RAMPAGE mode.
RRRRAAAGHH!
He's not listening to BRUCE BANNER-- especially not when my voice is coming out of a FLOATING ROBOT.
KING ARTHUR and his knights are getting SMACKED, and any SECOND...
...Arthur's going to call in his BIG GUN!
WHAT SORCERY...?
MERLIN! TO MY SIDE!

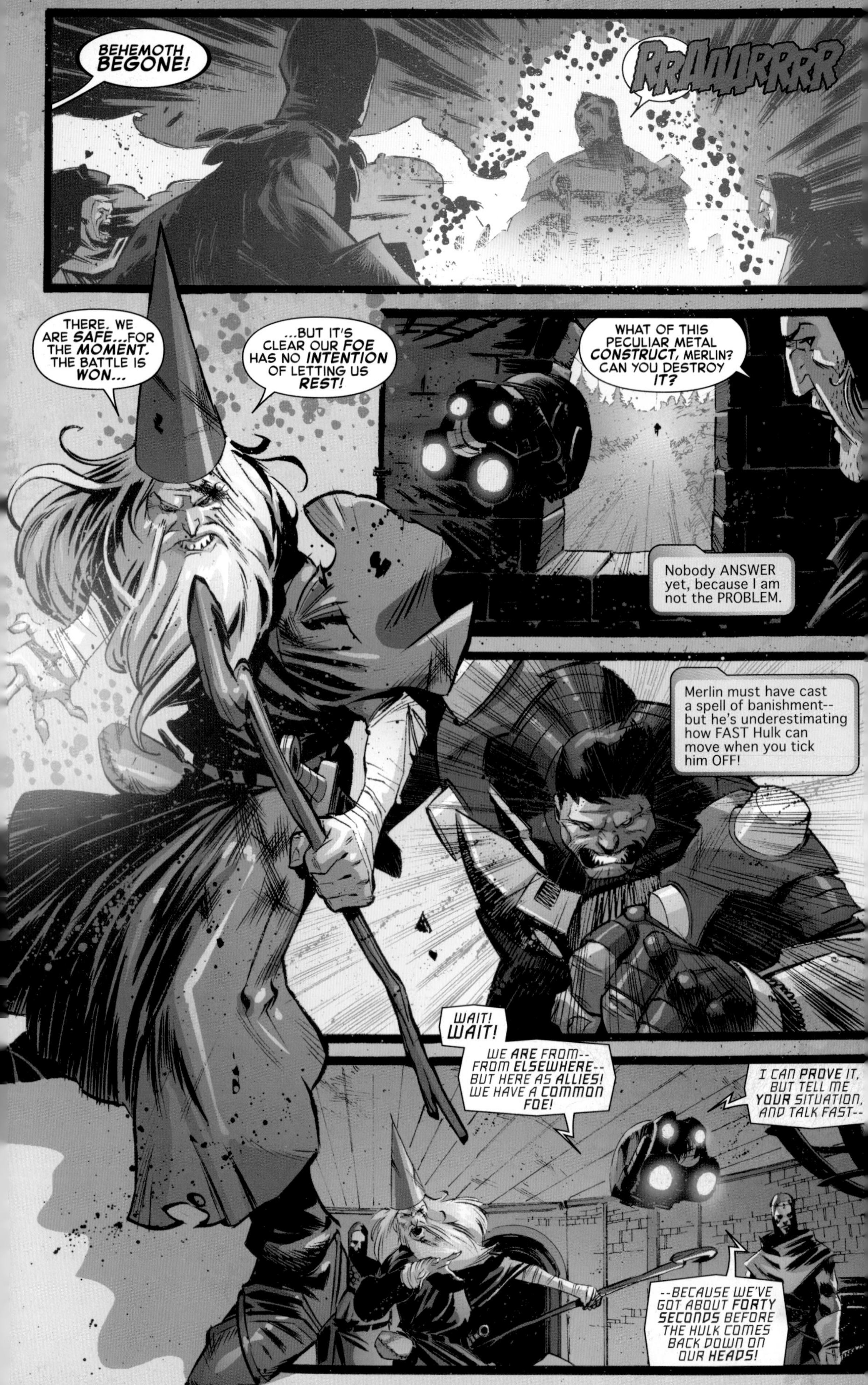
BEHEMOTH BEGONE!
RRAAARRRR
THERE. WE ARE SAFE...FOR THE MOMENT. THE BATTLE IS WON...
...BUT IT'S CLEAR OUR FOE HAS NO INTENTION OF LETTING US REST!
WHAT OF THIS PECULIAR METAL CONSTRUCT, MERLIN? CAN YOU DESTROY IT?
Nobody ANSWER yet, because I am not the PROBLEM.
Merlin must have cast a spell of banishment-- but he's underestimating how FAST Hulk can move when you tick him OFF!
WAIT! WAIT!
WE ARE FROM-- FROM ELSEWHERE-- BUT HERE AS ALLIES! WE HAVE A COMMON FOE!
I CAN PROVE IT, BUT TELL ME YOUR SITUATION, AND TALK FAST--
--BECAUSE WE'VE GOT ABOUT FORTY SECONDS BEFORE THE HULK COMES BACK DOWN ON OUR HEADS!

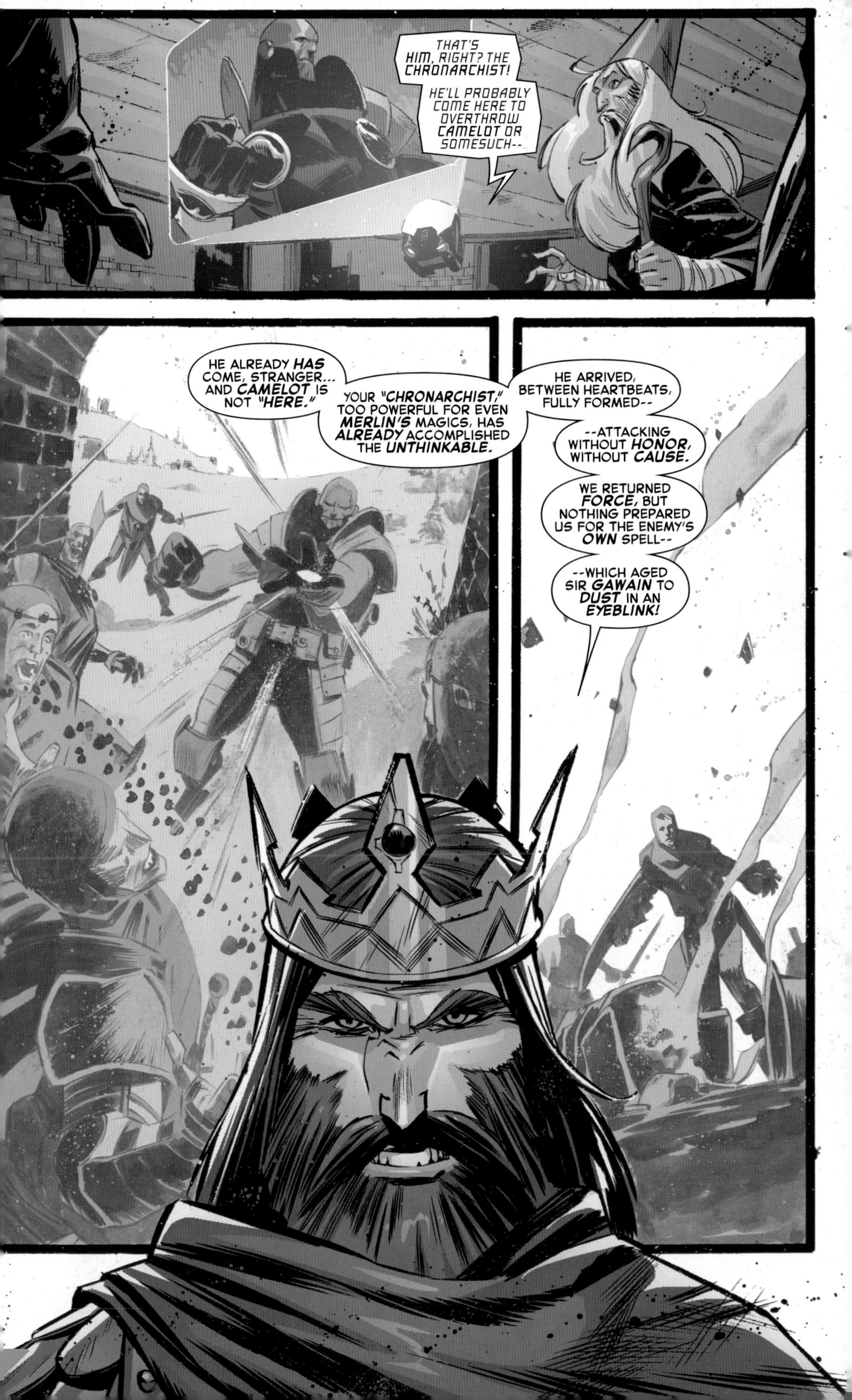
THAT'S HIM, RIGHT? THE CHRONARCHIST!
HE'LL PROBABLY COME HERE TO OVERTHROW CAMELOT OR SOMESUCH--
HE ALREADY HAS COME, STRANGER... AND CAMELOT IS NOT "HERE."
YOUR "CHRONARCHIST," TOO POWERFUL FOR EVEN MERLIN'S MAGICS, HAS ALREADY ACCOMPLISHED THE UNTHINKABLE.
HE ARRIVED, BETWEEN HEARTBEATS, FULLY FORMED--
--ATTACKING WITHOUT HONOR, WITHOUT CAUSE.
WE RETURNED FORCE, BUT NOTHING PREPARED US FOR THE ENEMY'S OWN SPELL--
--WHICH AGED SIR GAWAIN TO DUST IN AN EYEBLINK!

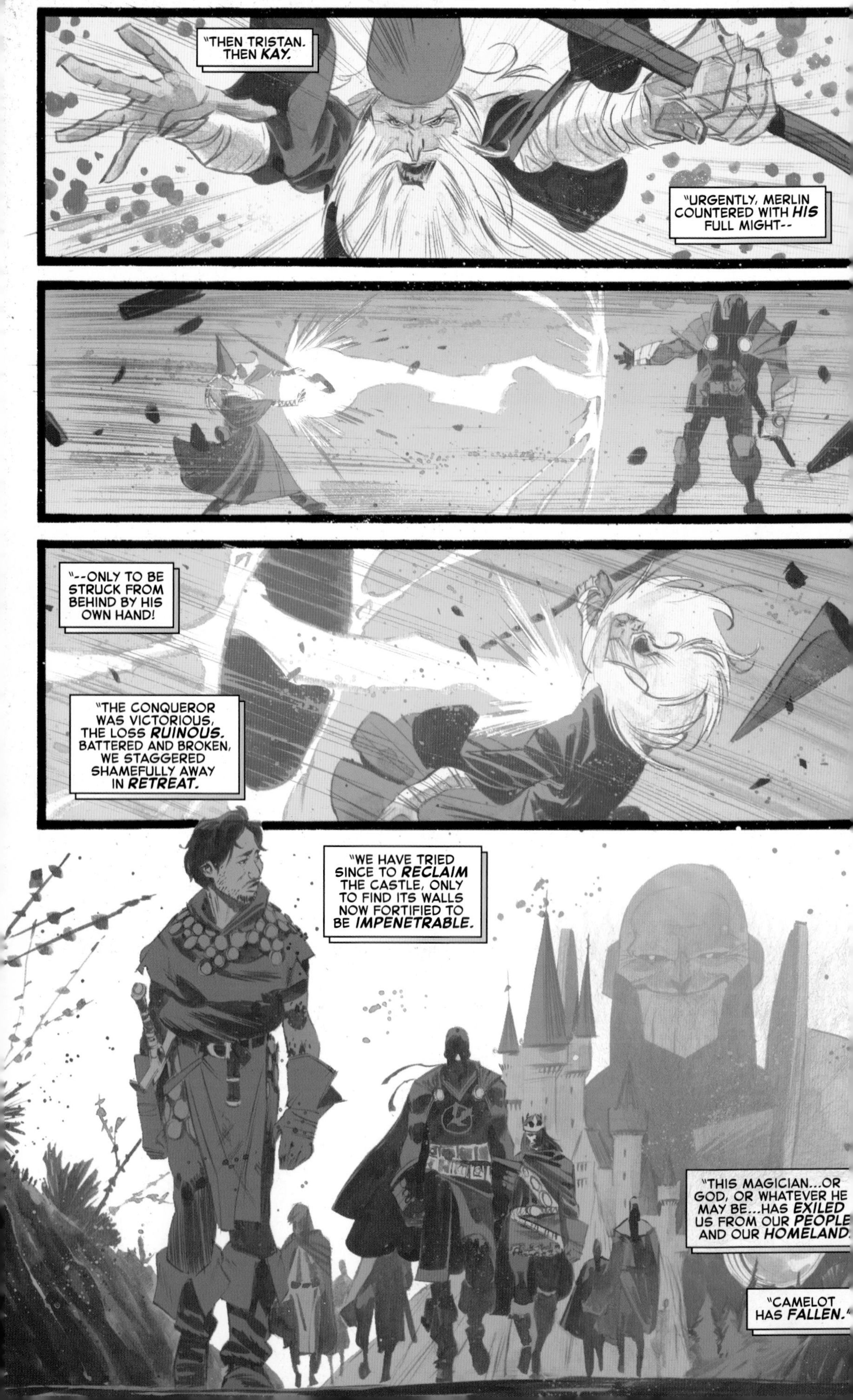
"THEN TRISTAN. THEN KAY.
"URGENTLY, MERLIN COUNTERED WITH HIS FULL MIGHT--
"--ONLY TO BE STRUCK FROM BEHIND BY HIS OWN HAND!
"THE CONQUEROR WAS VICTORIOUS, THE LOSS RUINOUS. BATTERED AND BROKEN, WE STAGGERED SHAMEFULLY AWAY IN RETREAT.
"WE HAVE TRIED SINCE TO RECLAIM THE CASTLE, ONLY TO FIND ITS WALLS NOW FORTIFIED TO BE IMPENETRABLE.
"THIS MAGICIAN...OR GOD, OR WHATEVER HE MAY BE...HAS EXILED US FROM OUR PEOPLE AND OUR HOMELAND.
"CAMELOT HAS FALLEN."

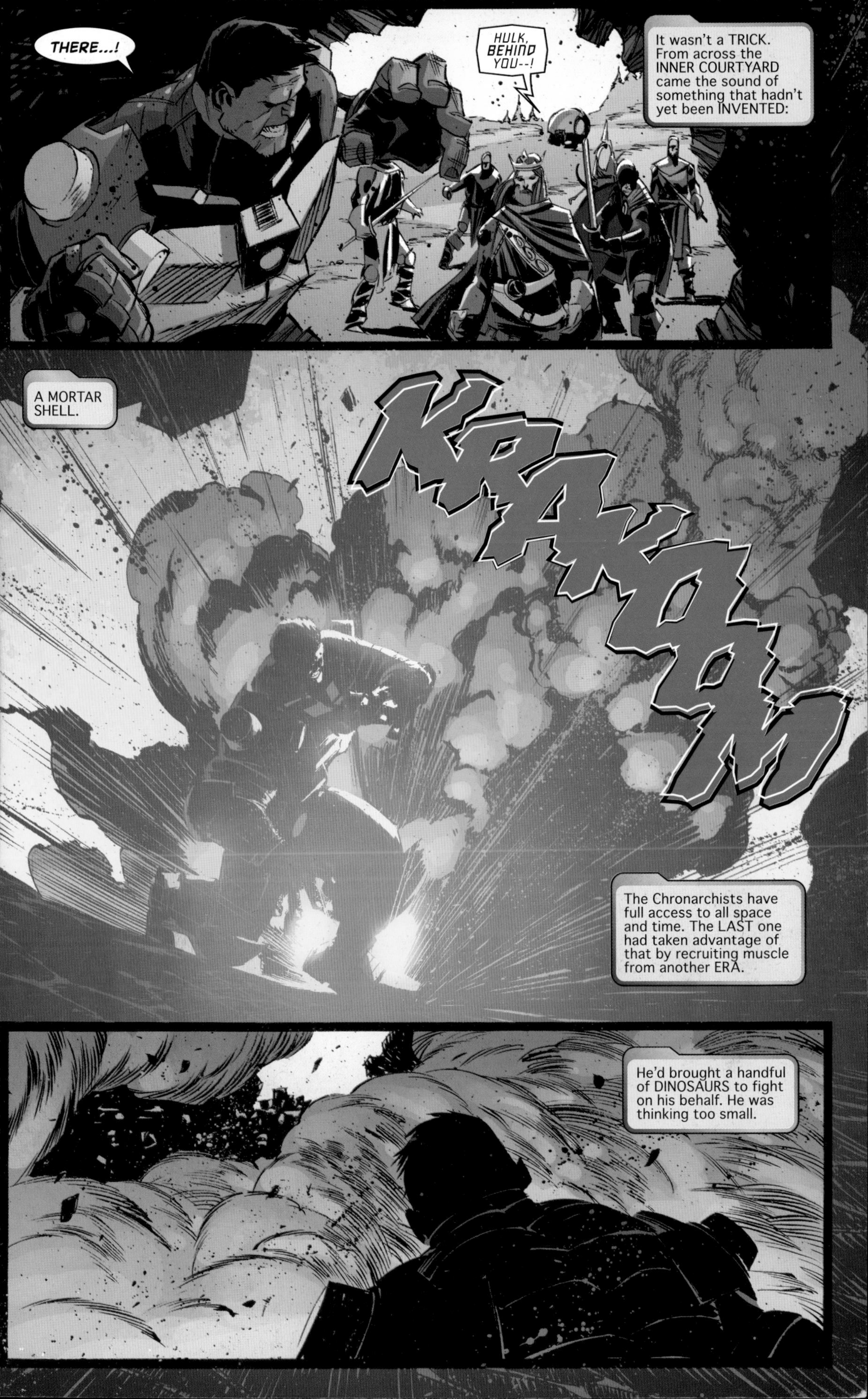
THERE...!
HULK, BEHIND YOU--!
It wasn't a TRICK. From across the INNER COURTYARD came the sound of something that hadn't yet been INVENTED:
A MORTAR SHELL.
KRAKOOM
The Chronarchists have full access to all space and time. The LAST one had taken advantage of that by recruiting muscle from another ERA.
He'd brought a handful of DINOSAURS to fight on his behalf. He was thinking too small.

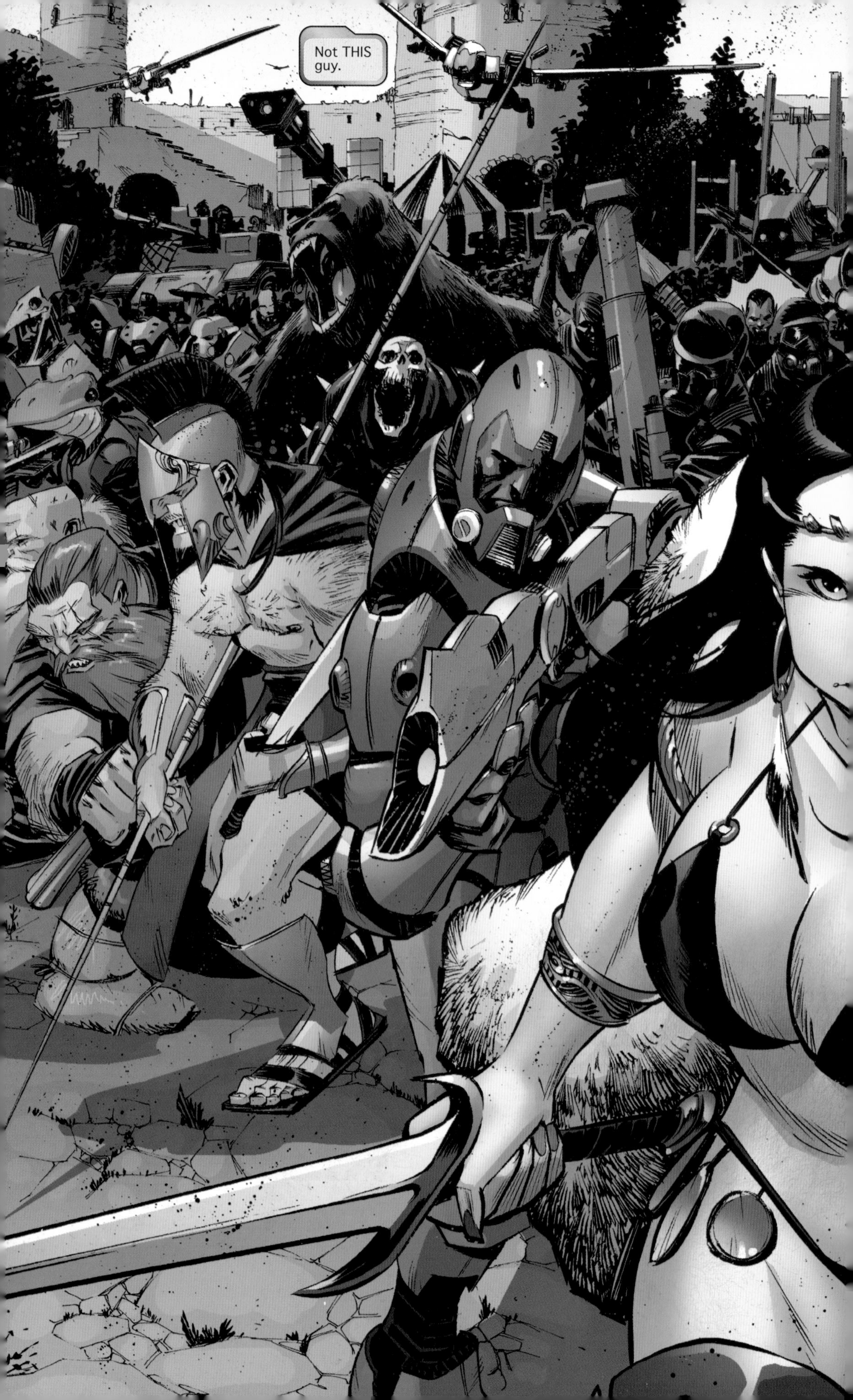
Not THIS guy.

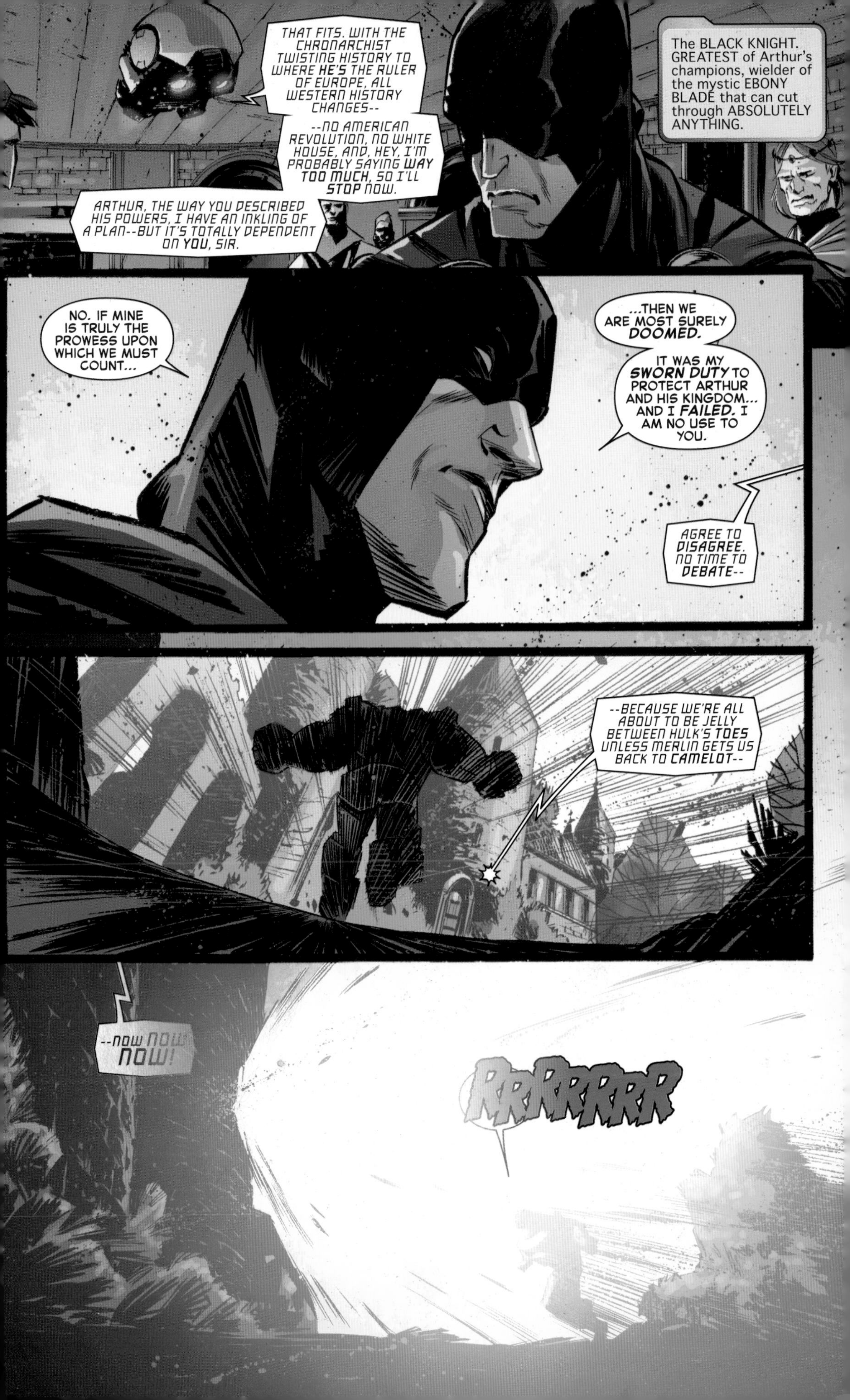
THAT FITS. WITH THE CHRONARCHIST TWISTING HISTORY TO WHERE HE'S THE RULER OF EUROPE, ALL WESTERN HISTORY CHANGES--
--NO AMERICAN REVOLUTION, NO WHITE HOUSE, AND, HEY, I'M PROBABLY SAYING WAY TOO MUCH, SO I'LL STOP NOW.
The BLACK KNIGHT. GREATEST of Arthur's champions, wielder of the mystic EBONY BLADE that can cut through ABSOLUTELY ANYTHING.
ARTHUR, THE WAY YOU DESCRIBED HIS POWERS, I HAVE AN INKLING OF A PLAN--BUT IT'S TOTALLY DEPENDENT ON YOU, SIR.
NO. IF MINE IS TRULY THE PROWESS UPON WHICH WE MUST COUNT...
...THEN WE ARE MOST SURELY DOOMED.
IT WAS MY SWORN DUTY TO PROTECT ARTHUR AND HIS KINGDOM... AND I FAILED. I AM NO USE TO YOU.
AGREE TO DISAGREE. NO TIME TO DEBATE--
--BECAUSE WE'RE ALL ABOUT TO BE JELLY BETWEEN HULK'S TOES UNLESS MERLIN GETS US BACK TO CAMELOT--
--now NOW NOW!
RRRRRRR

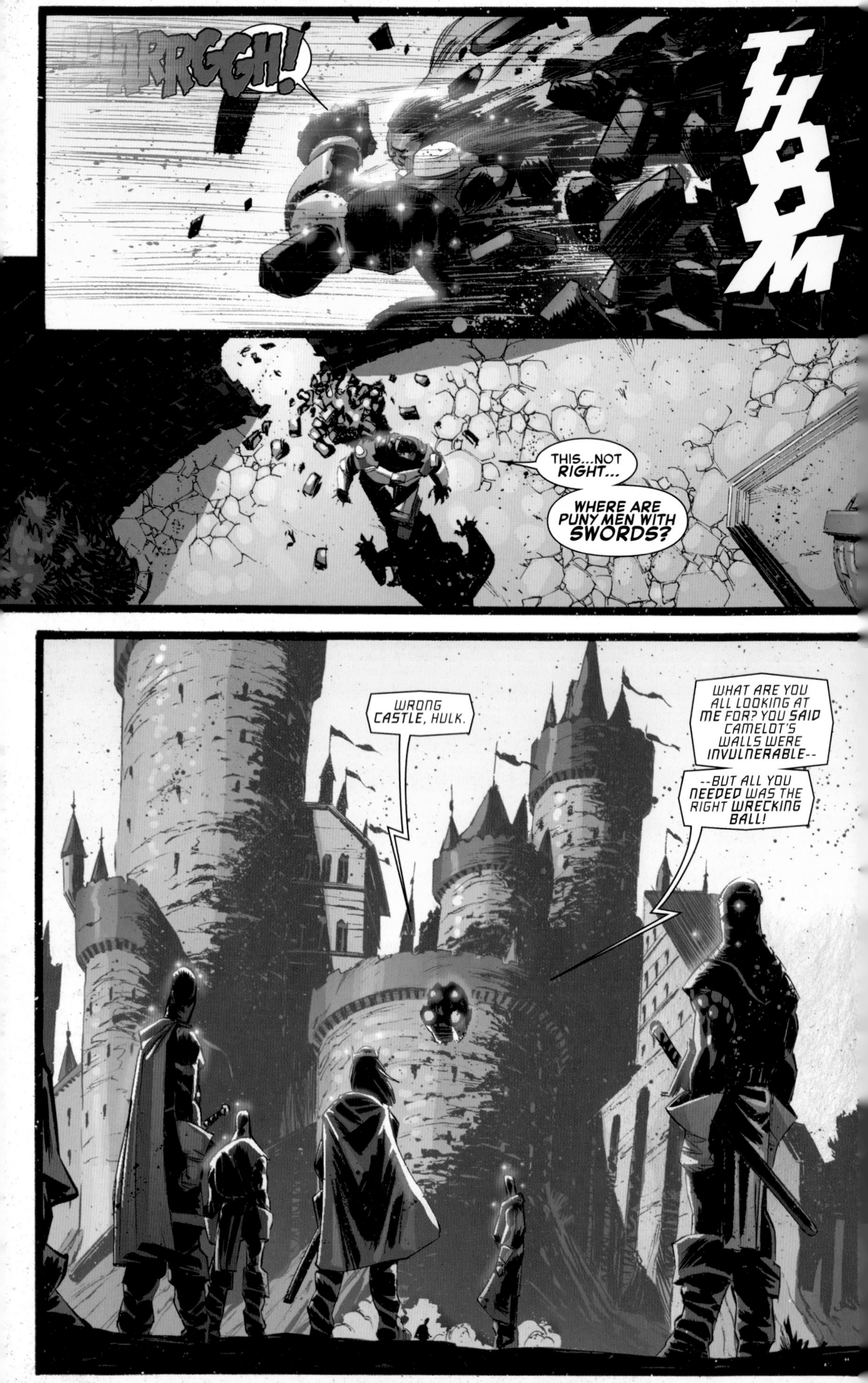
ARRGGH!
THOOM
THIS...NOT RIGHT...
WHERE ARE PUNY MEN WITH SWORDS?
WRONG CASTLE, HULK.
WHAT ARE YOU ALL LOOKING AT ME FOR? YOU SAID CAMELOT'S WALLS WERE INVULNERABLE--
--BUT ALL YOU NEEDED WAS THE RIGHT WRECKING BALL!

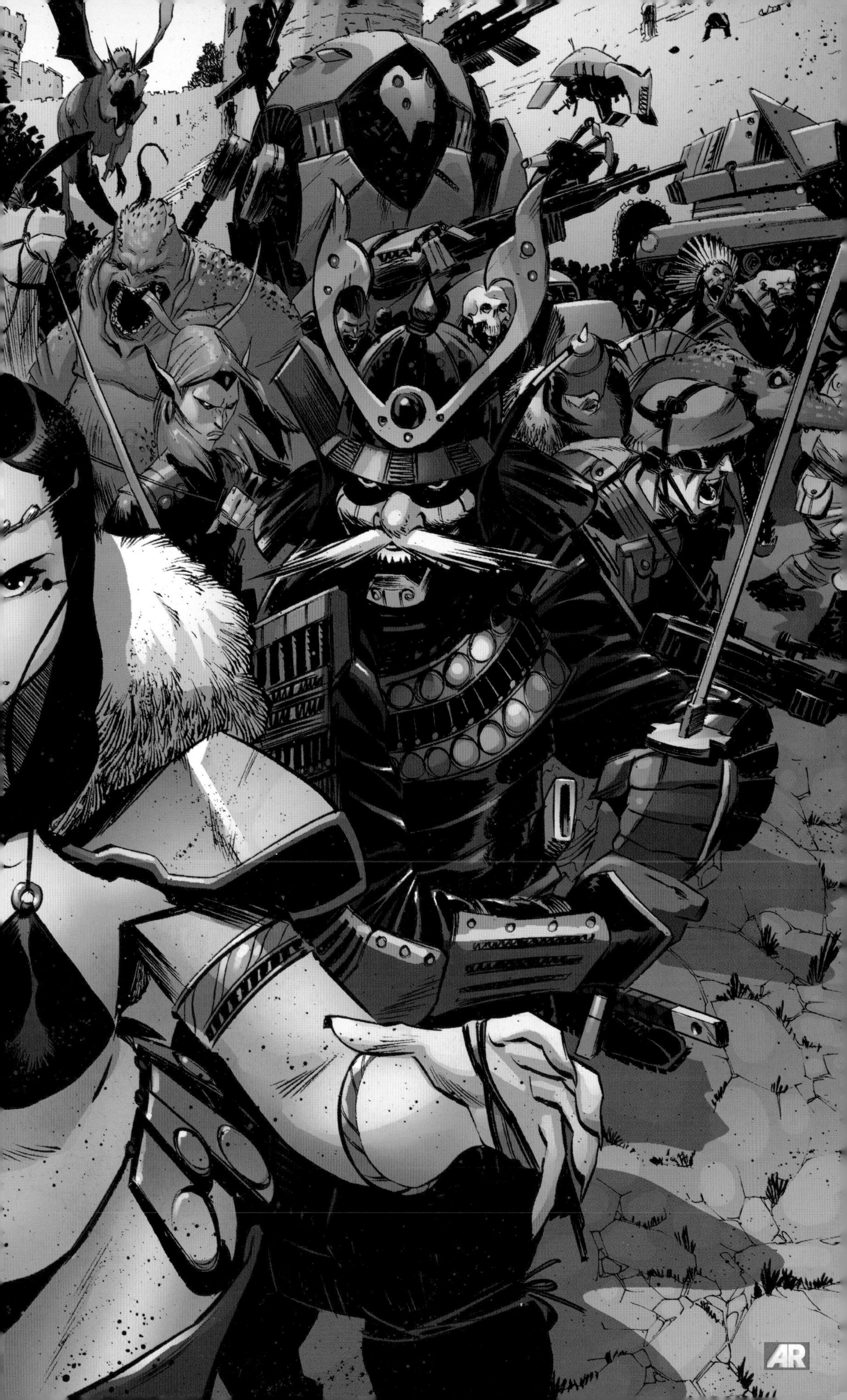

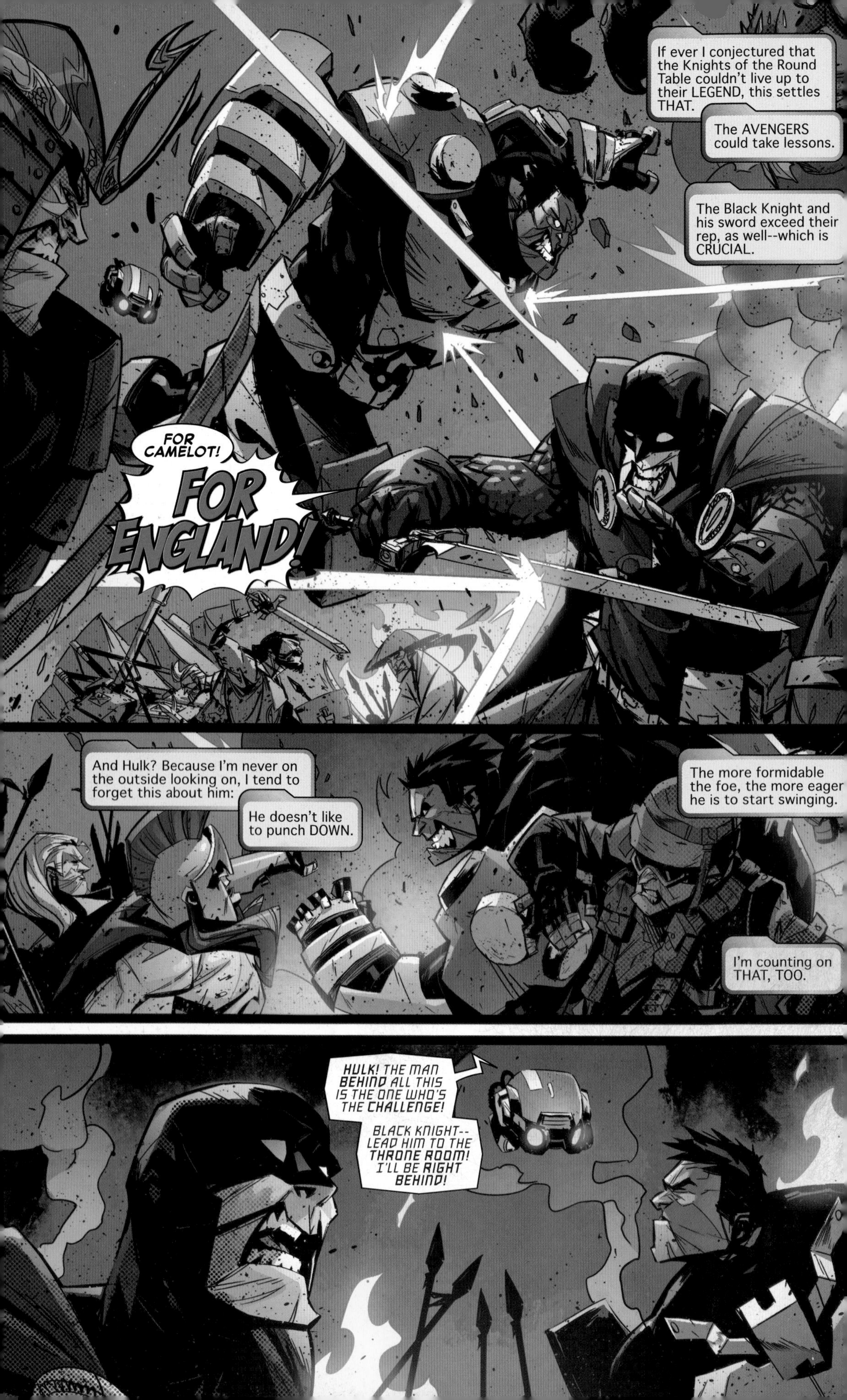

If ever I conjectured that the Knights of the Round Table couldn't live up to their LEGEND, this settles THAT.
The AVENGERS could take lessons.
The Black Knight and his sword exceed their rep, as well--which is CRUCIAL.
FOR CAMELOT!
FOR ENGLAND!
And Hulk? Because I'm never on the outside looking on, I tend to forget this about him:
He doesn't like to punch DOWN.
The more formidable the foe, the more eager he is to start swinging.
I'm counting on THAT, TOO.
HULK! THE MAN BEHIND ALL THIS IS THE ONE WHO'S THE CHALLENGE!
BLACK KNIGHT-- LEAD HIM TO THE THRONE ROOM! I'LL BE RIGHT BEHIND!

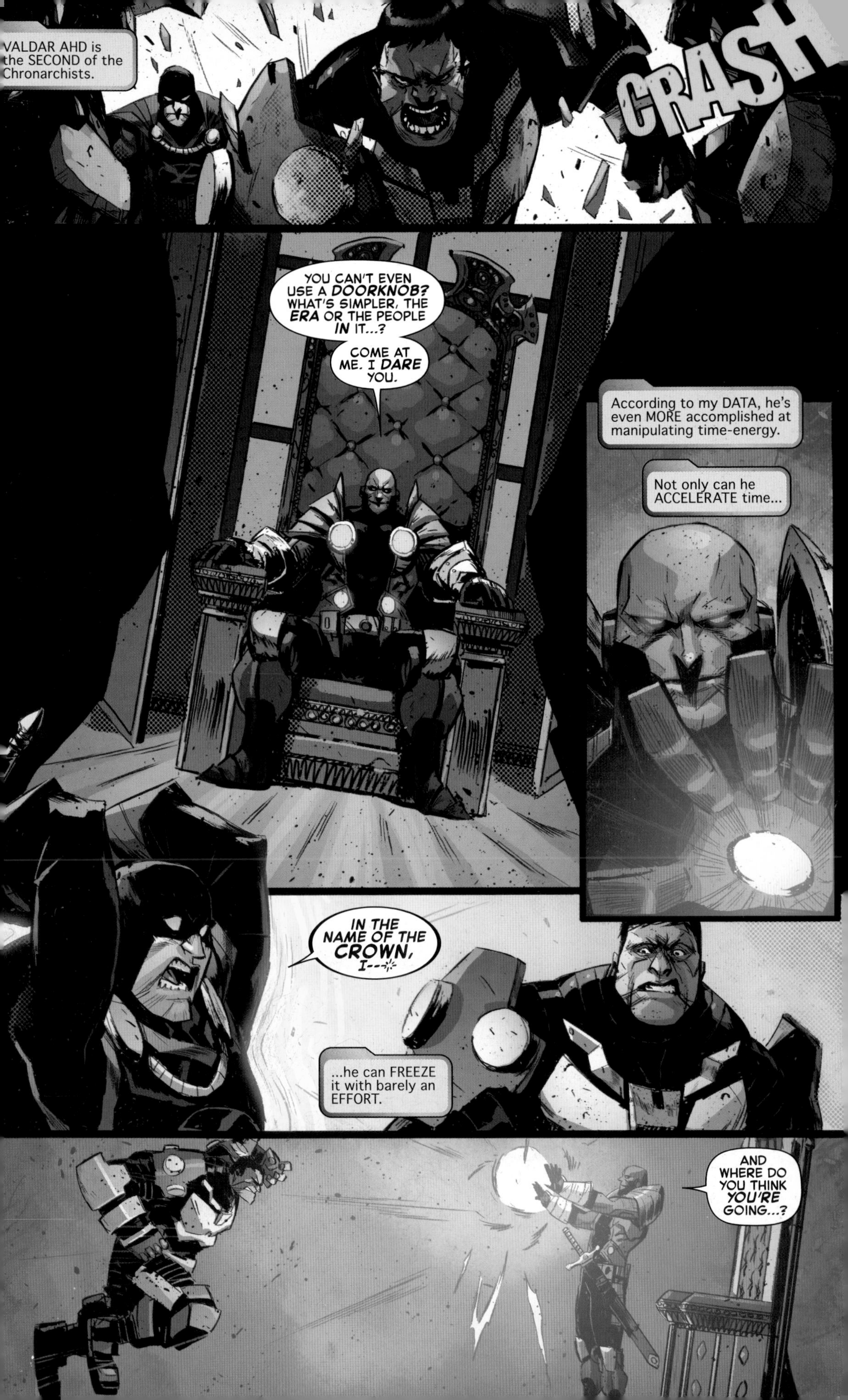
VALDAR AHD is the SECOND of the Chronarchists.
CRASH
YOU CAN'T EVEN USE A DOORKNOB? WHAT'S SIMPLER, THE ERA OR THE PEOPLE IN IT...?
COME AT ME. I DARE YOU.
According to my DATA, he's even MORE accomplished at manipulating time-energy.
Not only can he ACCELERATE time...
IN THE NAME OF THE CROWN, I--
...he can FREEZE it with barely an EFFORT.
AND WHERE DO YOU THINK YOU'RE GOING...?

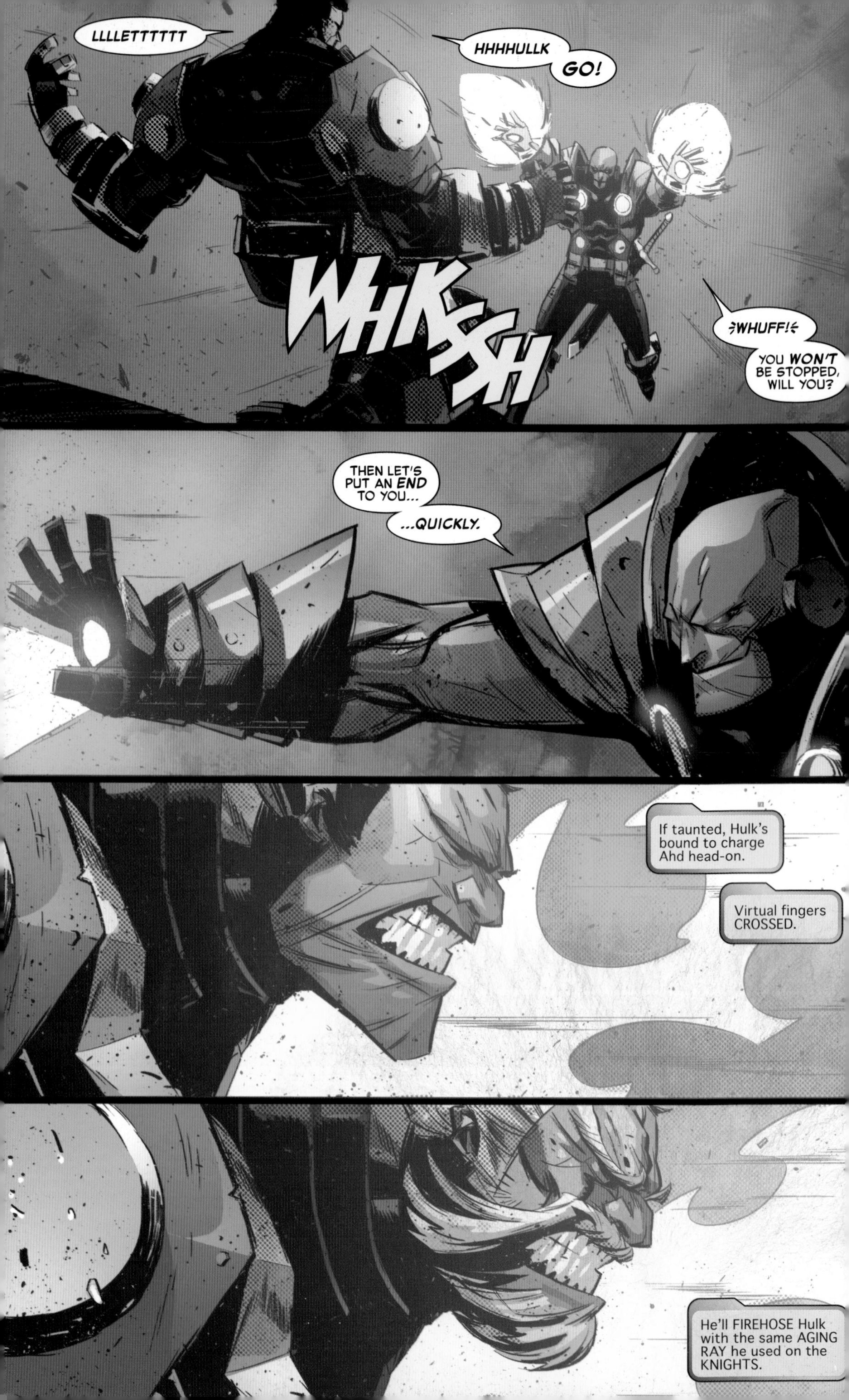
LLLLETTTTTT
HHHHULLK
GO!
WHKSSH
⪢WHUFF!⪡
YOU WON'T BE STOPPED, WILL YOU?
THEN LET'S PUT AN END TO YOU...
...QUICKLY.
If taunted, Hulk's bound to charge Ahd head-on.
Virtual fingers CROSSED.
He'll FIREHOSE Hulk with the same AGING RAY he used on the KNIGHTS.

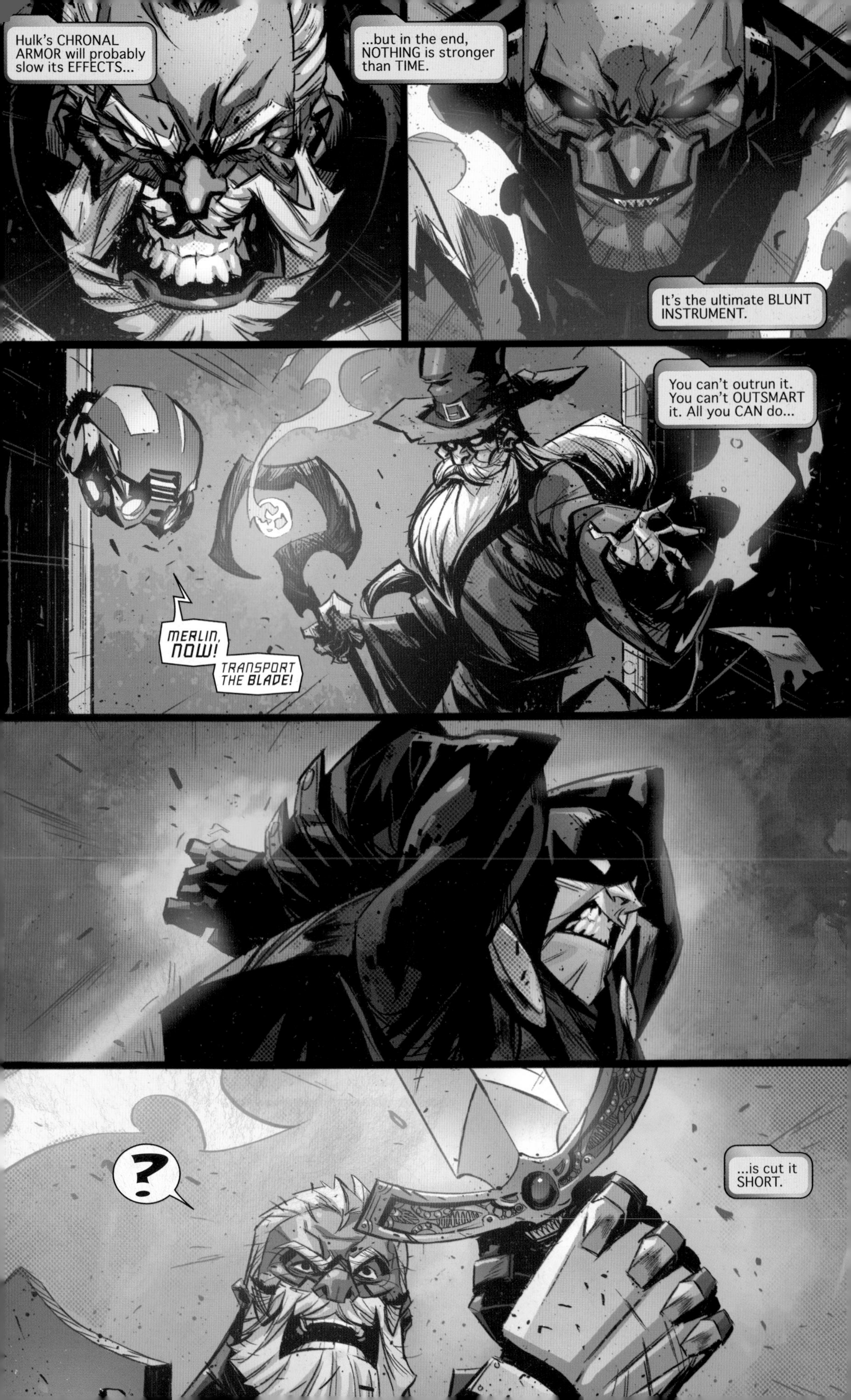
Hulk's CHRONAL ARMOR will probably slow its EFFECTS...
...but in the end, NOTHING is stronger than TIME.
It's the ultimate BLUNT INSTRUMENT.
You can't outrun it. You can't OUTSMART it. All you CAN do...
MERLIN, NOW!
TRANSPORT THE BLADE!
?
...is cut it SHORT.

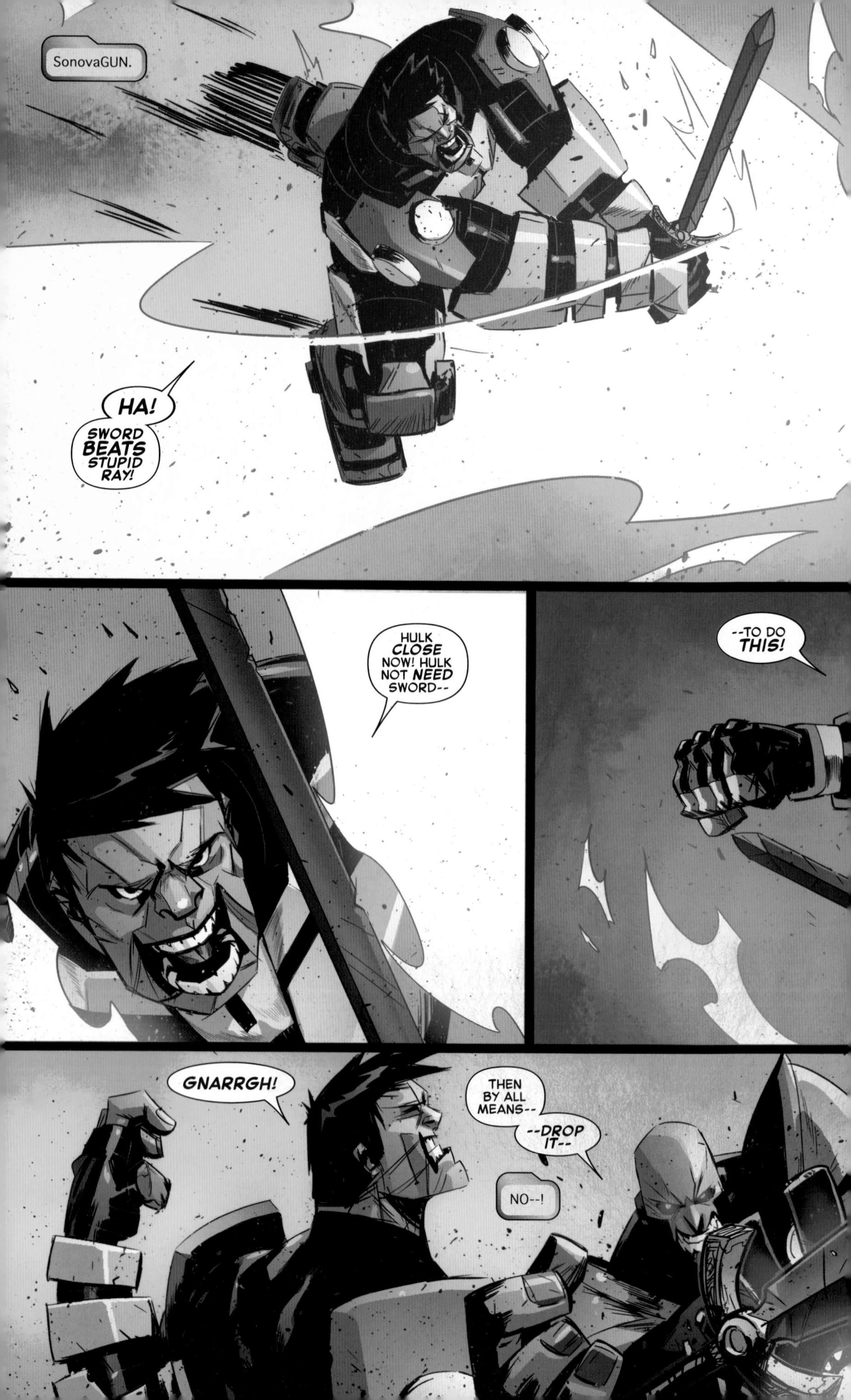
SonovaGUN.
HA! SWORD BEATS STUPID RAY!
HULK CLOSE NOW! HULK NOT NEED SWORD--
--TO DO THIS!
GNARRGH!
THEN BY ALL MEANS--
--DROP IT--
NO--!

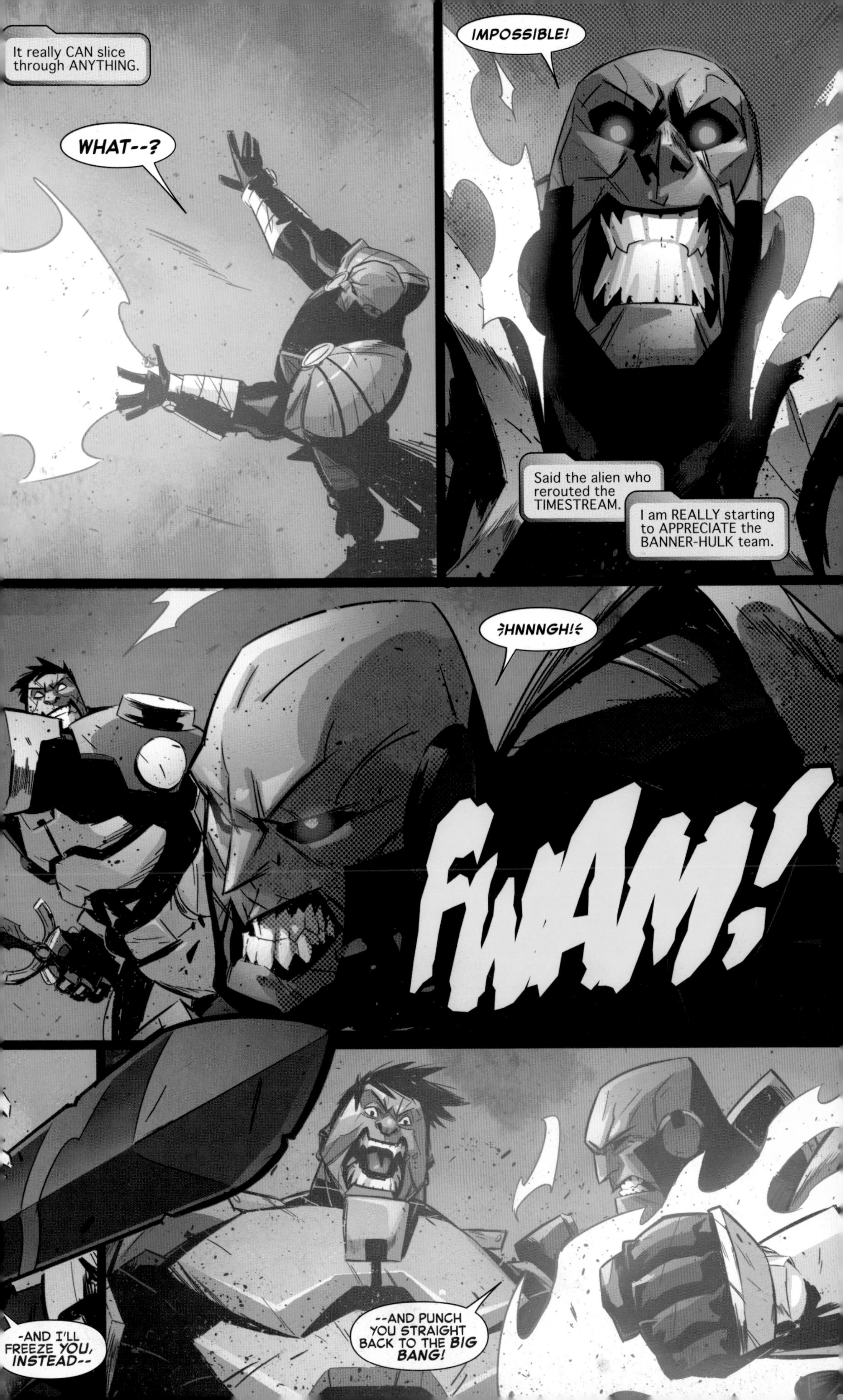
It really CAN slice through ANYTHING.
WHAT--?
IMPOSSIBLE!
Said the alien who rerouted the TIMESTREAM.
I am REALLY starting to APPRECIATE the BANNER-HULK team.
HNNNGH!
FWAM!
-AND I'LL FREEZE YOU, INSTEAD--
--AND PUNCH YOU STRAIGHT BACK TO THE BIG BANG!

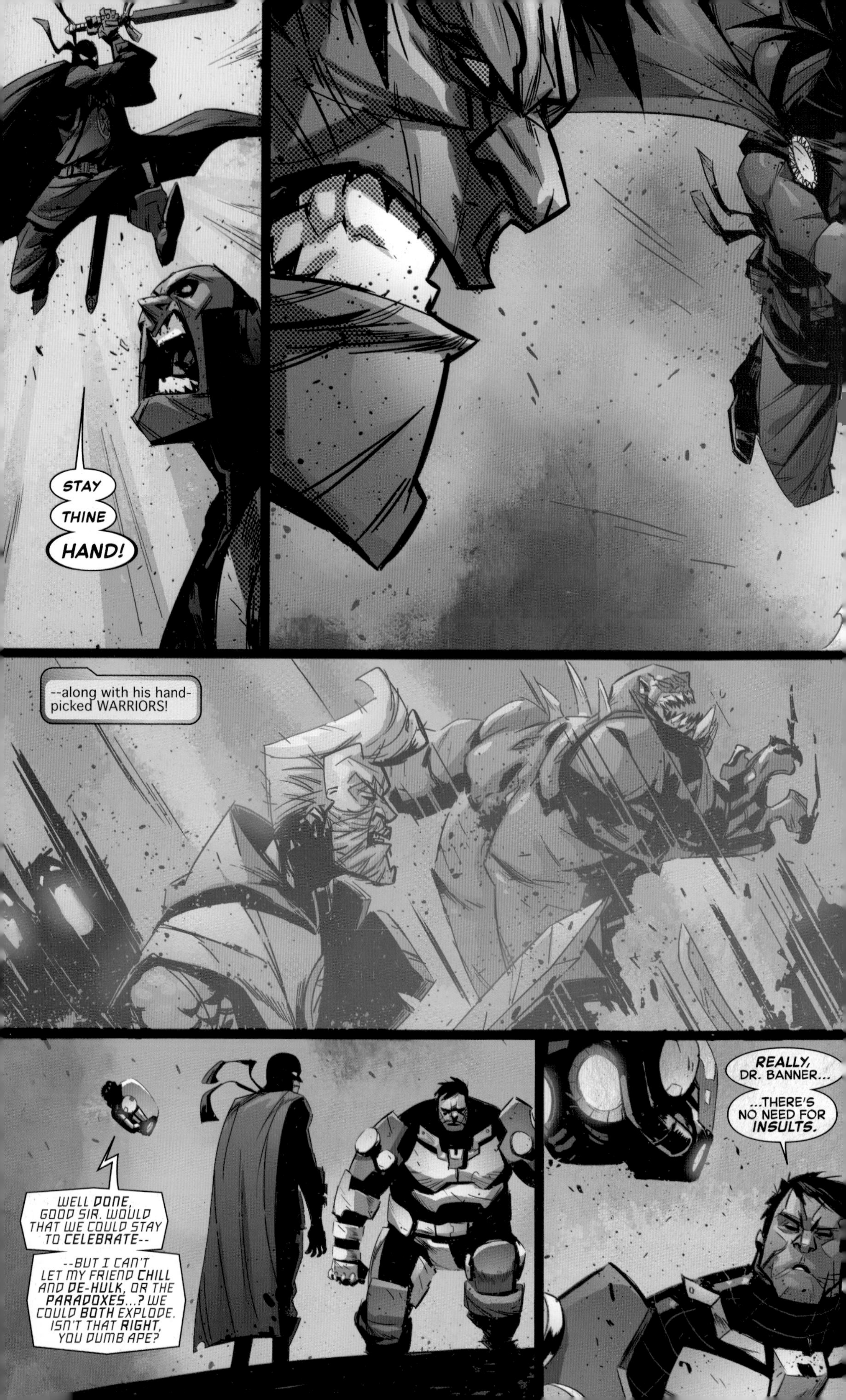
STAY THINE HAND!
--along with his hand-picked WARRIORS!
WELL DONE, GOOD SIR. WOULD THAT WE COULD STAY TO CELEBRATE--
--BUT I CAN'T LET MY FRIEND CHILL AND DE-HULK, OR THE PARADOXES...? WE COULD BOTH EXPLODE. ISN'T THAT RIGHT, YOU DUMB APE?
REALLY, DR. BANNER...
...THERE'S NO NEED FOR INSULTS.

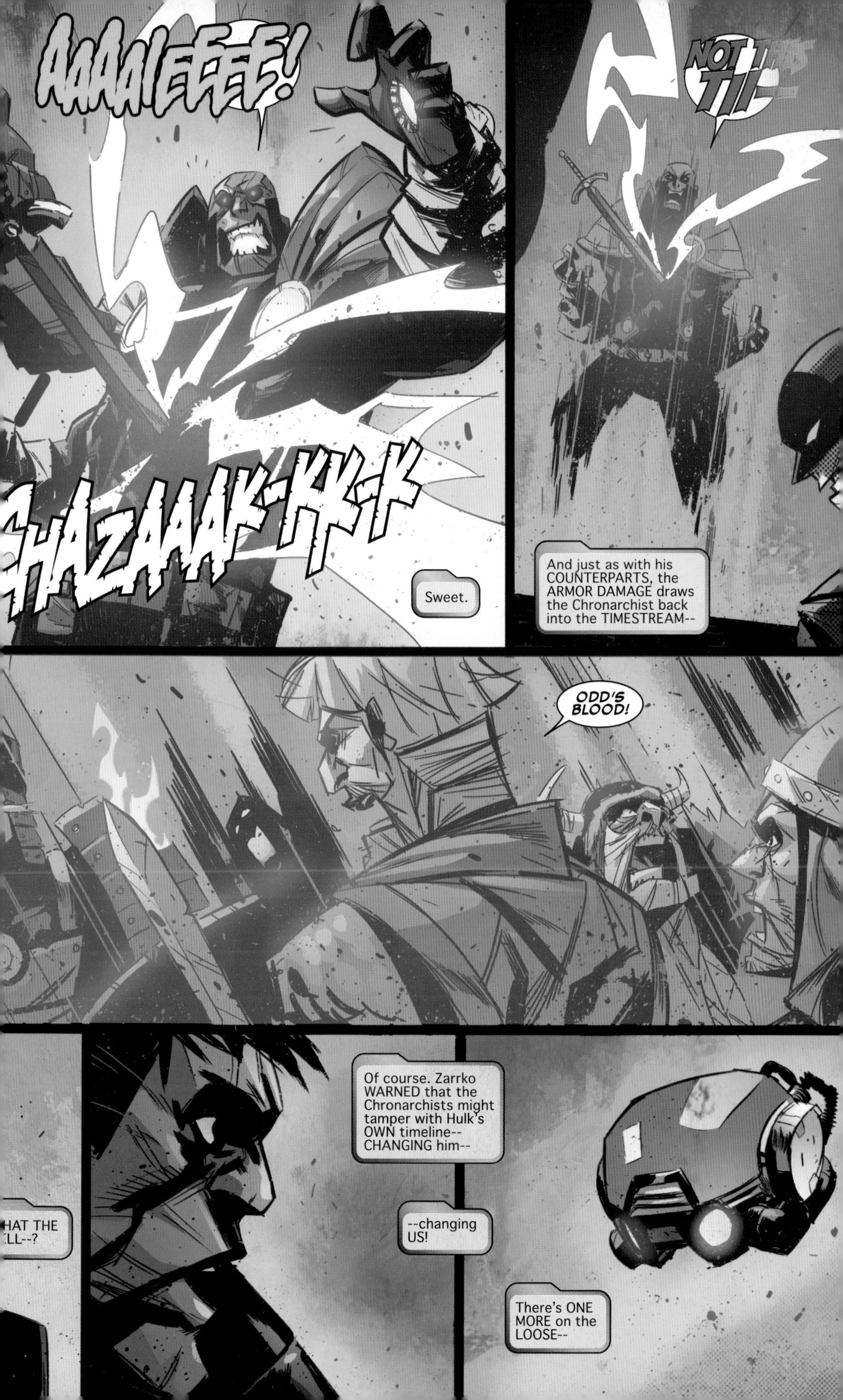
AAAAIEEEE!
CHAZAAAK-KK-K
Sweet.
NOT
And just as with his COUNTERPARTS, the ARMOR DAMAGE draws the Chronarchist back into the TIMESTREAM--
ODD'S BLOOD!
HAT THE
LL--?
Of course. Zarrko WARNED that the Chronarchists might tamper with Hulk's OWN timeline-- CHANGING him--
--changing US!
There's ONE MORE on the LOOSE--

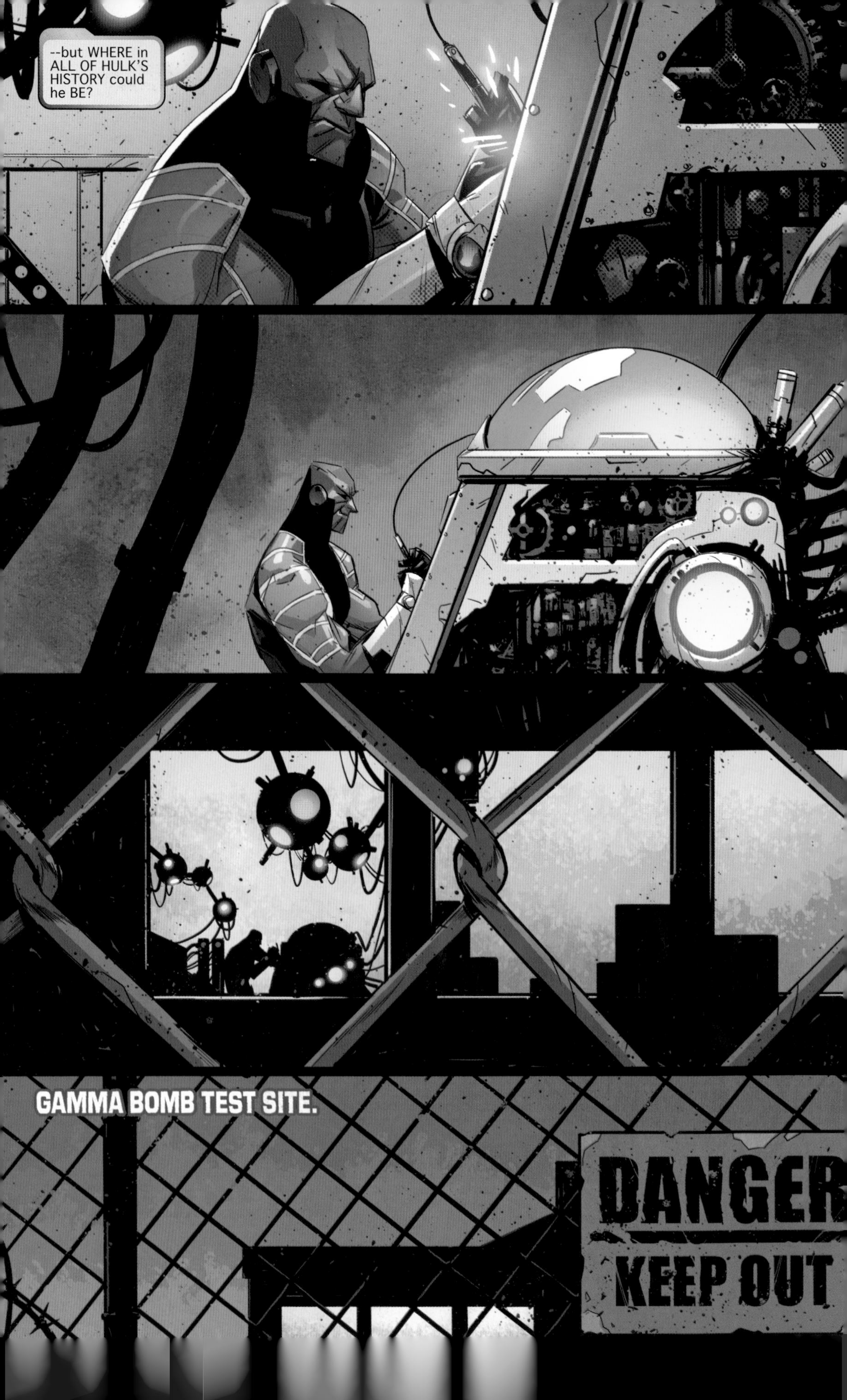
--but WHERE in ALL OF HULK'S HISTORY could he BE?
GAMMA BOMB TEST SITE.
DANGER
KEEP OUT

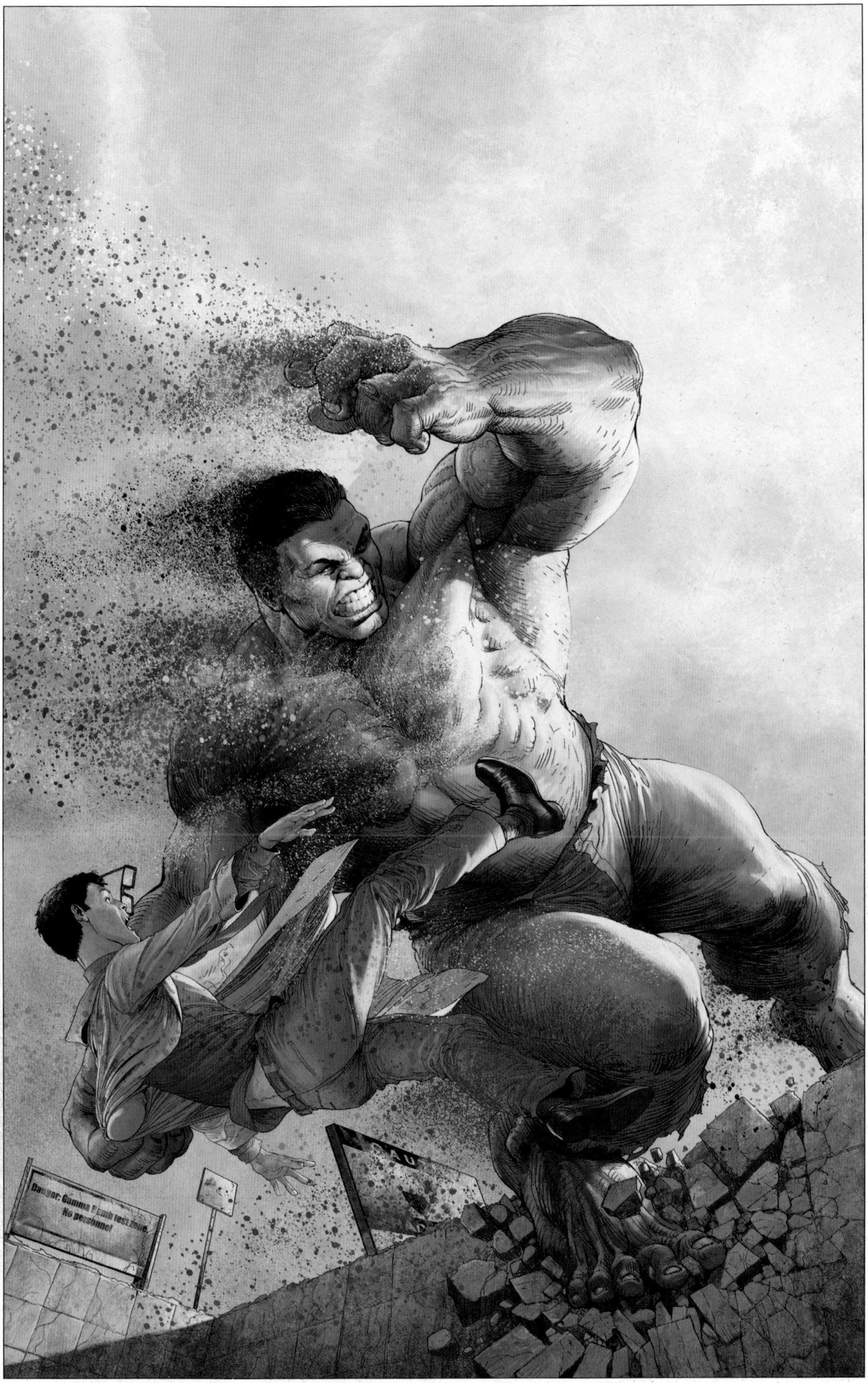

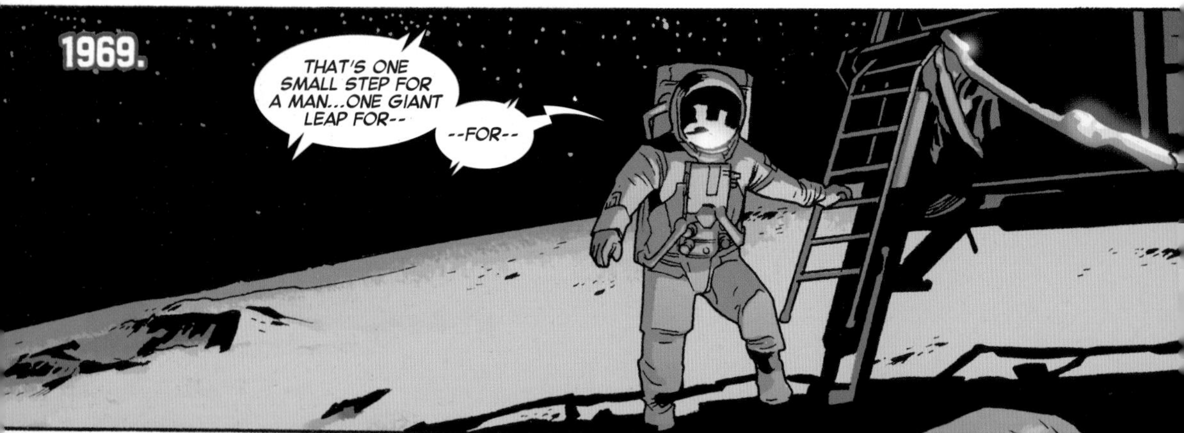
1969.
THAT'S ONE SMALL STEP FOR A MAN...ONE GIANT LEAP FOR--
--FOR--

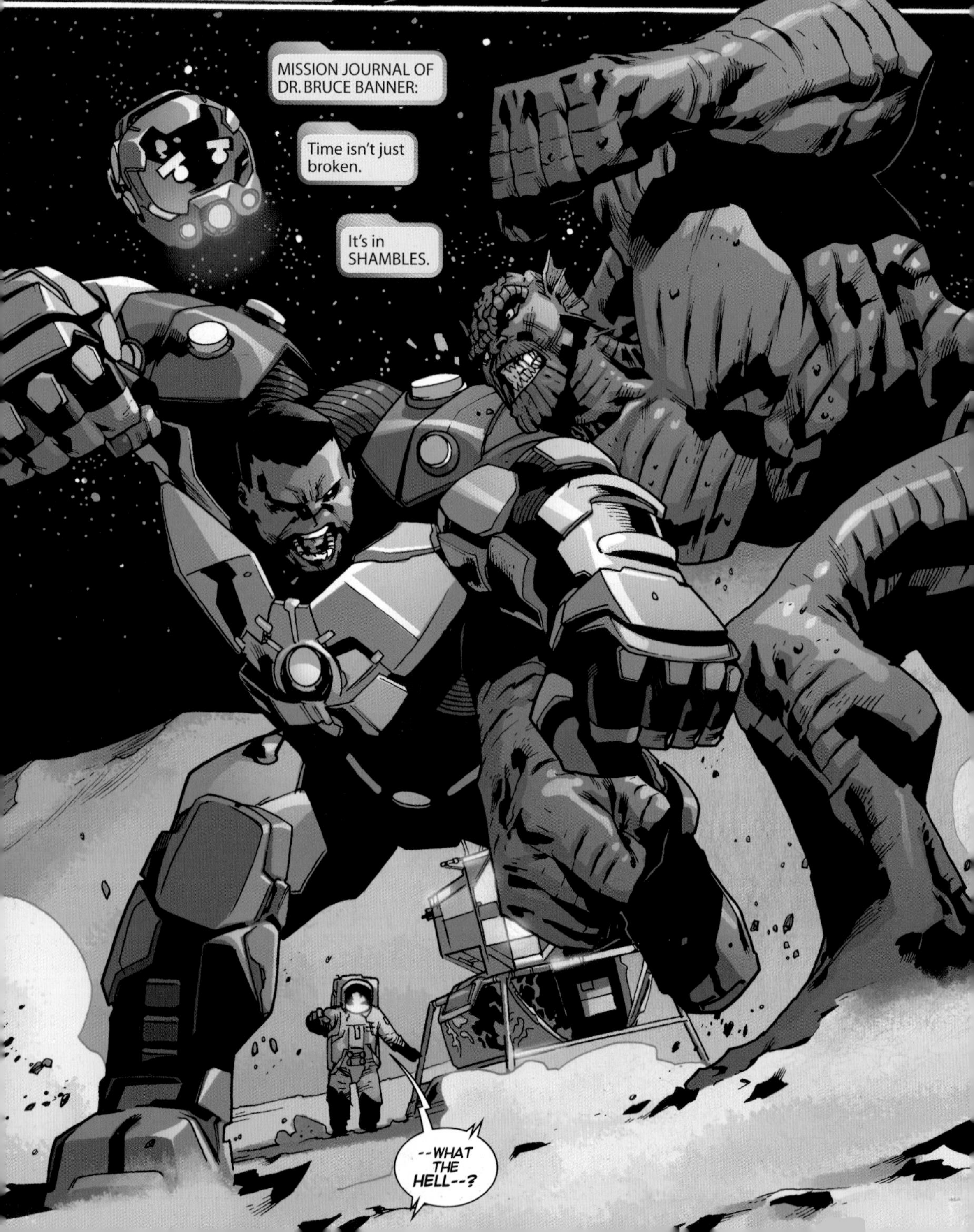
MISSION JOURNAL OF DR. BRUCE BANNER:
Time isn't just broken.
It's in SHAMBLES.
--WHAT THE HELL--?

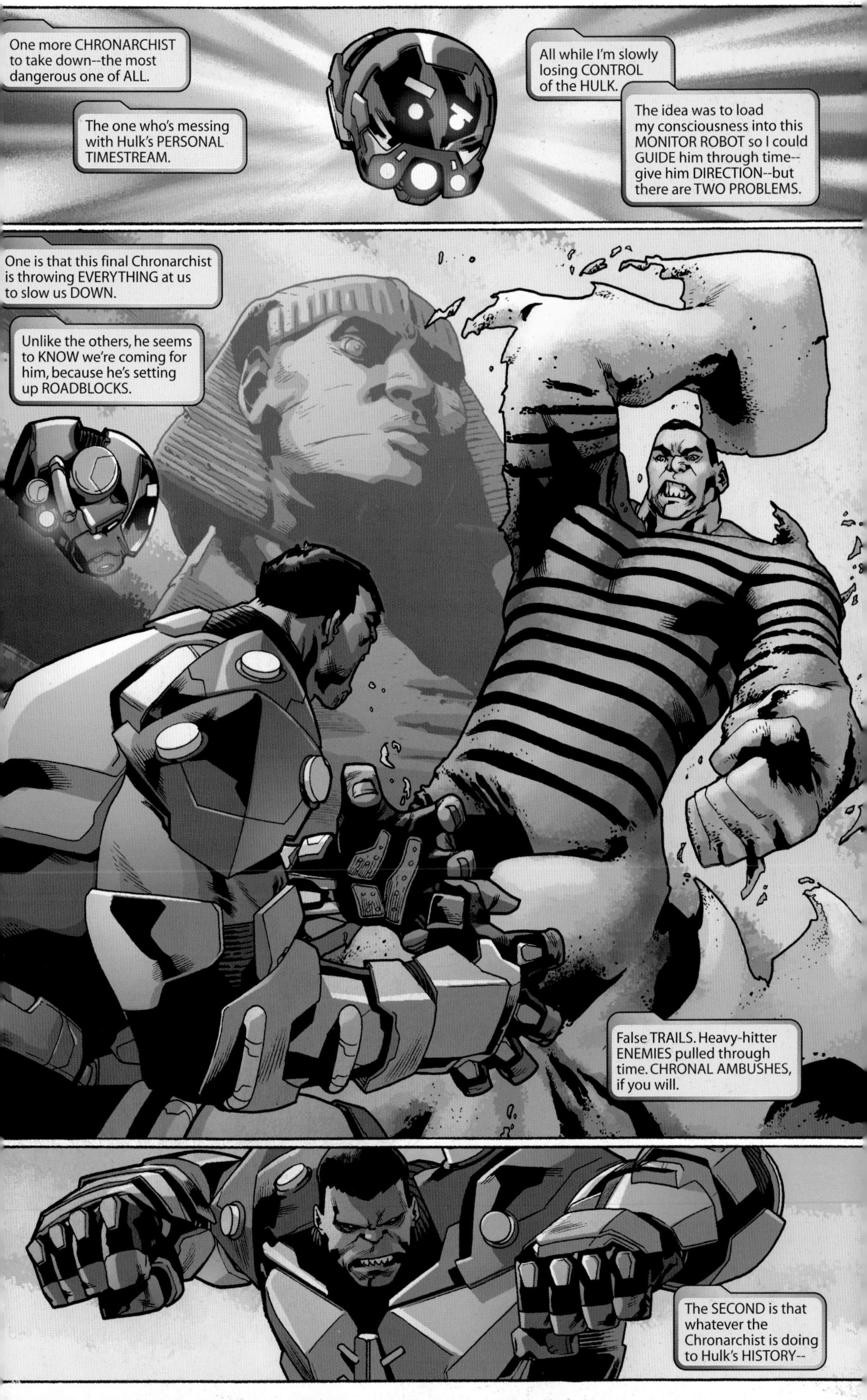
One more CHRONARCHIST to take down--the most dangerous one of ALL.
The one who's messing with Hulk's PERSONAL TIMESTREAM.
All while I'm slowly losing CONTROL of the HULK.
The idea was to load my consciousness into this MONITOR ROBOT so I could GUIDE him through time--give him DIRECTION--but there are TWO PROBLEMS.
One is that this final Chronarchist is throwing EVERYTHING at us to slow us DOWN.
Unlike the others, he seems to KNOW we're coming for him, because he's setting up ROADBLOCKS.
False TRAILS. Heavy-hitter ENEMIES pulled through time. CHRONAL AMBUSHES, if you will.
The SECOND is that whatever the Chronarchist is doing to Hulk's HISTORY--

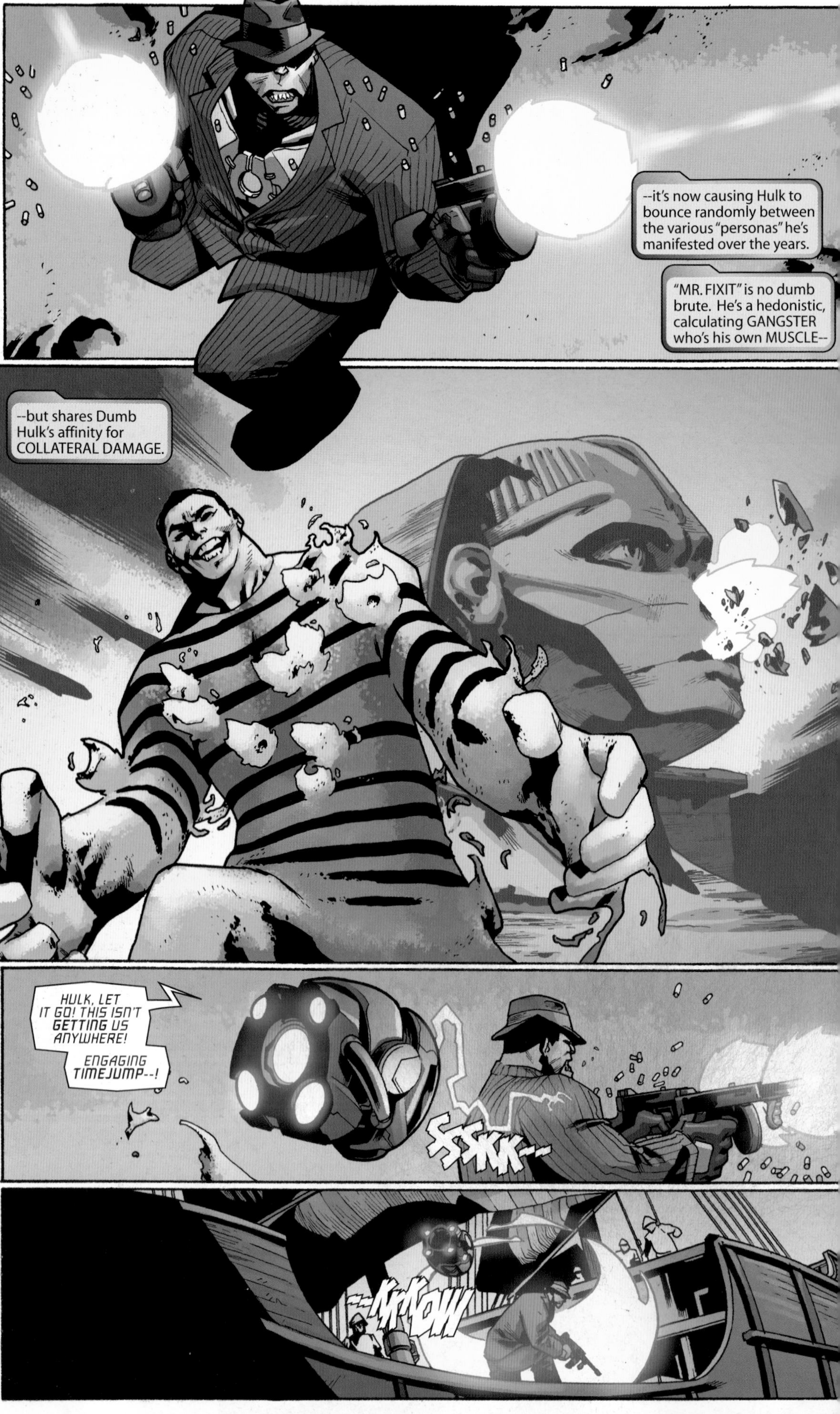
--it's now causing Hulk to bounce randomly between the various "personas" he's manifested over the years.
"MR. FIXIT" is no dumb brute. He's a hedonistic, calculating GANGSTER who's his own MUSCLE--
--but shares Dumb Hulk's affinity for COLLATERAL DAMAGE.
HULK, LET IT GO! THIS ISN'T GETTING US ANYWHERE!
ENGAGING TIMEJUMP--!
SSSKK--
--KRKOW

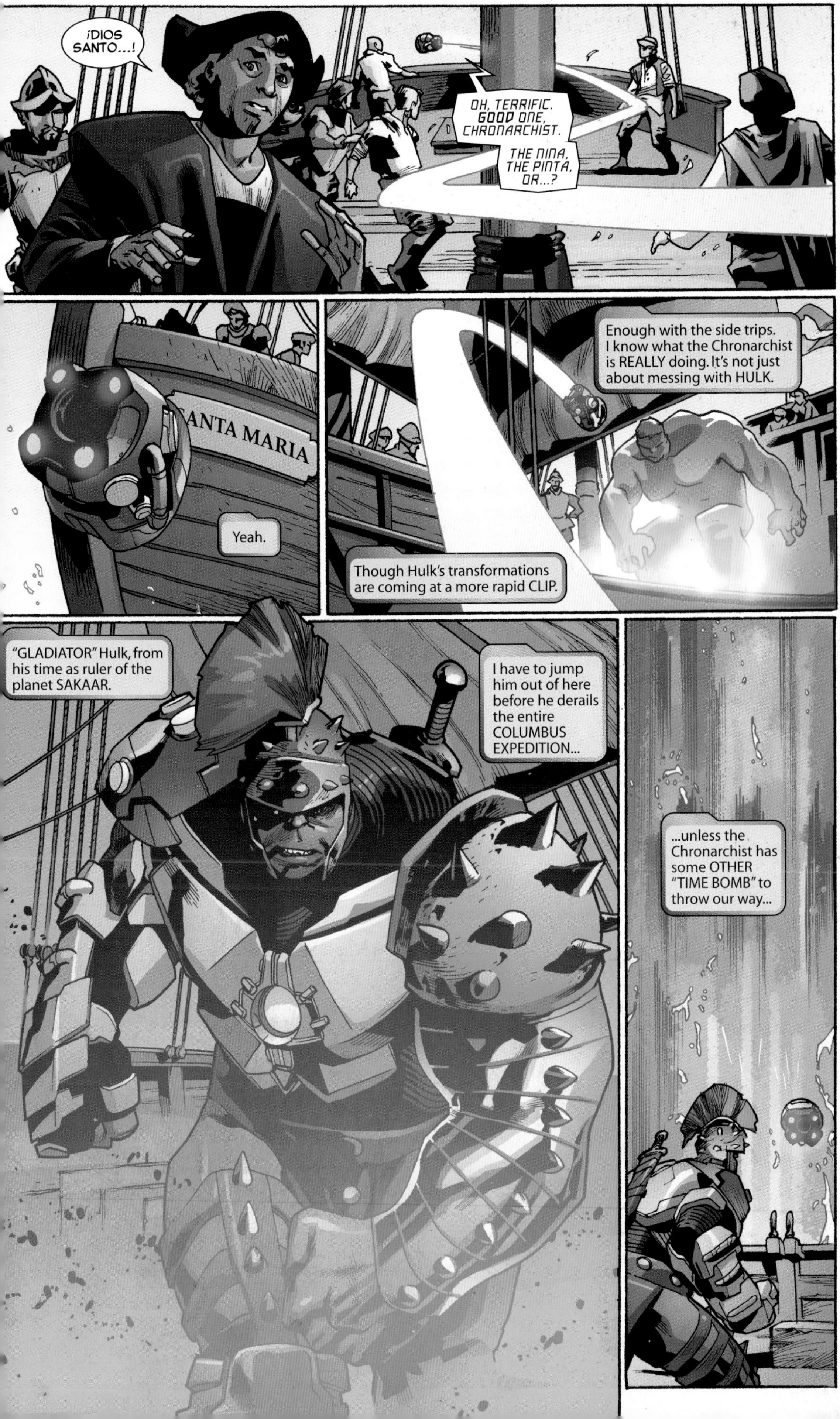

¡DIOS SANTO...!
OH, TERRIFIC. GOOD ONE, CHRONARCHIST.
THE NINA, THE PINTA, OR...?
SANTA MARIA
Yeah.
Enough with the side trips. I know what the Chronarchist is REALLY doing. It's not just about messing with HULK.
Though Hulk's transformations are coming at a more rapid CLIP.
"GLADIATOR" Hulk, from his time as ruler of the planet SAKAAR.
I have to jump him out of here before he derails the entire COLUMBUS EXPEDITION...
...unless the Chronarchist has some OTHER "TIME BOMB" to throw our way...

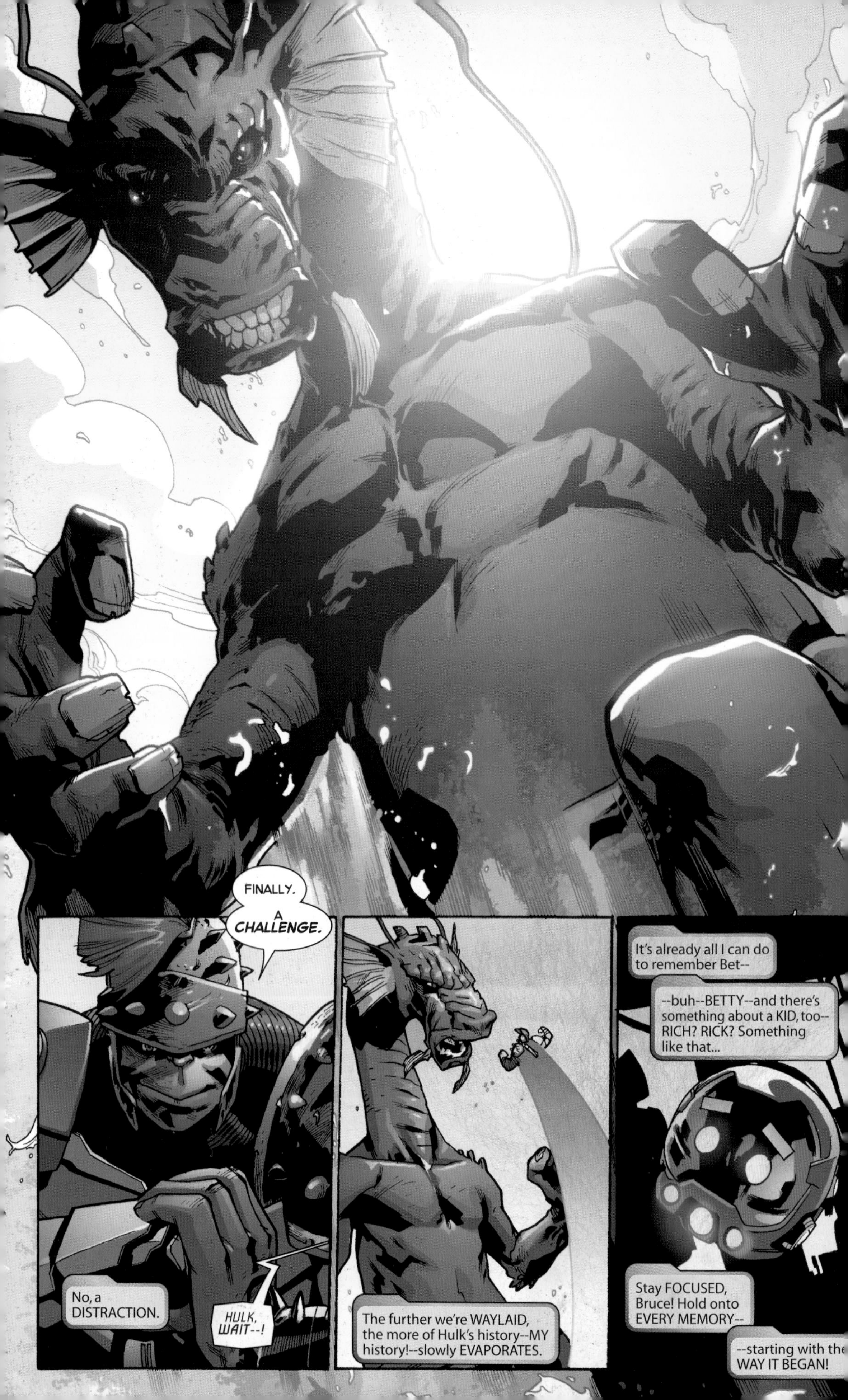
FINALLY.
A CHALLENGE.
No, a DISTRACTION.
HULK, WAIT--!
The further we're WAYLAID, the more of Hulk's history--MY history!--slowly EVAPORATES.
It's already all I can do to remember Bet--
--buh--BETTY--and there's something about a KID, too--RICH? RICK? Something like that...
Stay FOCUSED, Bruce! Hold onto EVERY MEMORY--
--starting with the WAY IT BEGAN!

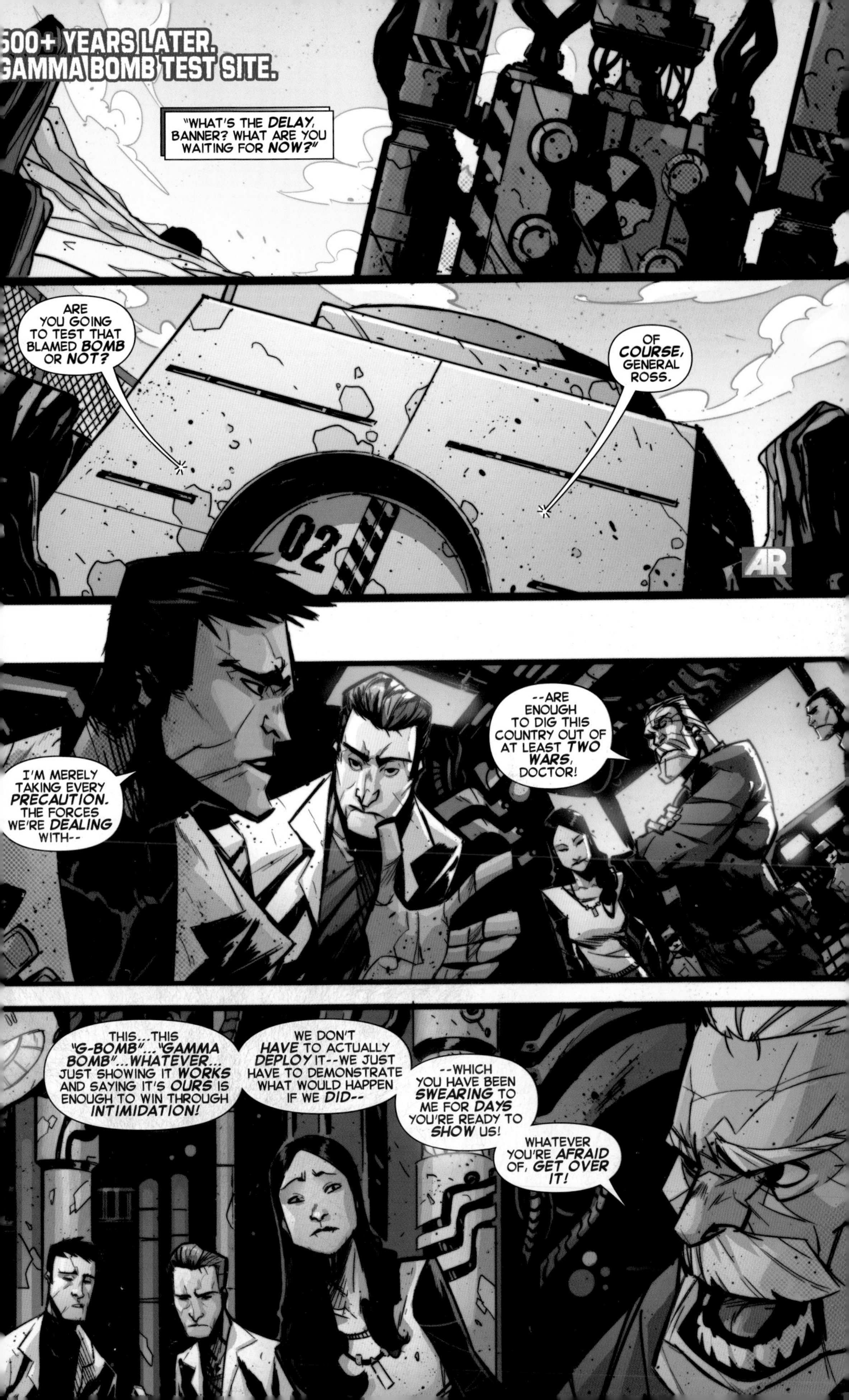
500+ YEARS LATER. GAMMA BOMB TEST SITE.
"WHAT'S THE DELAY, BANNER? WHAT ARE YOU WAITING FOR NOW?"
ARE YOU GOING TO TEST THAT BLAMED BOMB OR NOT?
OF COURSE, GENERAL ROSS.
02
I'M MERELY TAKING EVERY PRECAUTION. THE FORCES WE'RE DEALING WITH--
--ARE ENOUGH TO DIG THIS COUNTRY OUT OF AT LEAST TWO WARS, DOCTOR!
THIS...THIS "G-BOMB"..."GAMMA BOMB"...WHATEVER... JUST SHOWING IT WORKS AND SAYING IT'S OURS IS ENOUGH TO WIN THROUGH INTIMIDATION!
WE DON'T HAVE TO ACTUALLY DEPLOY IT--WE JUST HAVE TO DEMONSTRATE WHAT WOULD HAPPEN IF WE DID--
--WHICH YOU HAVE BEEN SWEARING TO ME FOR DAYS YOU'RE READY TO SHOW US!
WHATEVER YOU'RE AFRAID OF, GET OVER IT!

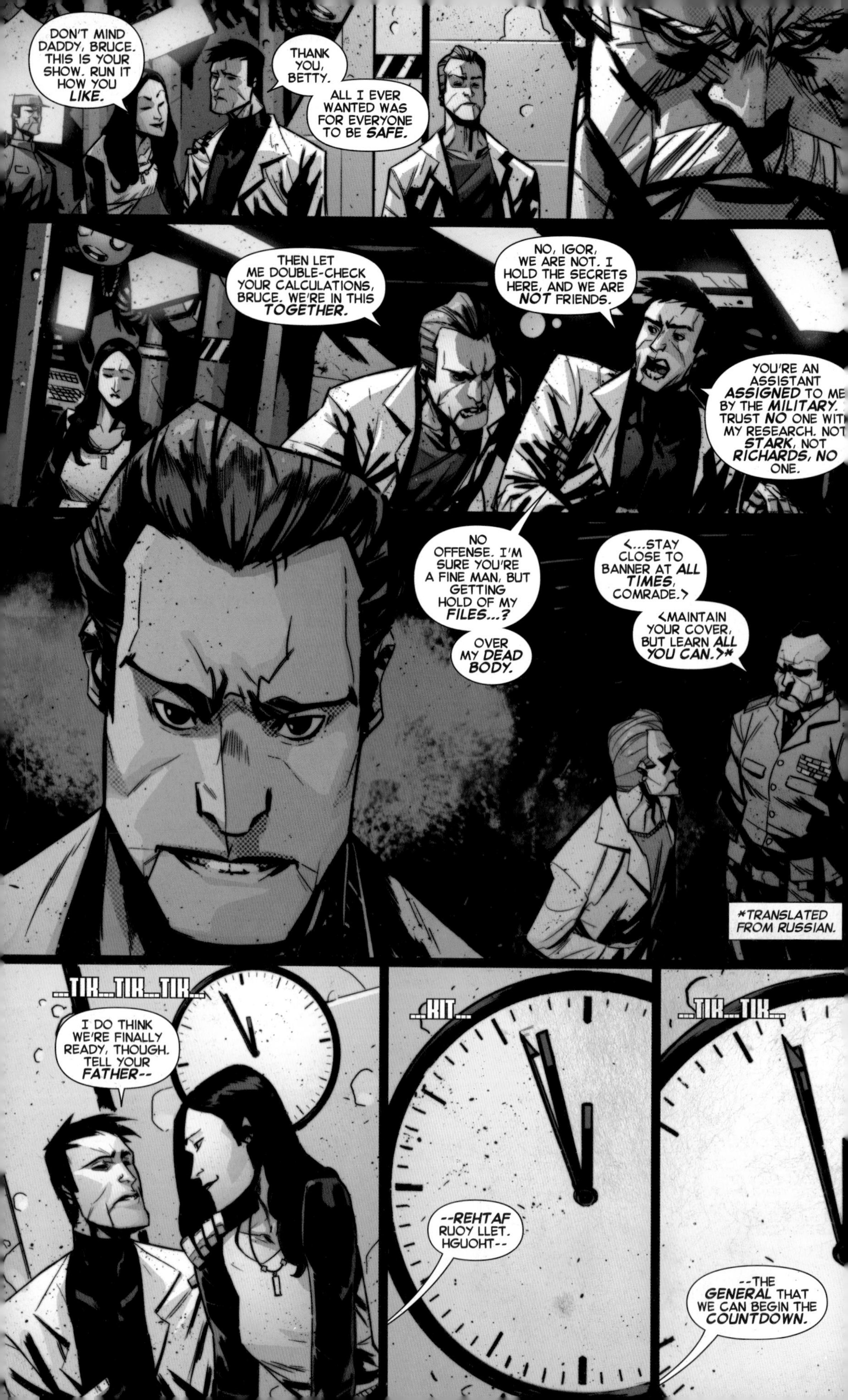
DON'T MIND DADDY, BRUCE. THIS IS YOUR SHOW. RUN IT HOW YOU LIKE.
THANK YOU, BETTY.
ALL I EVER WANTED WAS FOR EVERYONE TO BE SAFE.
THEN LET ME DOUBLE-CHECK YOUR CALCULATIONS, BRUCE. WE'RE IN THIS TOGETHER.
NO, IGOR, WE ARE NOT. I HOLD THE SECRETS HERE, AND WE ARE NOT FRIENDS.
YOU'RE AN ASSISTANT ASSIGNED TO ME BY THE MILITARY. TRUST NO ONE WITH MY RESEARCH. NOT STARK, NOT RICHARDS, NO ONE.
NO OFFENSE. I'M SURE YOU'RE A FINE MAN, BUT GETTING HOLD OF MY FILES...?
OVER MY DEAD BODY.
<...STAY CLOSE TO BANNER AT ALL TIMES, COMRADE.>
<MAINTAIN YOUR COVER, BUT LEARN ALL YOU CAN.>*
*TRANSLATED FROM RUSSIAN.
...TIK...TIK...TIK...
I DO THINK WE'RE FINALLY READY, THOUGH. TELL YOUR FATHER--
...KIT...
--REHTAF RUOY LLET. HGUOHT--
...TIK...TIK...
--THE GENERAL THAT WE CAN BEGIN THE COUNTDOWN.

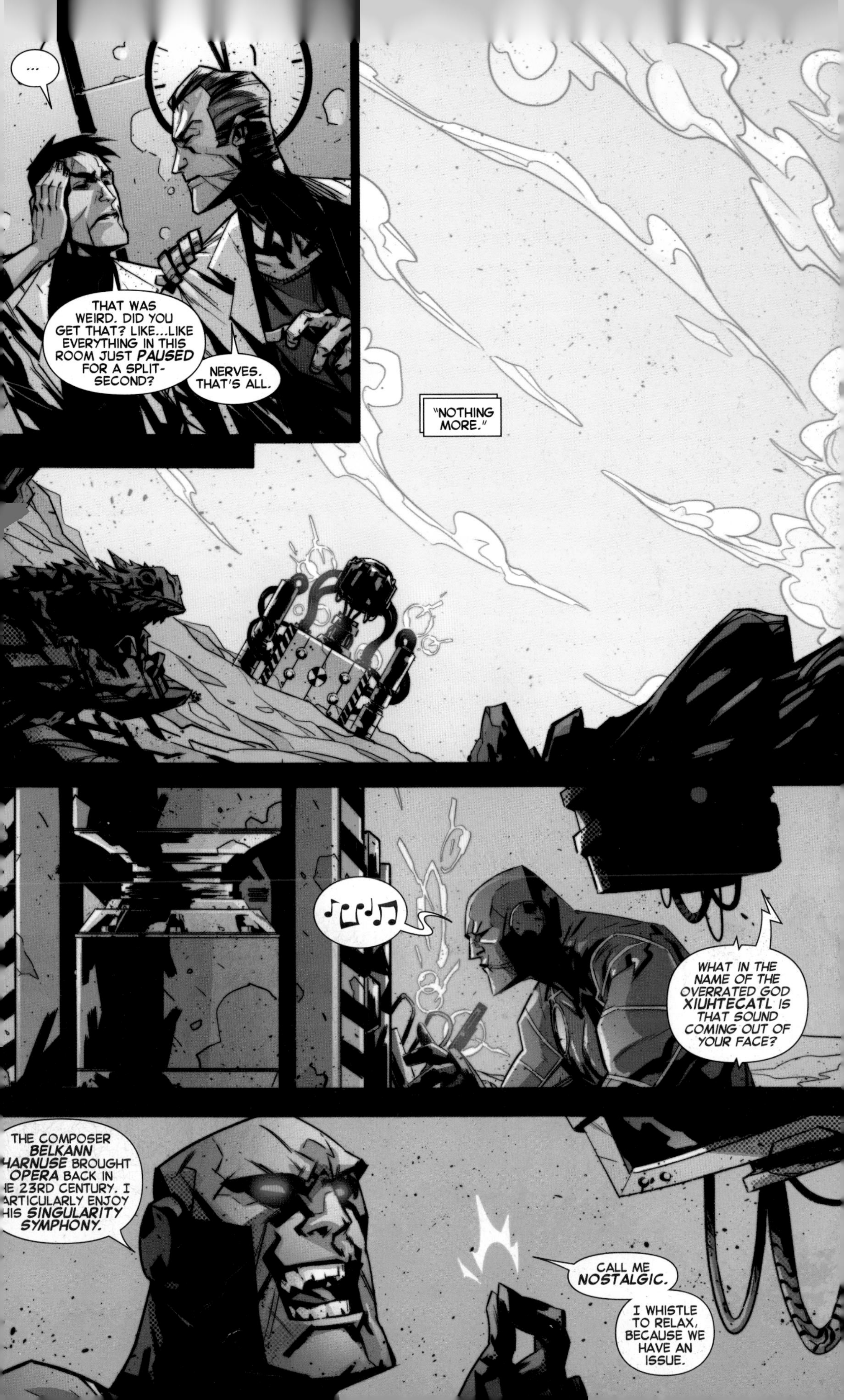
...
THAT WAS WEIRD. DID YOU GET THAT? LIKE...LIKE EVERYTHING IN THIS ROOM JUST PAUSED FOR A SPLIT-SECOND?
NERVES. THAT'S ALL.
"NOTHING MORE."
WHAT IN THE NAME OF THE OVERRATED GOD XIUHTECATL IS THAT SOUND COMING OUT OF YOUR FACE?
THE COMPOSER BELKANN HARNUSE BROUGHT OPERA BACK IN THE 23RD CENTURY. I PARTICULARLY ENJOY HIS SINGULARITY SYMPHONY.
CALL ME NOSTALGIC.
I WHISTLE TO RELAX, BECAUSE WE HAVE AN ISSUE.

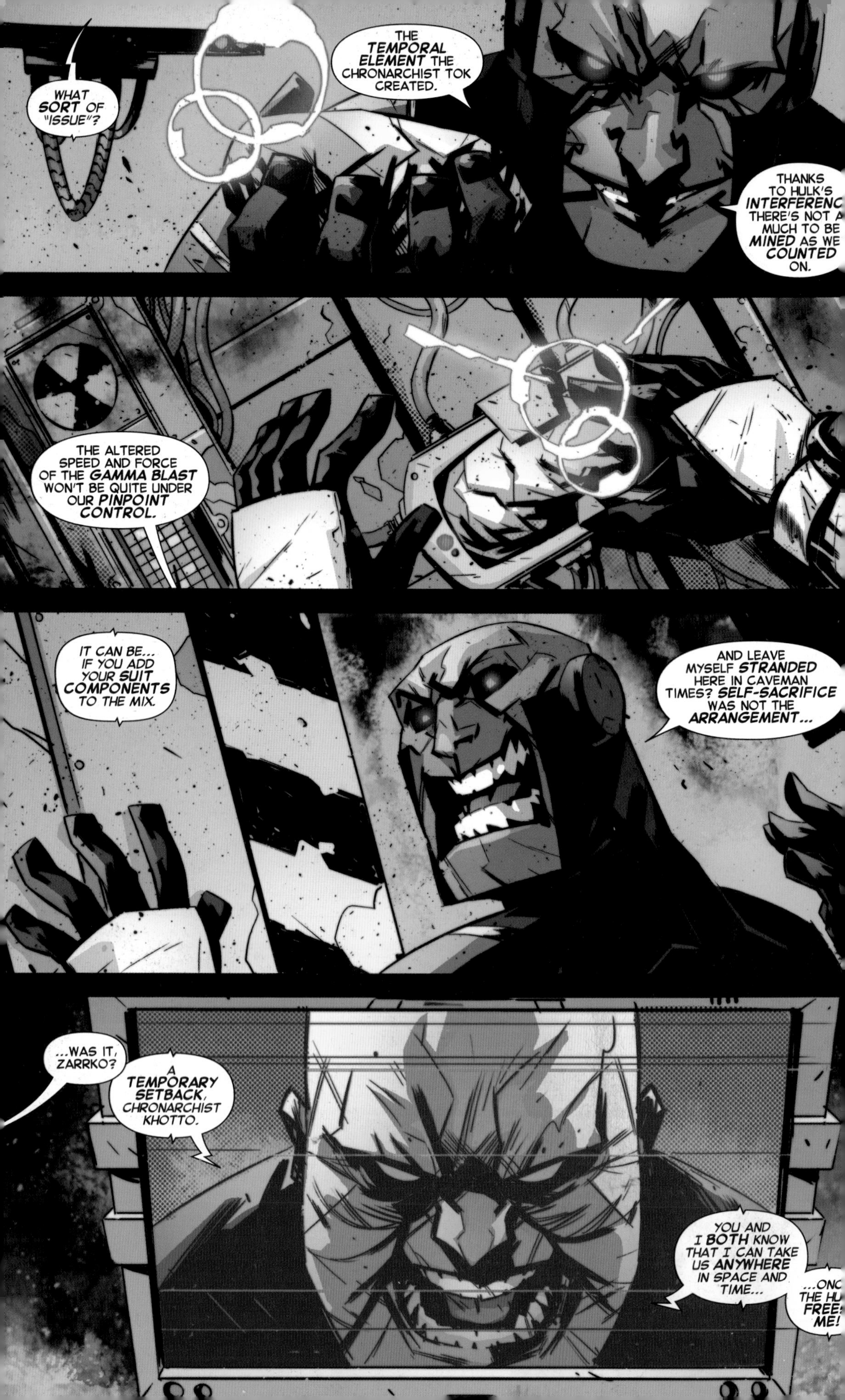
WHAT SORT OF "ISSUE"?
THE TEMPORAL ELEMENT THE CHRONARCHIST TOK CREATED.
THANKS TO HULK'S INTERFERENC THERE'S NOT A MUCH TO BE MINED AS WE COUNTED ON.
THE ALTERED SPEED AND FORCE OF THE GAMMA BLAST WON'T BE QUITE UNDER OUR PINPOINT CONTROL.
IT CAN BE... IF YOU ADD YOUR SUIT COMPONENTS TO THE MIX.
AND LEAVE MYSELF STRANDED HERE IN CAVEMAN TIMES? SELF-SACRIFICE WAS NOT THE ARRANGEMENT...
...WAS IT, ZARRKO?
A TEMPORARY SETBACK, CHRONARCHIST KHOTTO.
YOU AND I BOTH KNOW THAT I CAN TAKE US ANYWHERE IN SPACE AND TIME...

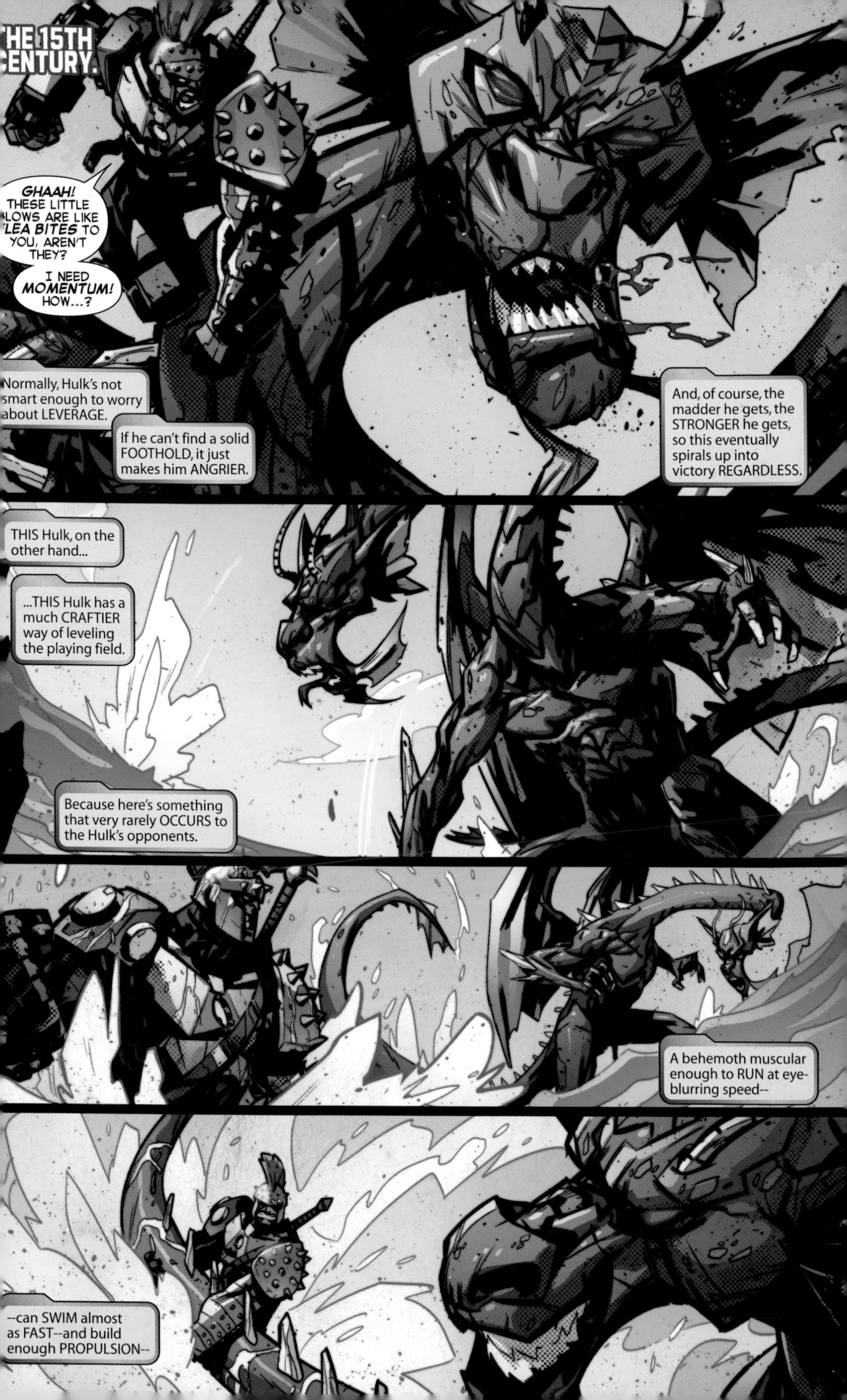

HE 15TH
ENTURY.
GHAAH! THESE LITTLE LOWS ARE LIKE LEA BITES TO YOU, AREN'T THEY?
I NEED MOMENTUM! HOW...?
Normally, Hulk's not smart enough to worry about LEVERAGE.
If he can't find a solid FOOTHOLD, it just makes him ANGRIER.
And, of course, the madder he gets, the STRONGER he gets, so this eventually spirals up into victory REGARDLESS.
THIS Hulk, on the other hand...
...THIS Hulk has a much CRAFTIER way of leveling the playing field.
Because here's something that very rarely OCCURS to the Hulk's opponents.
A behemoth muscular enough to RUN at eye-blurring speed--
--can SWIM almost as FAST--and build enough PROPULSION--

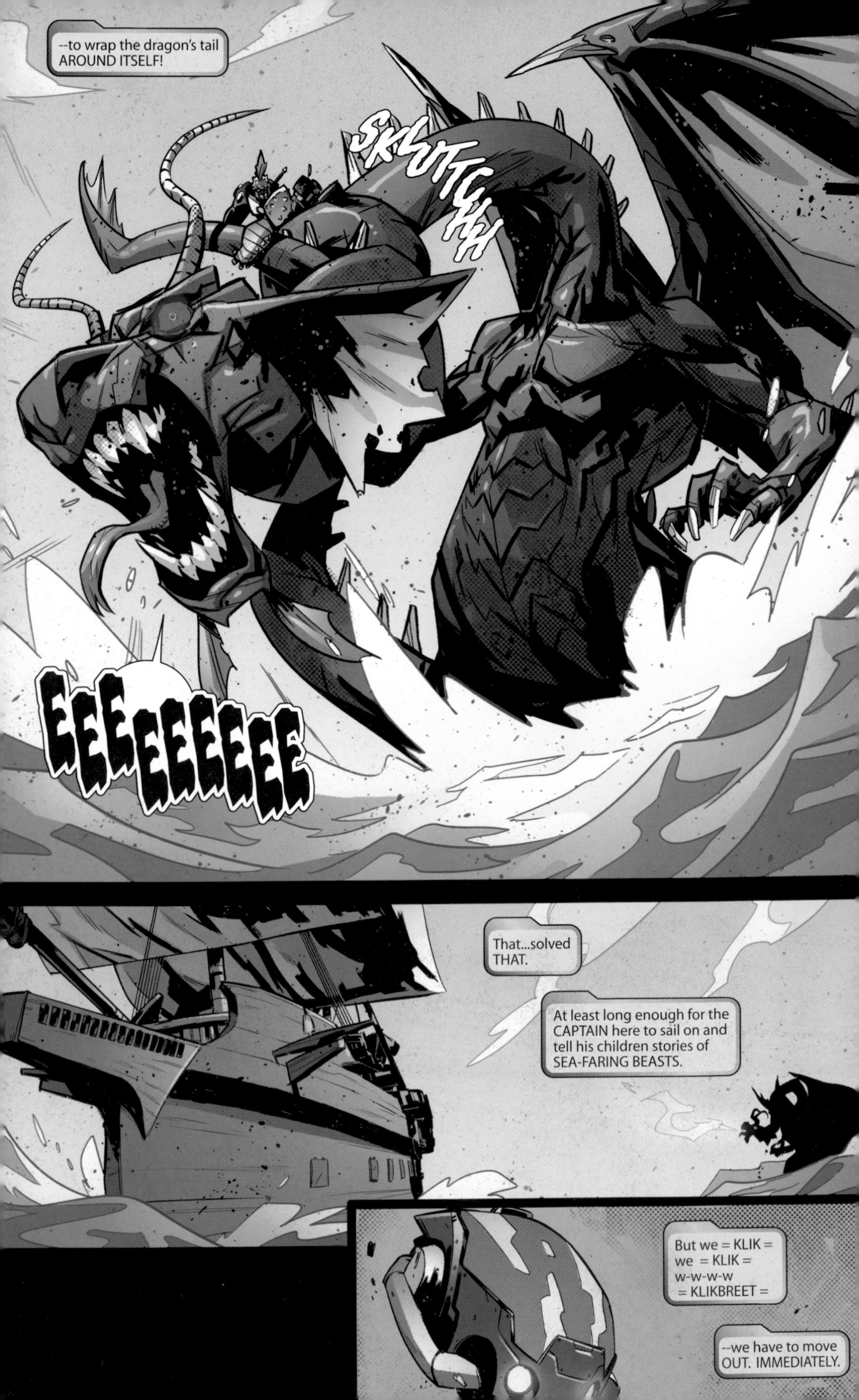
--to wrap the dragon's tail AROUND ITSELF!
SKLUTCHH
EEEEEEEEEE
That...solved THAT.
At least long enough for the CAPTAIN here to sail on and tell his children stories of SEA-FARING BEASTS.
But we = KLIK = we = KLIK = w-w-w-w = KLIKBREET =
--we have to move OUT. IMMEDIATELY.

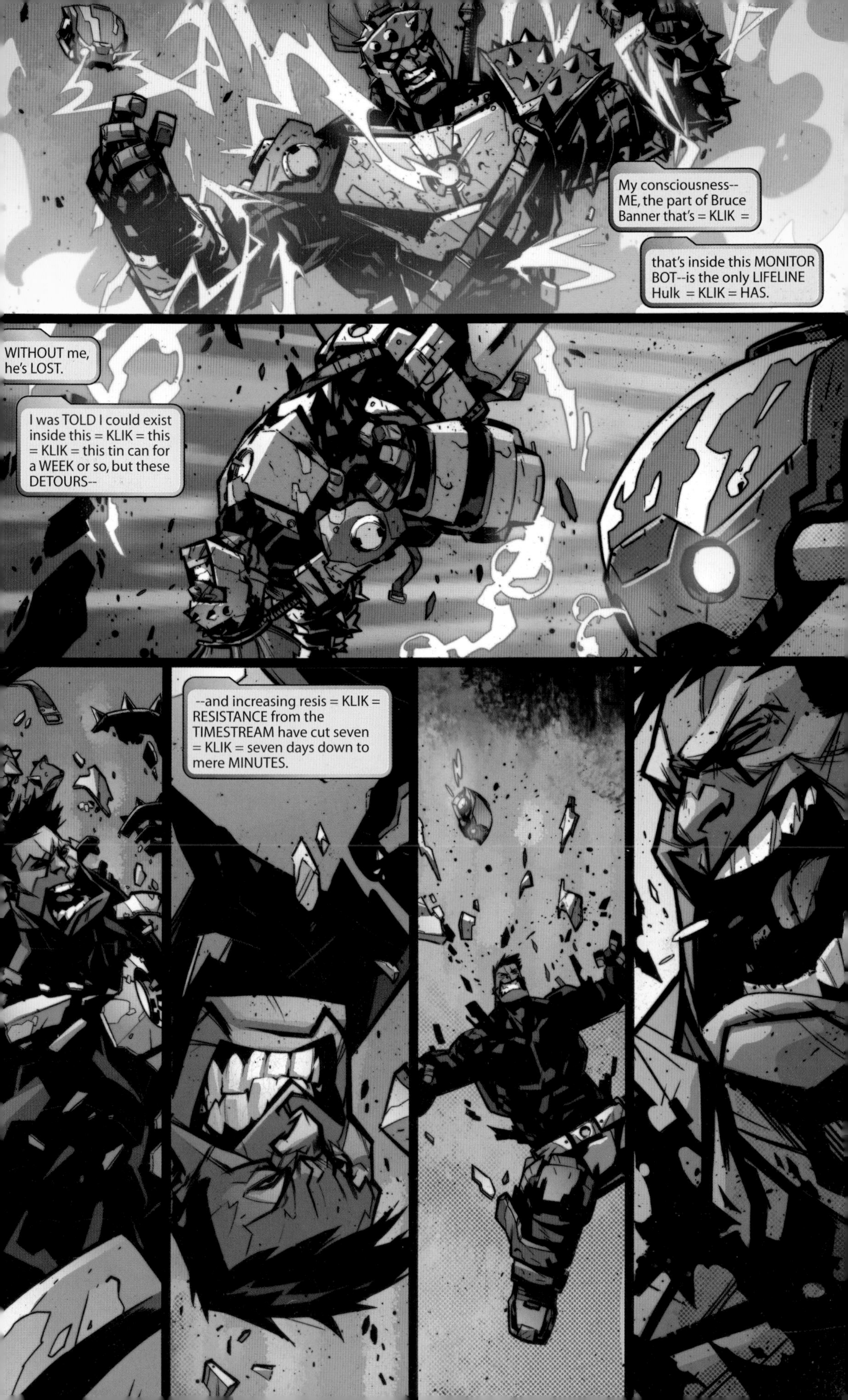
My consciousness-- ME, the part of Bruce Banner that's = KLIK =
that's inside this MONITOR BOT--is the only LIFELINE Hulk = KLIK = HAS.
WITHOUT me, he's LOST.
I was TOLD I could exist inside this = KLIK = this = KLIK = this tin can for a WEEK or so, but these DETOURS--
--and increasing resis = KLIK = RESISTANCE from the TIMESTREAM have cut seven = KLIK = seven days down to mere MINUTES.

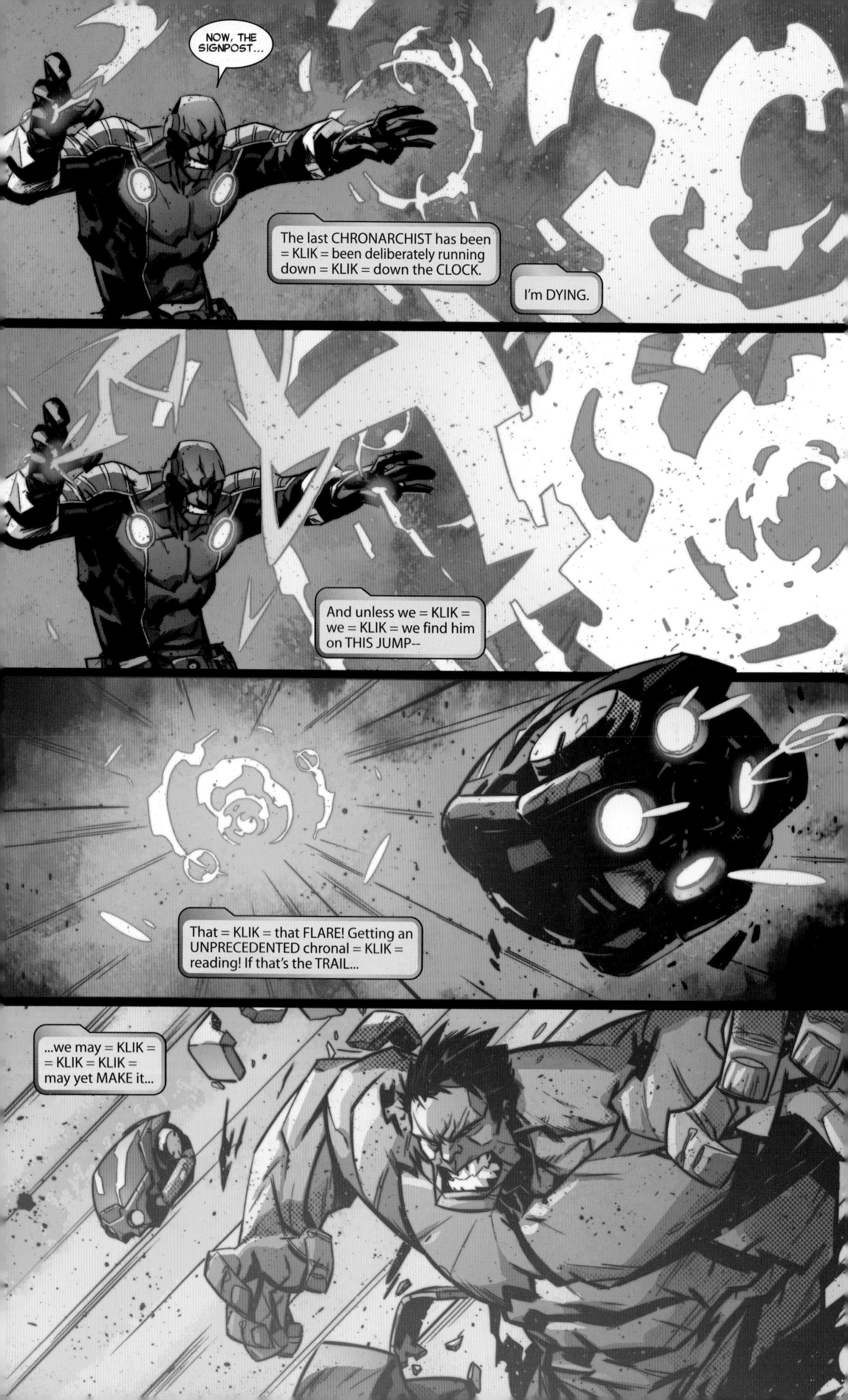
NOW, THE SIGNPOST...
The last CHRONARCHIST has been = KLIK = been deliberately running down = KLIK = down the CLOCK.
I'm DYING.
And unless we = KLIK = we = KLIK = we find him on THIS JUMP--
That = KLIK = that FLARE! Getting an UNPRECEDENTED chronal = KLIK = reading! If that's the TRAIL...
...we may = KLIK = = KLIK = KLIK = may yet MAKE it...

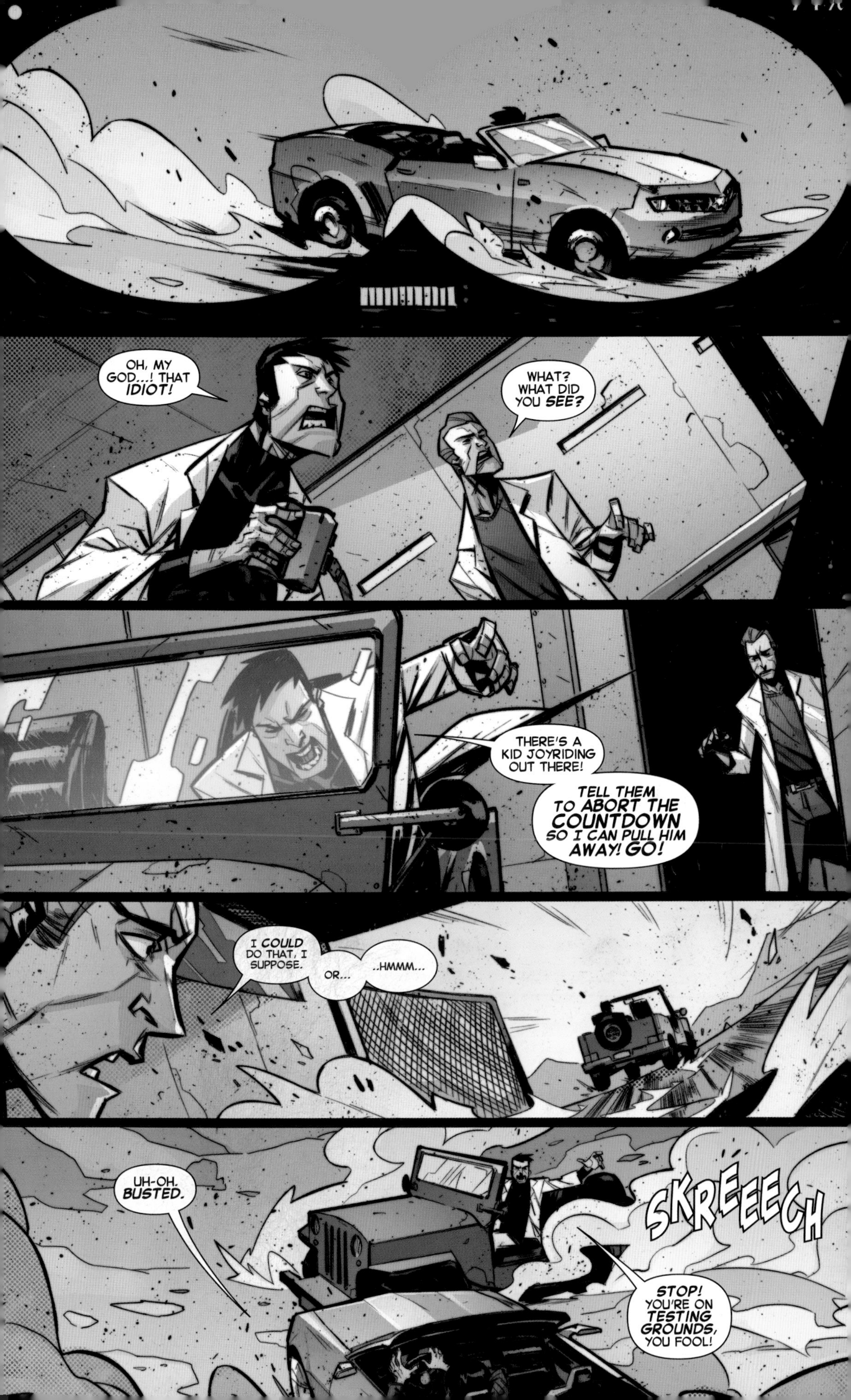
OH, MY GOD...! THAT IDIOT!
WHAT? WHAT DID YOU SEE?
THERE'S A KID JOYRIDING OUT THERE!
TELL THEM TO ABORT THE COUNTDOWN SO I CAN PULL HIM AWAY! GO!
I COULD DO THAT, I SUPPOSE.
OR...
..HMMM...
UH-OH. BUSTED.
SKREEECH
STOP! YOU'RE ON TESTING GROUNDS, YOU FOOL!

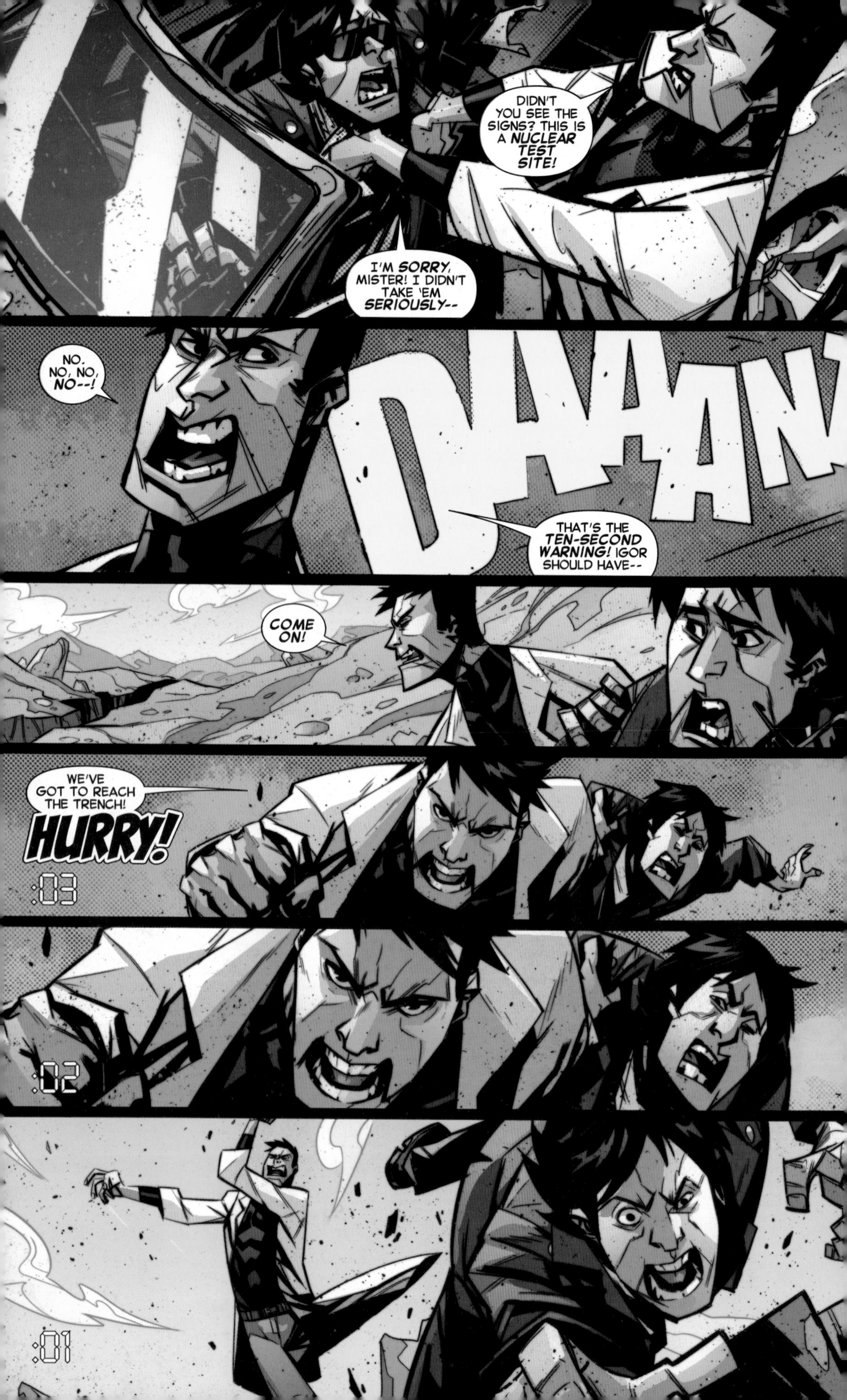

DIDN'T YOU SEE THE SIGNS? THIS IS A NUCLEAR TEST SITE!
I'M SORRY, MISTER! I DIDN'T TAKE 'EM SERIOUSLY--
NO. NO, NO, NO--!
DWAAN
THAT'S THE TEN-SECOND WARNING! IGOR SHOULD HAVE--
COME ON!
WE'VE GOT TO REACH THE TRENCH!
HURRY!
:03
:02
:01

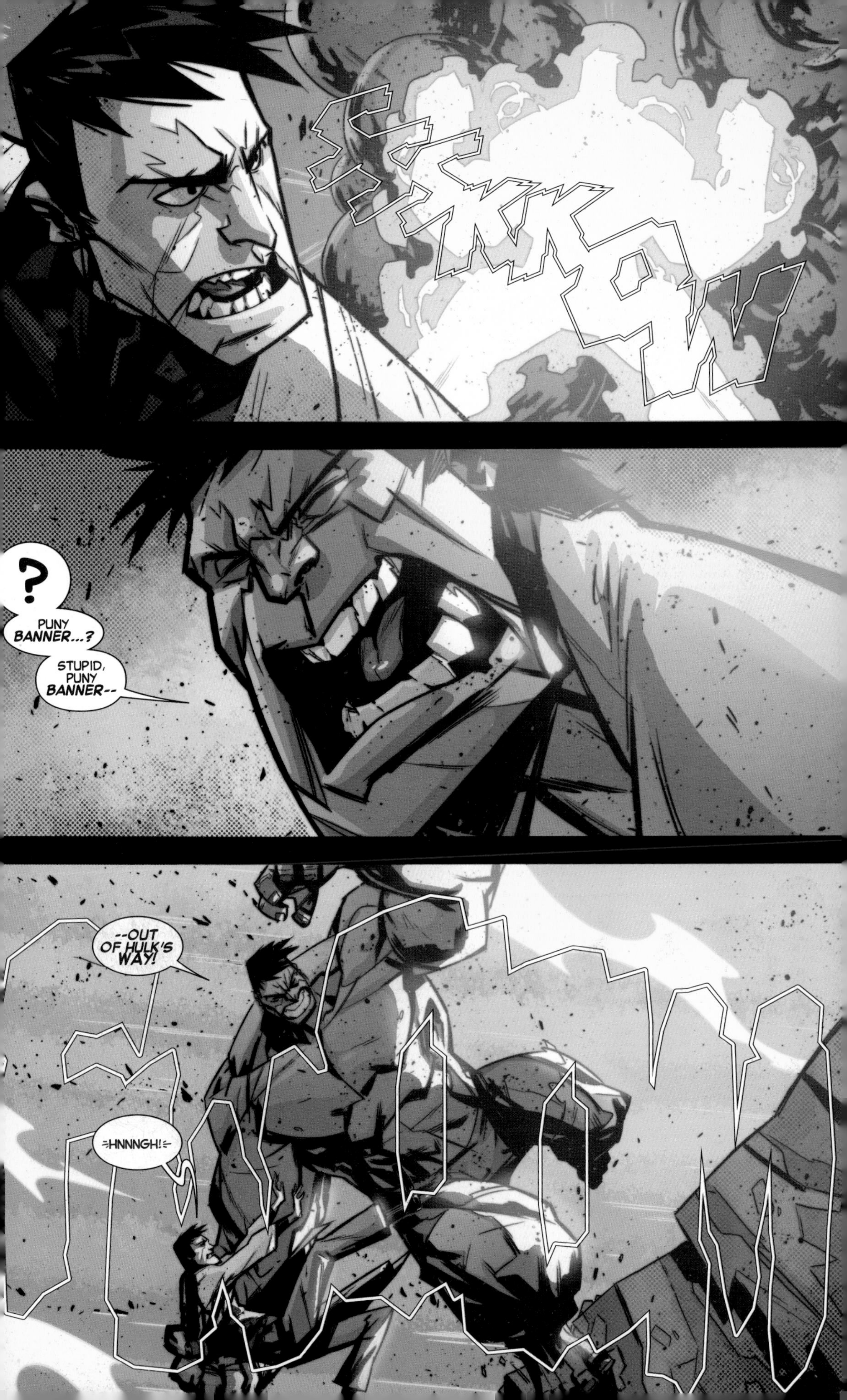
?
PUNY BANNER...?
STUPID, PUNY BANNER--
--OUT OF HULK'S WAY!
HNNNGH!

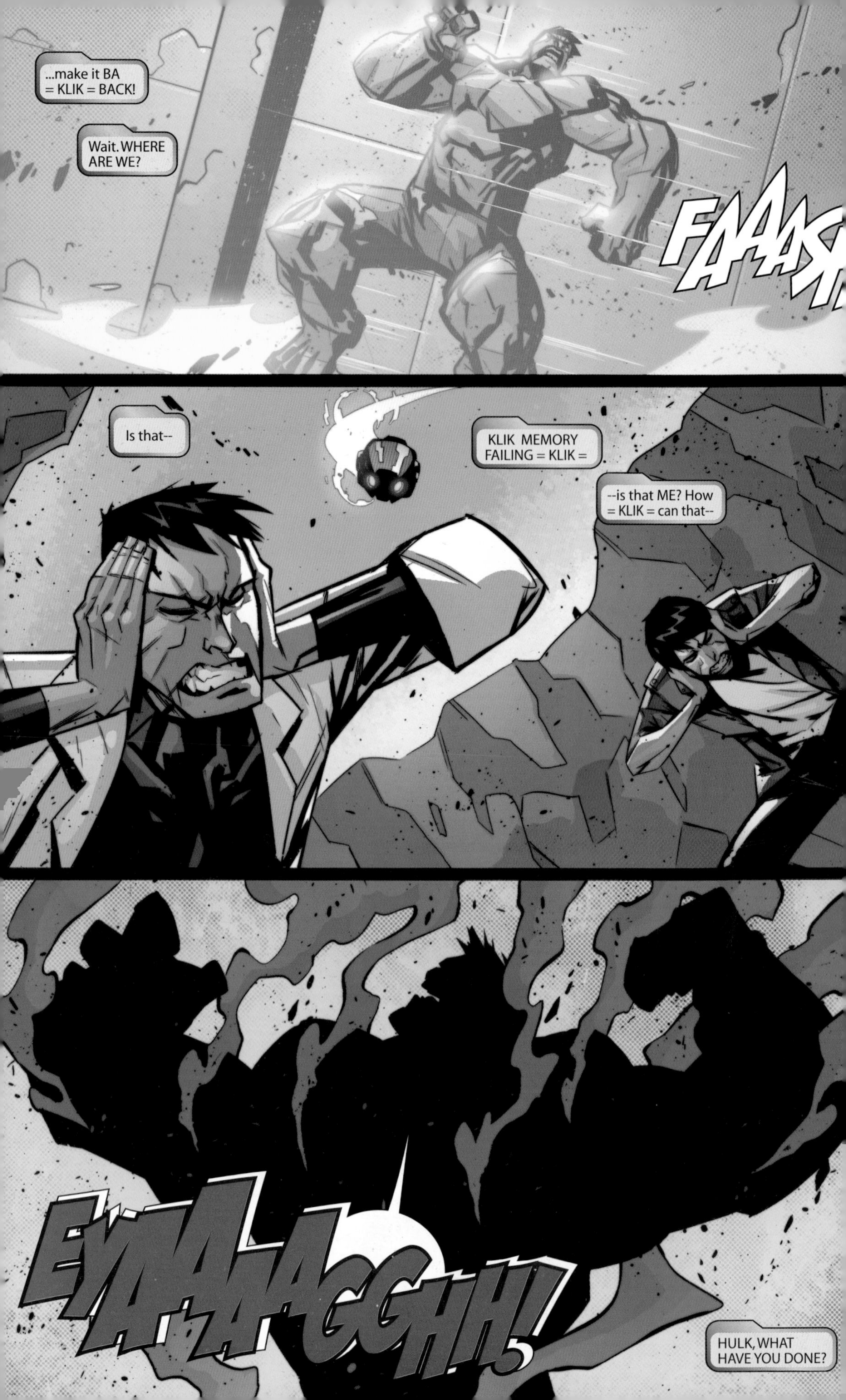
...make it BA = KLIK = BACK!
Wait. WHERE ARE WE?
FAAASH
Is that--
KLIK MEMORY FAILING = KLIK =
--is that ME? How = KLIK = can that--
EYAAAAGGHH!
HULK, WHAT HAVE YOU DONE?

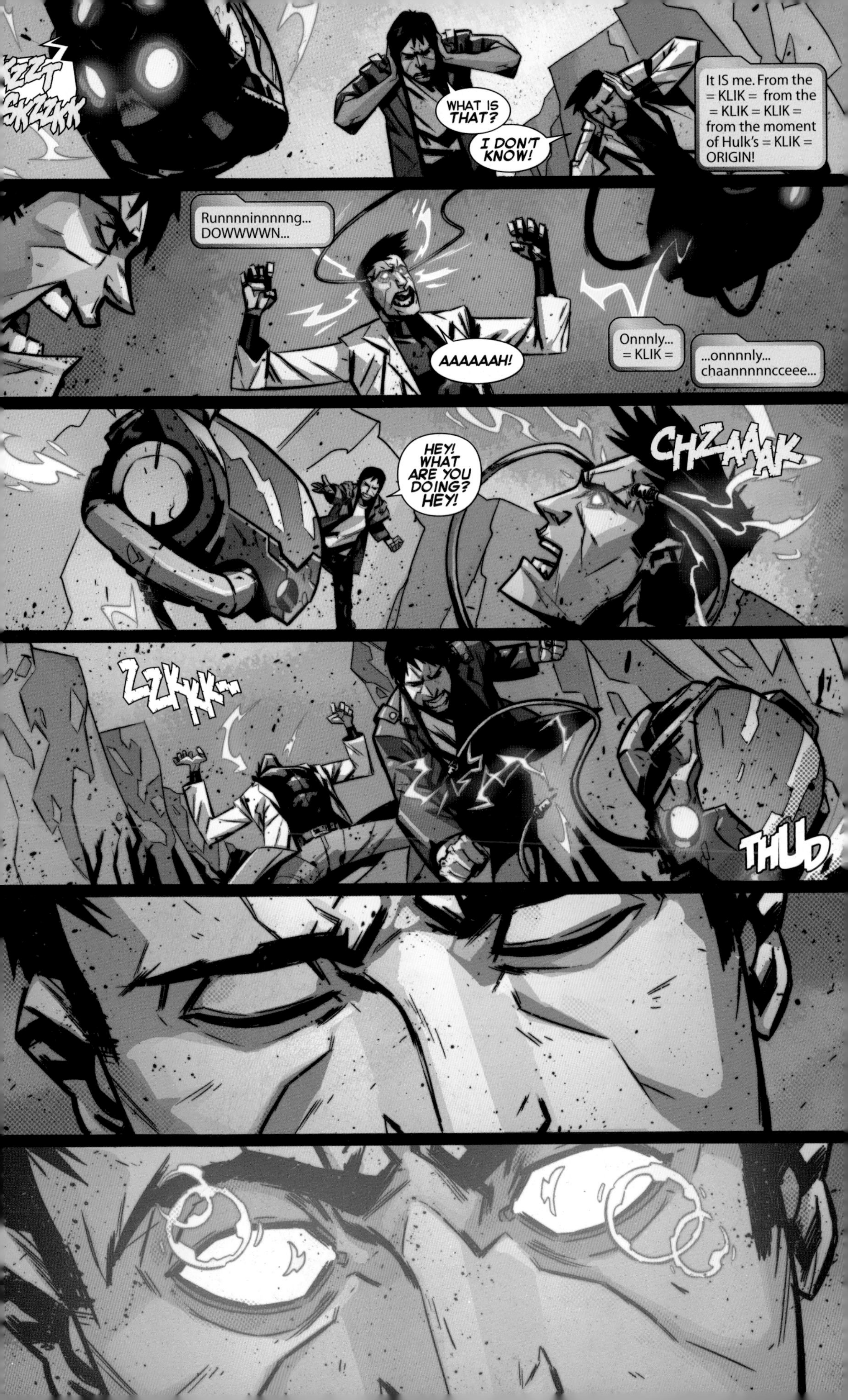
ZZT
SKZZAKK
WHAT IS THAT?
I DON'T KNOW!
It IS me. From the = KLIK = from the = KLIK = KLIK = from the moment of Hulk's = KLIK = ORIGIN!
Runnnninnnnng... DOWWWWN...
AAAAAAH!
Onnnly... = KLIK =
...onnnnly... chaannnnncceee...
HEY! WHAT ARE YOU DOING? HEY!
CHZAAAK
ZZKKK
THUD

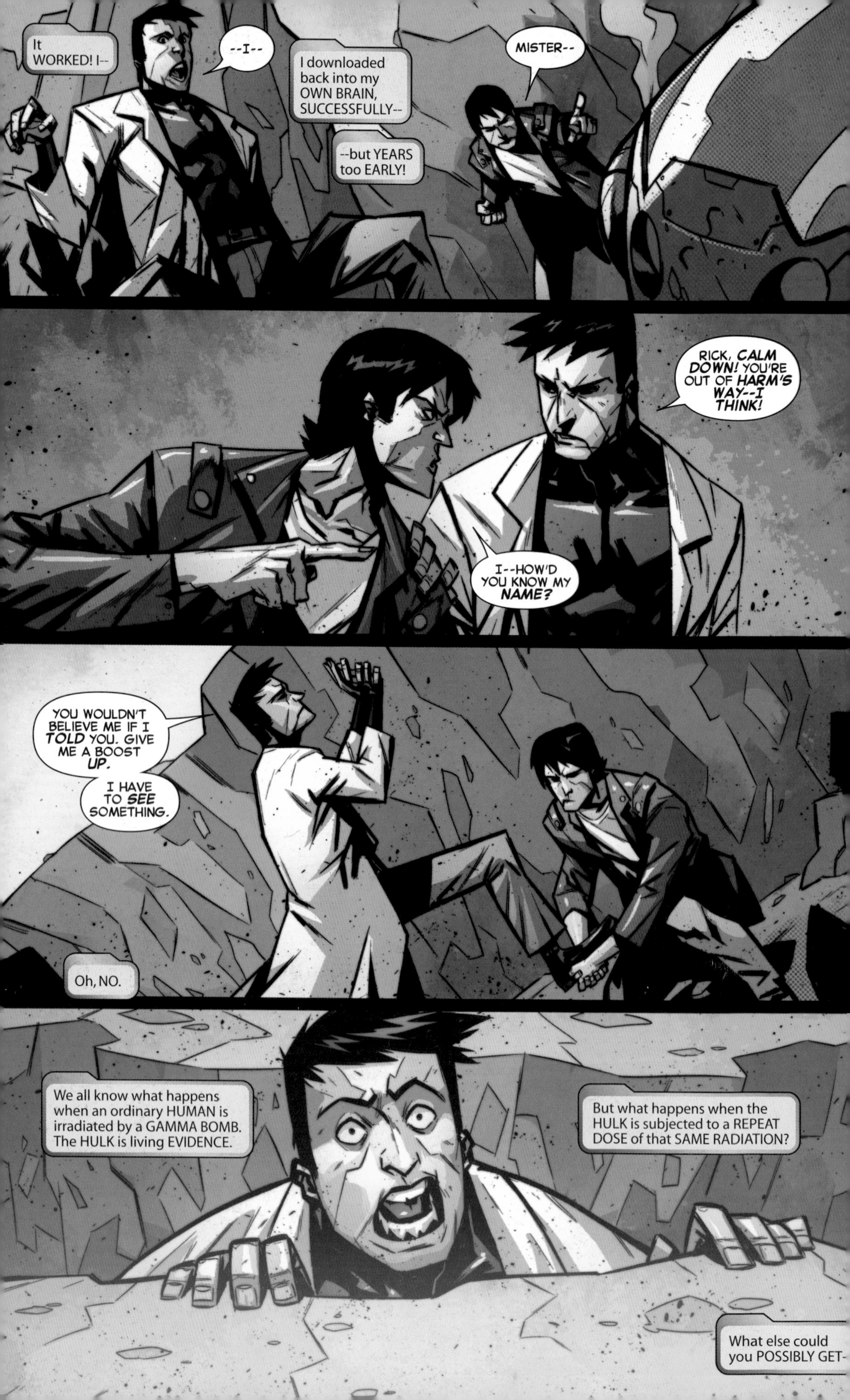
It WORKED! I--
--I--
I downloaded back into my OWN BRAIN, SUCCESSFULLY--
--but YEARS too EARLY!
MISTER--
RICK, CALM DOWN! YOU'RE OUT OF HARM'S WAY--I THINK!
I--HOW'D YOU KNOW MY NAME?
YOU WOULDN'T BELIEVE ME IF I TOLD YOU. GIVE ME A BOOST UP.
I HAVE TO SEE SOMETHING.
Oh, NO.
We all know what happens when an ordinary HUMAN is irradiated by a GAMMA BOMB. The HULK is living EVIDENCE.
But what happens when the HULK is subjected to a REPEAT DOSE of that SAME RADIATION?
What else could you POSSIBLY GET-

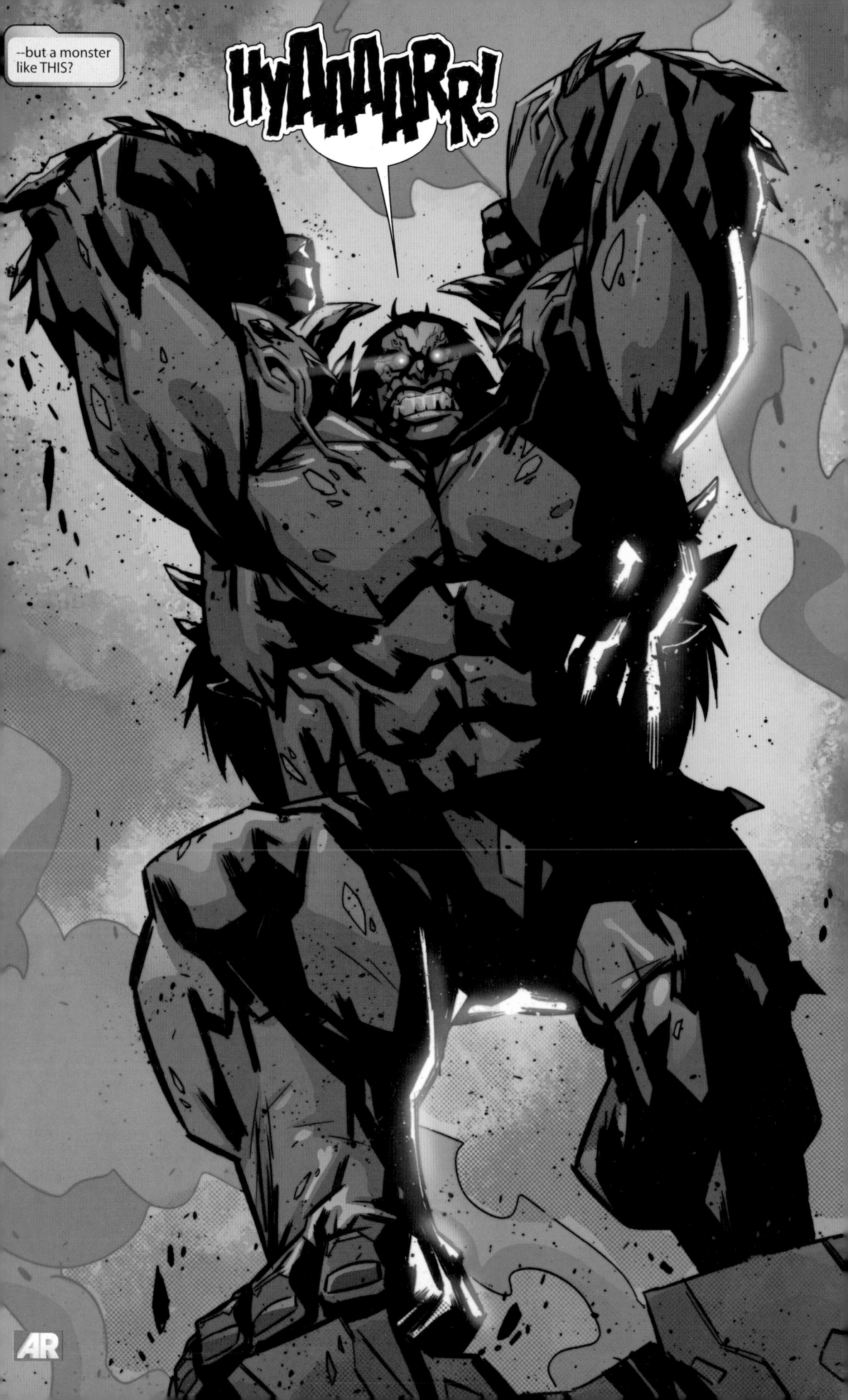
--but a monster like THIS?
HYAAAARRR!
AR

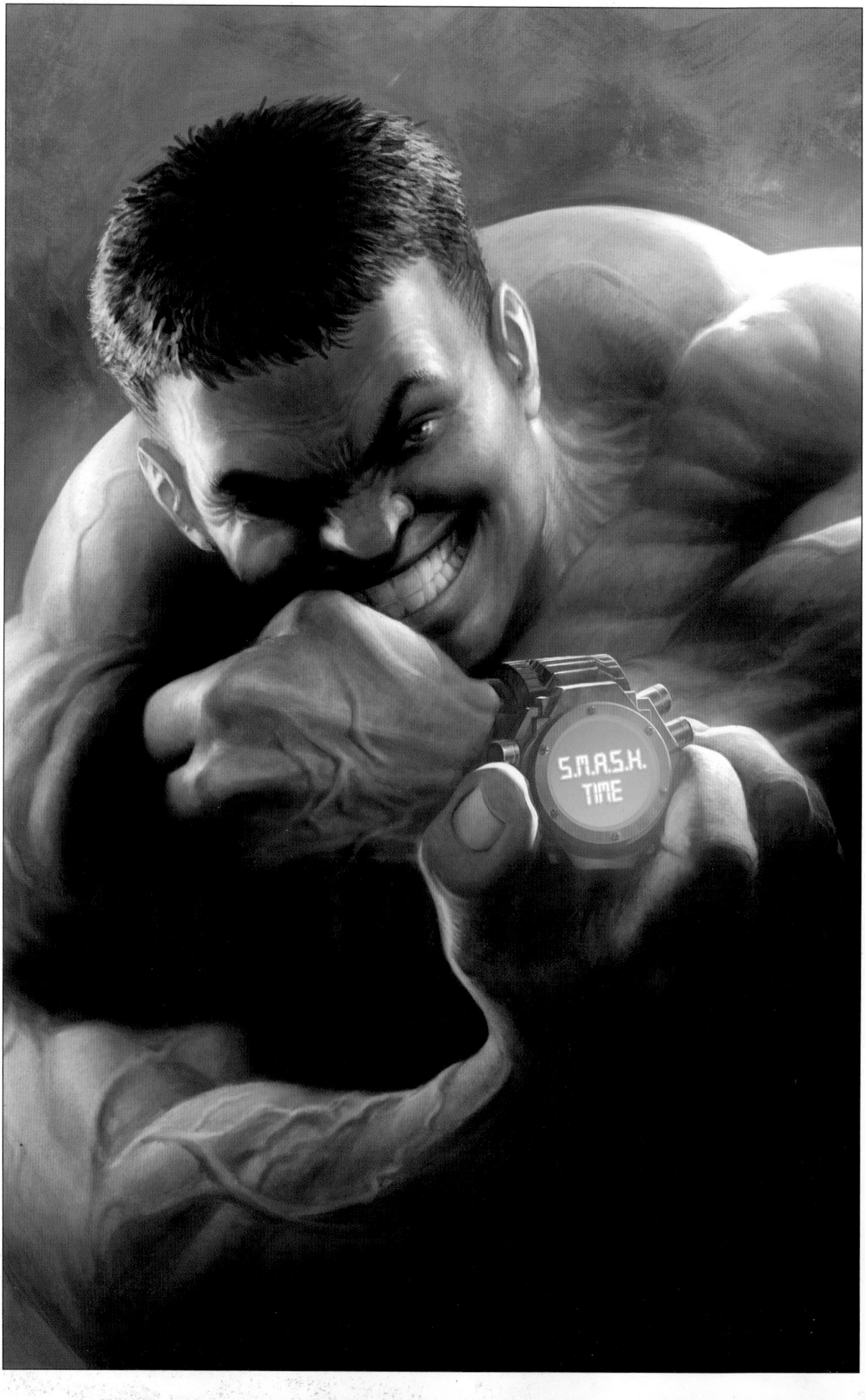
S.M.A.S.H.
TIME

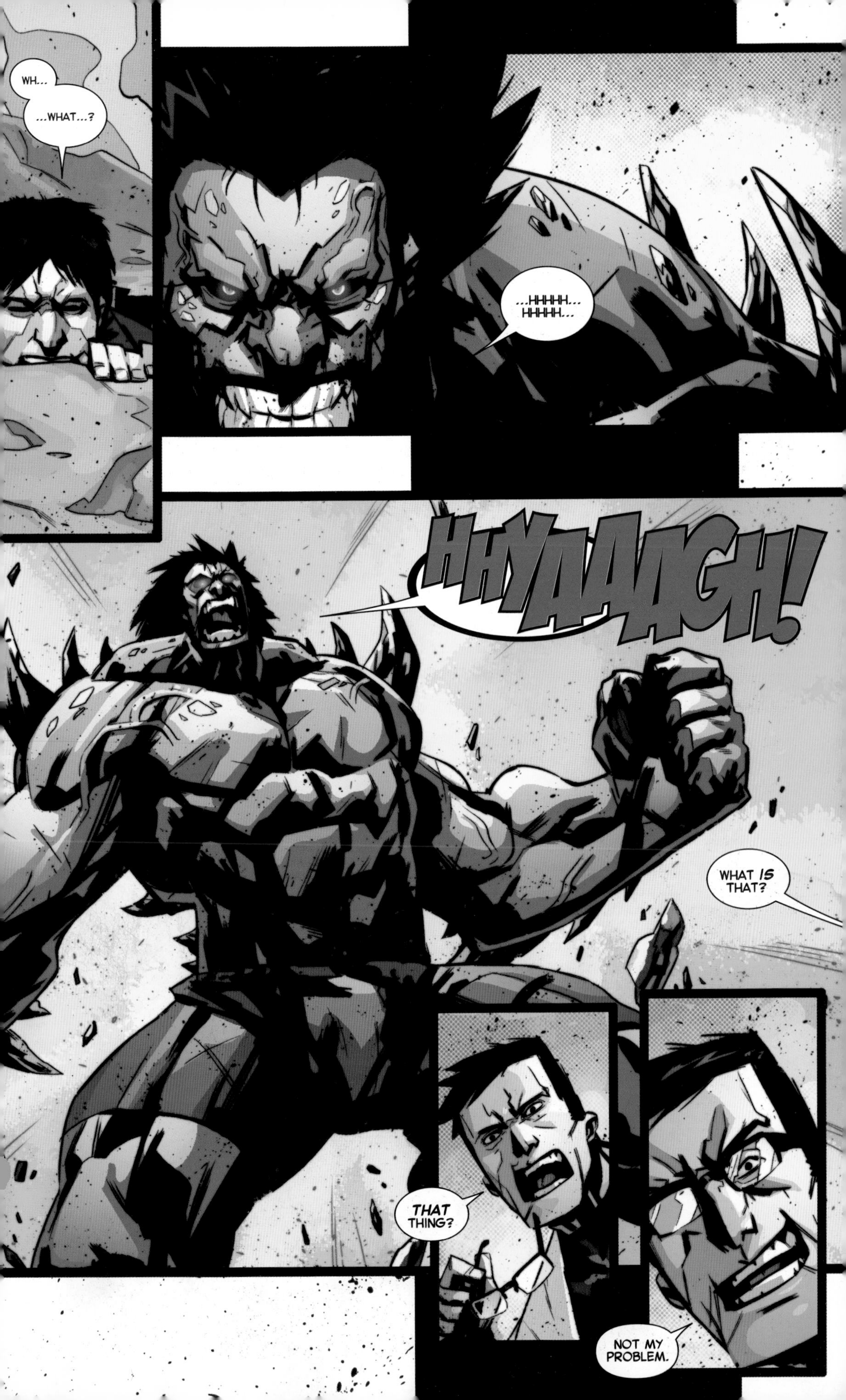

WH...
...WHAT...?
...HHHHH...
HHHHH...
HHYAAAGH!
WHAT IS THAT?
THAT THING?
NOT MY PROBLEM.

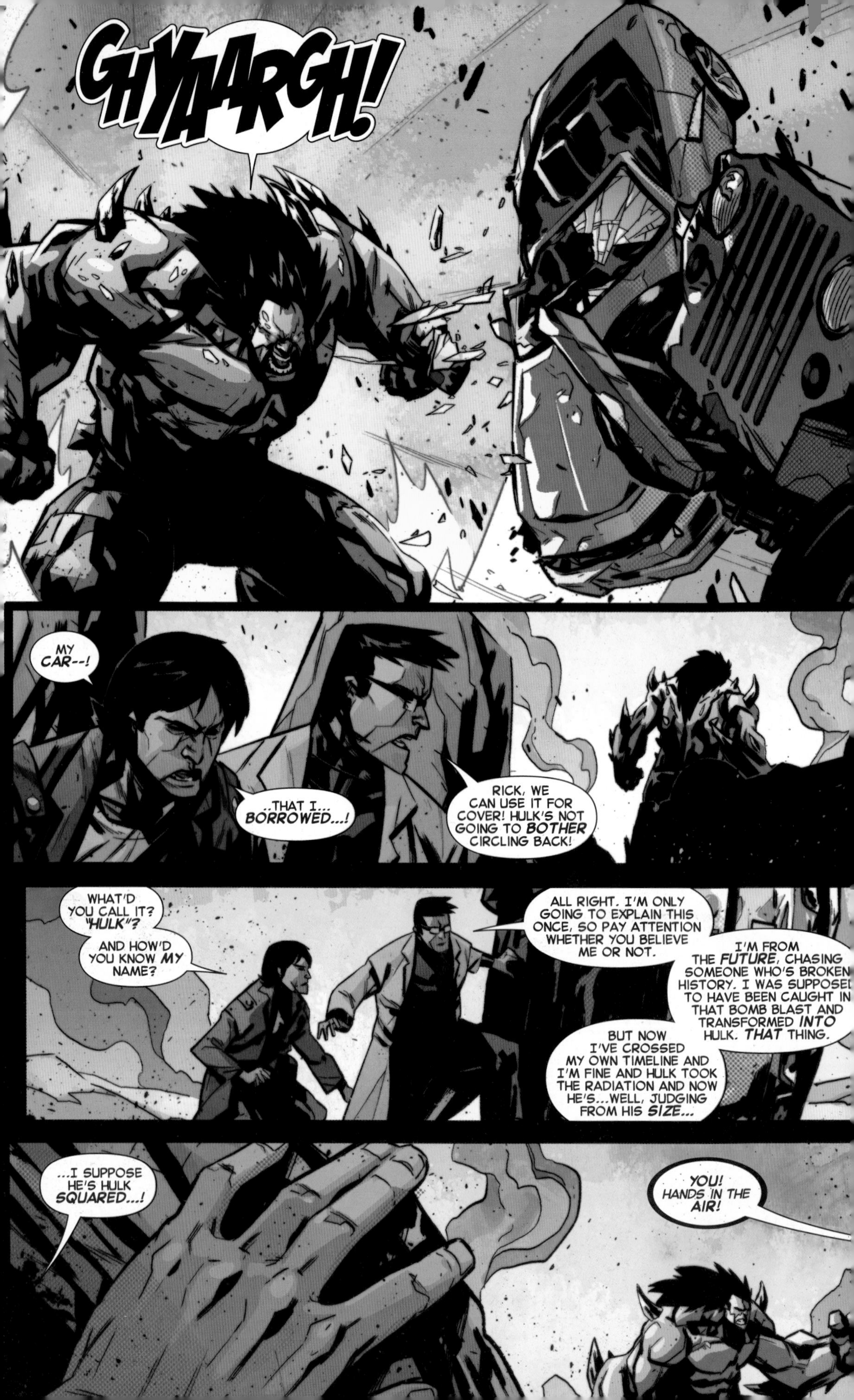
GHYAARGH!
MY CAR--!
..THAT I... BORROWED...!
RICK, WE CAN USE IT FOR COVER! HULK'S NOT GOING TO BOTHER CIRCLING BACK!
WHAT'D YOU CALL IT? "HULK"?
AND HOW'D YOU KNOW MY NAME?
ALL RIGHT. I'M ONLY GOING TO EXPLAIN THIS ONCE, SO PAY ATTENTION WHETHER YOU BELIEVE ME OR NOT.
I'M FROM THE FUTURE, CHASING SOMEONE WHO'S BROKEN HISTORY. I WAS SUPPOSED TO HAVE BEEN CAUGHT IN THAT BOMB BLAST AND TRANSFORMED INTO HULK. THAT THING.
BUT NOW I'VE CROSSED MY OWN TIMELINE AND I'M FINE AND HULK TOOK THE RADIATION AND NOW HE'S...WELL, JUDGING FROM HIS SIZE...
...I SUPPOSE HE'S HULK SQUARED...!
YOU! HANDS IN THE AIR!

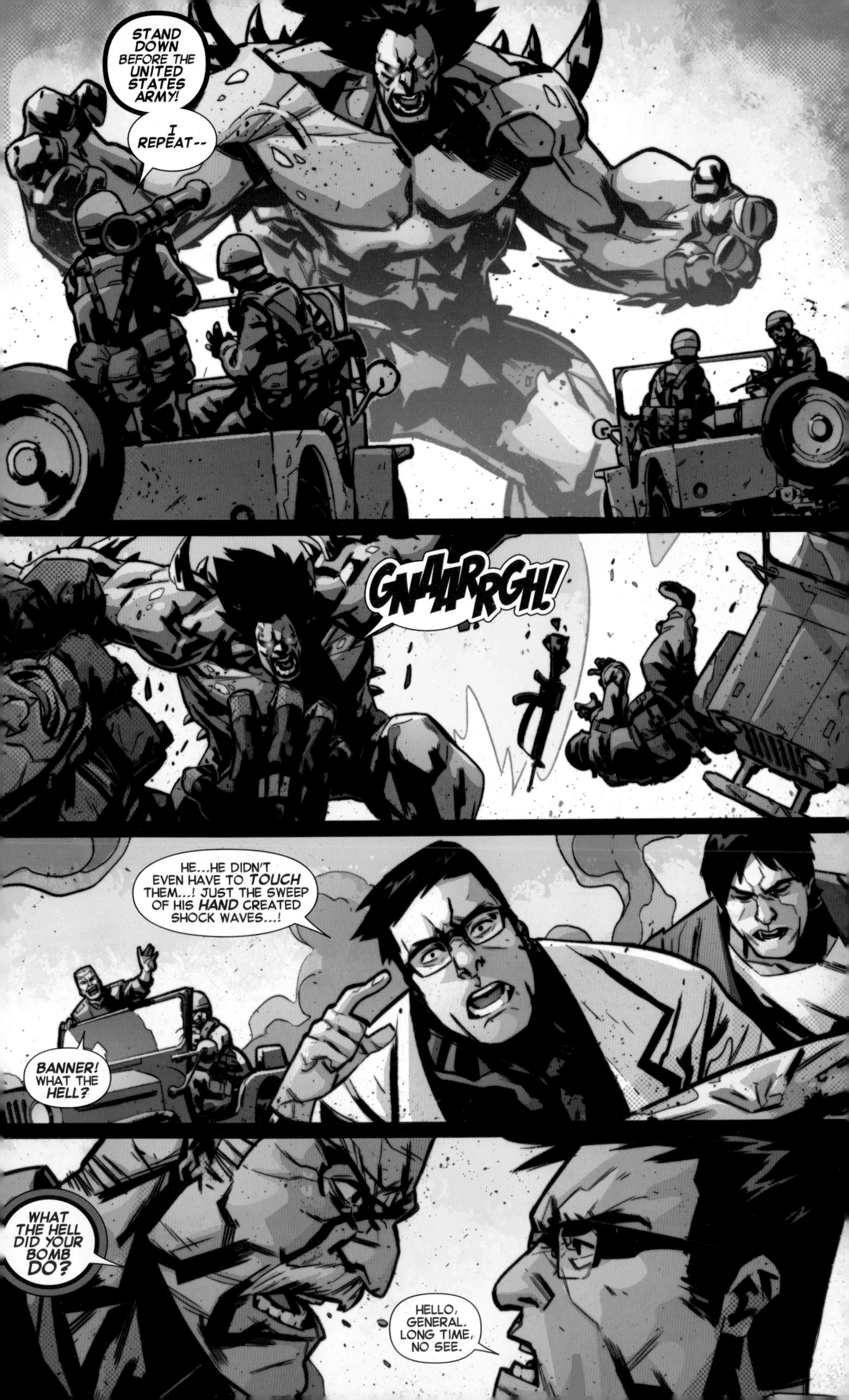
STAND DOWN BEFORE THE UNITED STATES ARMY!
I REPEAT--
GNAARRGH!
HE...HE DIDN'T EVEN HAVE TO TOUCH THEM...! JUST THE SWEEP OF HIS HAND CREATED SHOCK WAVES...!
BANNER! WHAT THE HELL?
WHAT THE HELL DID YOUR BOMB DO?
HELLO, GENERAL. LONG TIME, NO SEE.

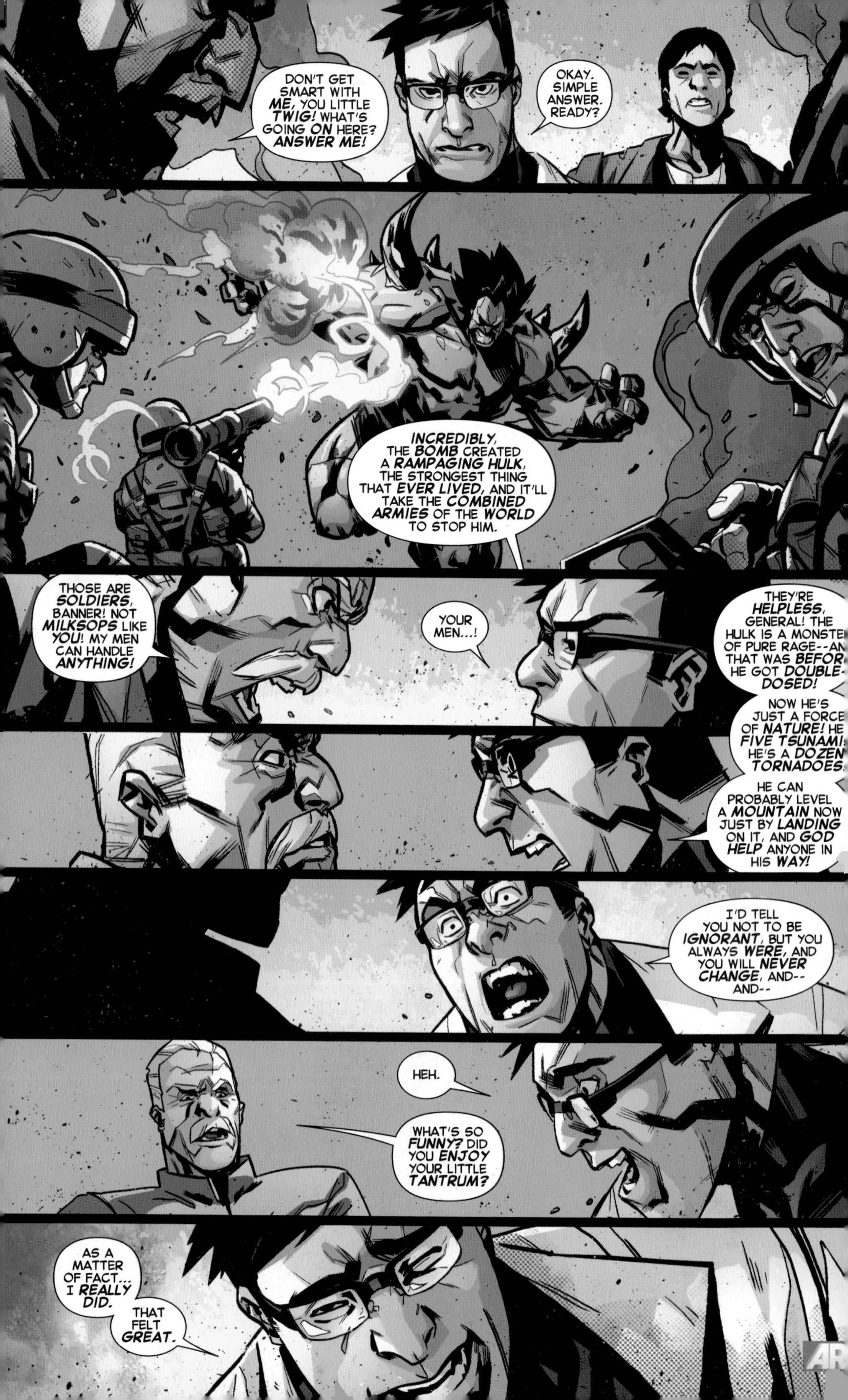
DON'T GET SMART WITH ME, YOU LITTLE TWIG! WHAT'S GOING ON HERE? ANSWER ME!
OKAY. SIMPLE ANSWER. READY?
INCREDIBLY, THE BOMB CREATED A RAMPAGING HULK, THE STRONGEST THING THAT EVER LIVED, AND IT'LL TAKE THE COMBINED ARMIES OF THE WORLD TO STOP HIM.
THOSE ARE SOLDIERS, BANNER! NOT MILKSOPS LIKE YOU! MY MEN CAN HANDLE ANYTHING!
YOUR MEN...!
THEY'RE HELPLESS, GENERAL! THE HULK IS A MONSTE OF PURE RAGE--AN THAT WAS BEFOR HE GOT DOUBLE-DOSED!
NOW HE'S JUST A FORCE OF NATURE! HE FIVE TSUNAMI HE'S A DOZEN TORNADOES
HE CAN PROBABLY LEVEL A MOUNTAIN NOW JUST BY LANDING ON IT, AND GOD HELP ANYONE IN HIS WAY!
I'D TELL YOU NOT TO BE IGNORANT, BUT YOU ALWAYS WERE, AND YOU WILL NEVER CHANGE, AND-- AND--
HEH.
WHAT'S SO FUNNY? DID YOU ENJOY YOUR LITTLE TANTRUM?
AS A MATTER OF FACT... I REALLY DID.
THAT FELT GREAT.

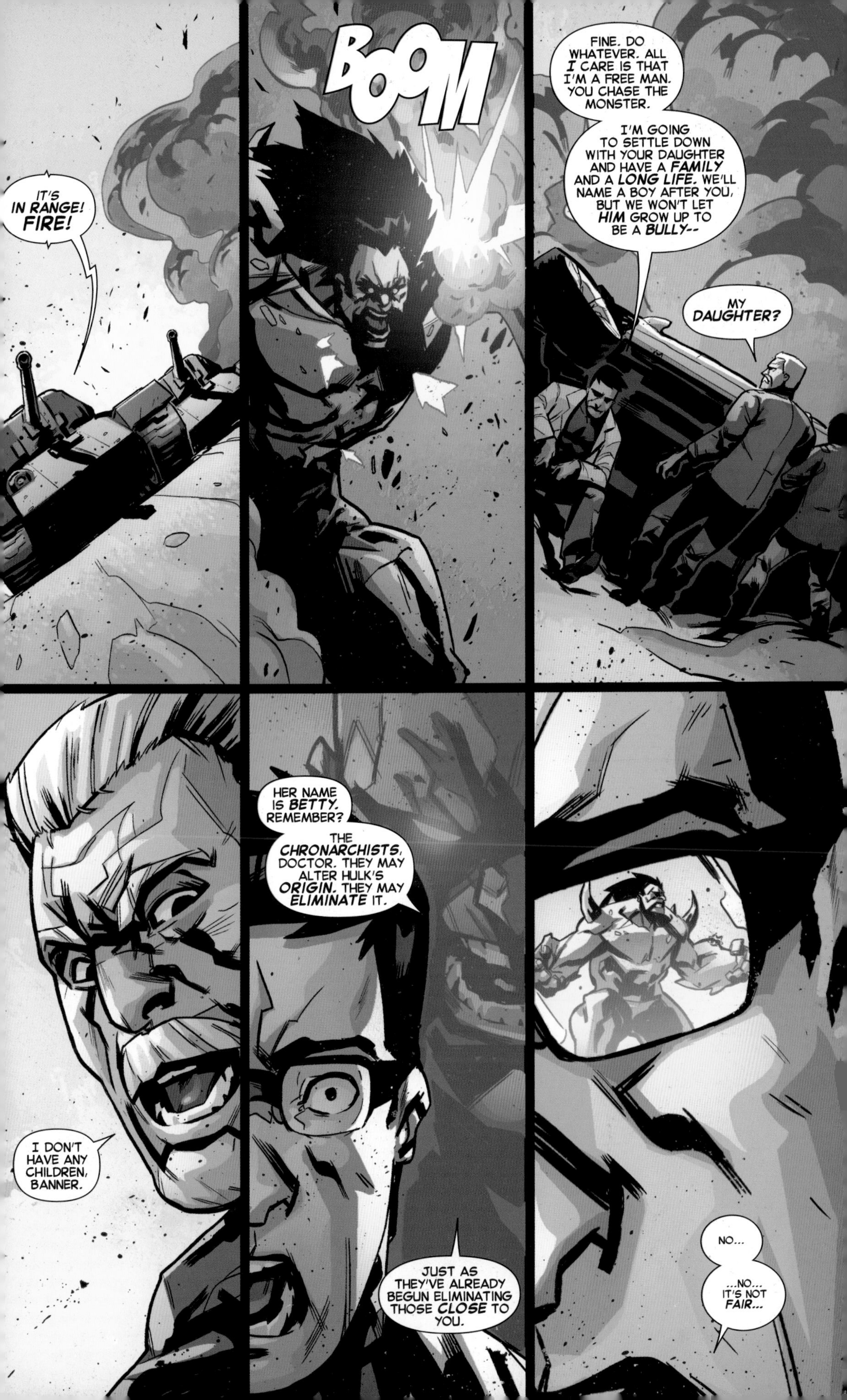
IT'S IN RANGE! FIRE!
BOOM
FINE. DO WHATEVER. ALL I CARE IS THAT I'M A FREE MAN. YOU CHASE THE MONSTER.
I'M GOING TO SETTLE DOWN WITH YOUR DAUGHTER AND HAVE A FAMILY AND A LONG LIFE. WE'LL NAME A BOY AFTER YOU, BUT WE WON'T LET HIM GROW UP TO BE A BULLY--
MY DAUGHTER?
I DON'T HAVE ANY CHILDREN, BANNER.
HER NAME IS BETTY. REMEMBER?
THE CHRONARCHISTS, DOCTOR. THEY MAY ALTER HULK'S ORIGIN. THEY MAY ELIMINATE IT.
JUST AS THEY'VE ALREADY BEGUN ELIMINATING THOSE CLOSE TO YOU.
NO...
...NO... IT'S NOT FAIR...

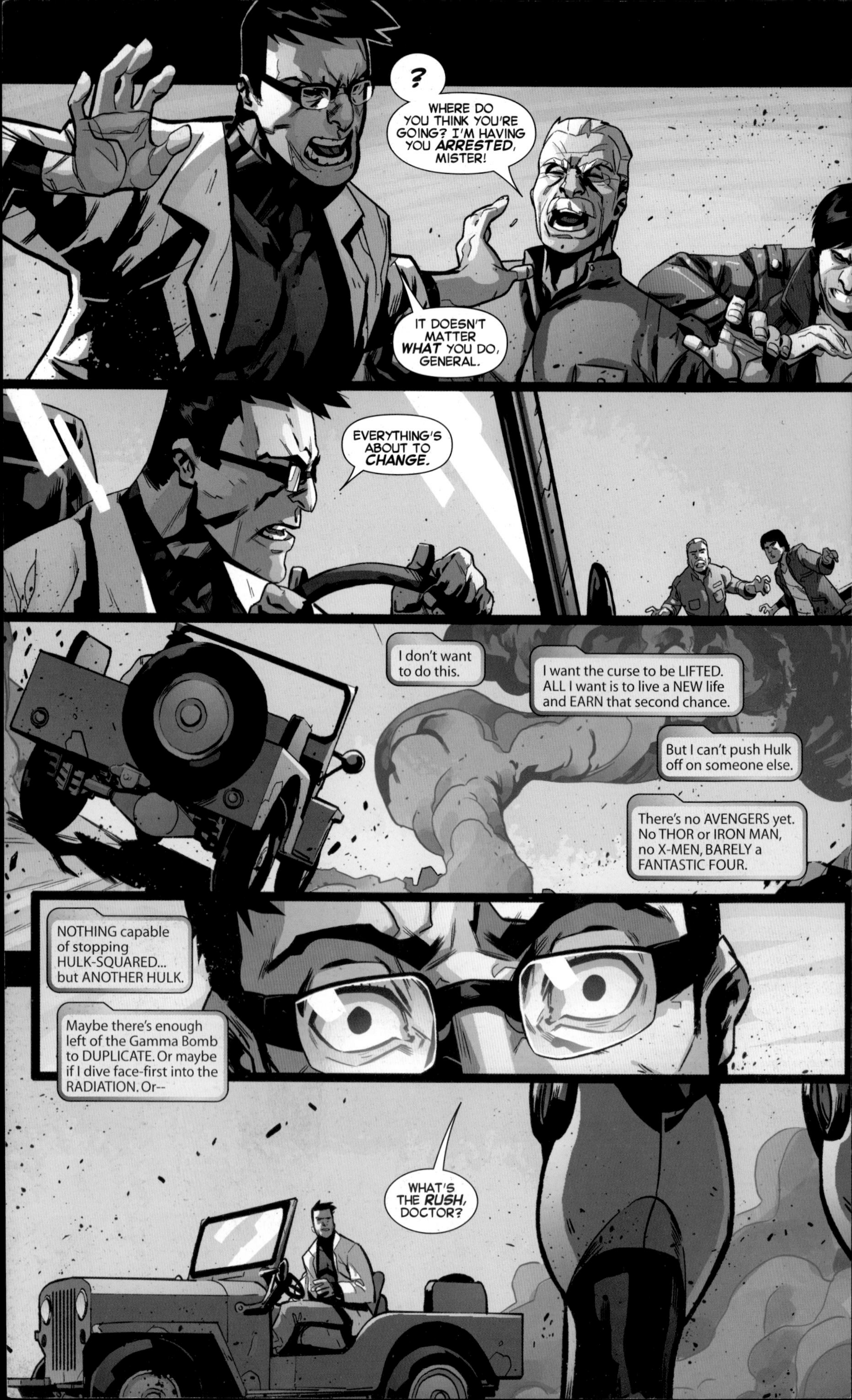
?
WHERE DO YOU THINK YOU'RE GOING? I'M HAVING YOU ARRESTED, MISTER!
IT DOESN'T MATTER WHAT YOU DO, GENERAL.
EVERYTHING'S ABOUT TO CHANGE.
I don't want to do this.
I want the curse to be LIFTED. ALL I want is to live a NEW life and EARN that second chance.
But I can't push Hulk off on someone else.
There's no AVENGERS yet. No THOR or IRON MAN, no X-MEN, BARELY a FANTASTIC FOUR.
NOTHING capable of stopping HULK-SQUARED... but ANOTHER HULK.
Maybe there's enough left of the Gamma Bomb to DUPLICATE. Or maybe if I dive face-first into the RADIATION. Or--
WHAT'S THE RUSH, DOCTOR?

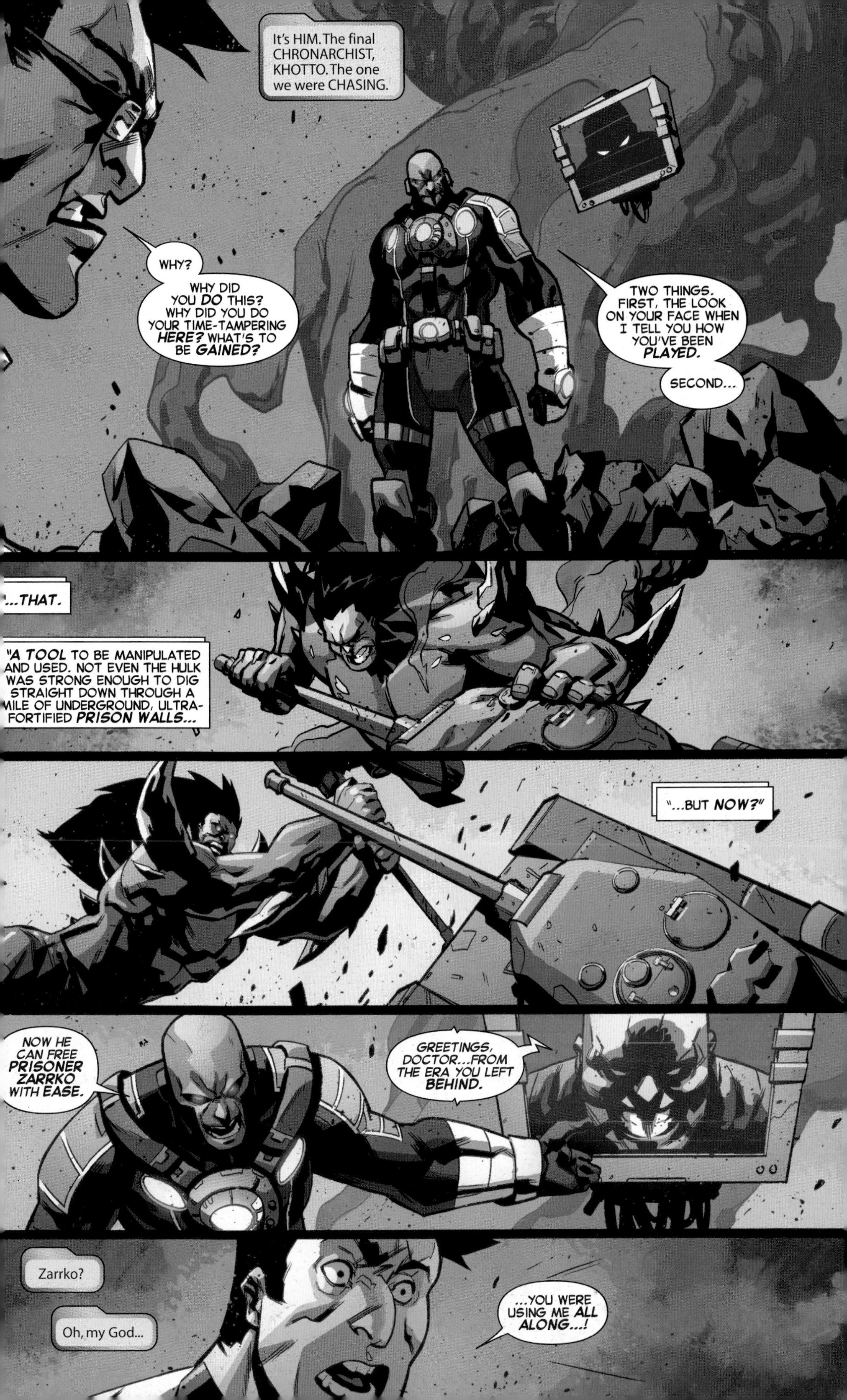
It's HIM. The final CHRONARCHIST, KHOTTO. The one we were CHASING.
WHY?
WHY DID YOU DO THIS? WHY DID YOU DO YOUR TIME-TAMPERING HERE? WHAT'S TO BE GAINED?
TWO THINGS. FIRST, THE LOOK ON YOUR FACE WHEN I TELL YOU HOW YOU'VE BEEN PLAYED.
SECOND...
"...THAT.
"A TOOL TO BE MANIPULATED AND USED. NOT EVEN THE HULK WAS STRONG ENOUGH TO DIG STRAIGHT DOWN THROUGH A MILE OF UNDERGROUND, ULTRA-FORTIFIED PRISON WALLS...
"...BUT NOW?"
NOW HE CAN FREE PRISONER ZARRKO WITH EASE.
GREETINGS, DOCTOR...FROM THE ERA YOU LEFT BEHIND.
Zarrko?
Oh, my God...
...YOU WERE USING ME ALL ALONG...!

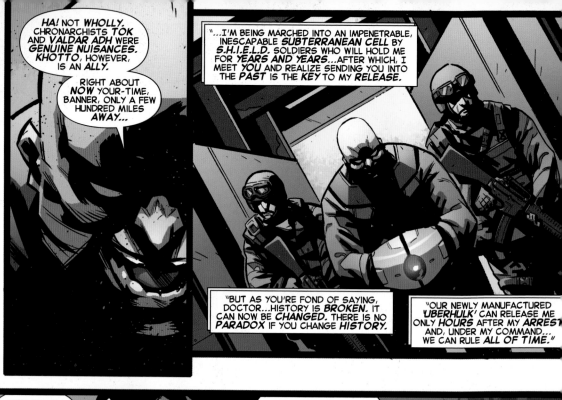

HA! NOT *WHOLLY.* CHRONARCHISTS *TOK* AND *VALDAR ADH* WERE GENUINE *NUISANCES.* *KHOTTO,* HOWEVER, IS AN *ALLY.*

RIGHT ABOUT *NOW* YOUR-TIME, BANNER, ONLY A FEW HUNDRED MILES *AWAY...*

"...I'M BEING MARCHED INTO AN IMPENETRABLE, INESCAPABLE *SUBTERRANEAN CELL* BY S.H.I.E.L.D. SOLDIERS WHO WILL HOLD ME FOR *YEARS AND YEARS...*AFTER WHICH, I MEET *YOU* AND REALIZE SENDING YOU INTO THE *PAST* IS THE *KEY* TO MY *RELEASE.*

"BUT AS YOU'RE FOND OF SAYING, DOCTOR...HISTORY IS *BROKEN.* IT CAN NOW BE *CHANGED.* THERE IS NO *PARADOX* IF YOU CHANGE *HISTORY.*

"OUR NEWLY MANUFACTURED *'UBERHULK'* CAN RELEASE ME ONLY *HOURS* AFTER MY *ARREST* AND, UNDER MY COMMAND... WE CAN RULE *ALL OF TIME.*"

YOU CAN'T CONTROL *THAT* HULK! *LOOK AT HIM!*

I *DISAGREE.* USING KHOTTO'S *TIMESUIT,* WE CAN BRING THE BEAST WHATEVER HE MAY *DESIRE* FROM ANYWHERE IN SPACE-TIME! OR WE CAN SIMPLY *STEER* HIM! WE CAN--

The TIMESUIT.

KHOTTO HAS A TIMESUIT.

DOCTOR, *CONTROL YOURSELF!* YOU'RE SO *PRACTICED* AT IT!

NNNGGHHH--!

THWAM

WHAT ARE YOU--?

STOP TEARING AT MY *SUIT!*

GHAAAAHH!

I'm NOT "tearing." I STUDIED reference on Khotto before I STARTED this timetrip--

--and I know how his TIMESUIT *WORKS!*

=HFFF=

BANNER, *STOP!*

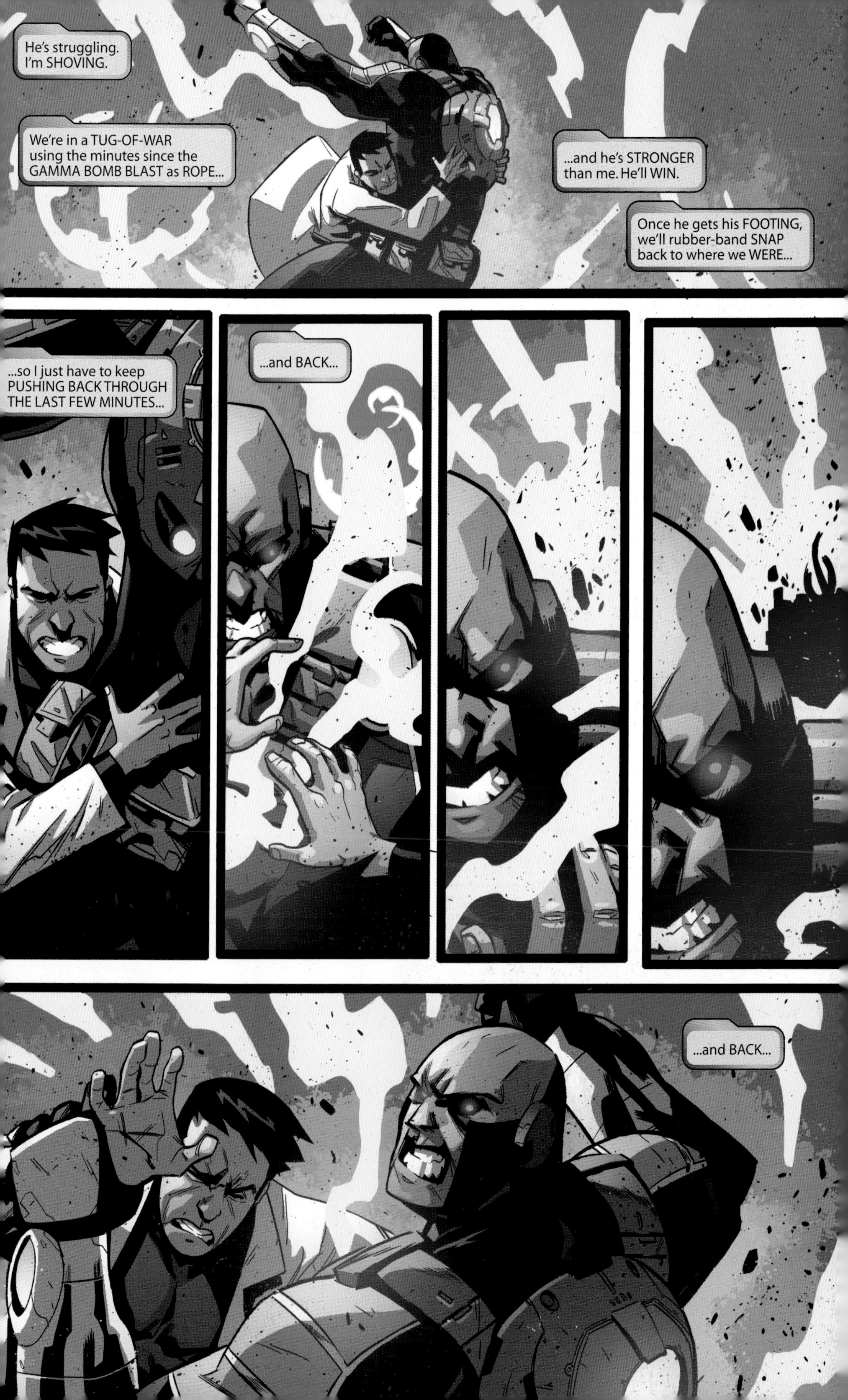
He's struggling. I'm SHOVING.
We're in a TUG-OF-WAR using the minutes since the GAMMA BOMB BLAST as ROPE...
...and he's STRONGER than me. He'll WIN.
Once he gets his FOOTING, we'll rubber-band SNAP back to where we WERE...
...so I just have to keep PUSHING BACK THROUGH THE LAST FEW MINUTES...
...and BACK...
...and BACK...

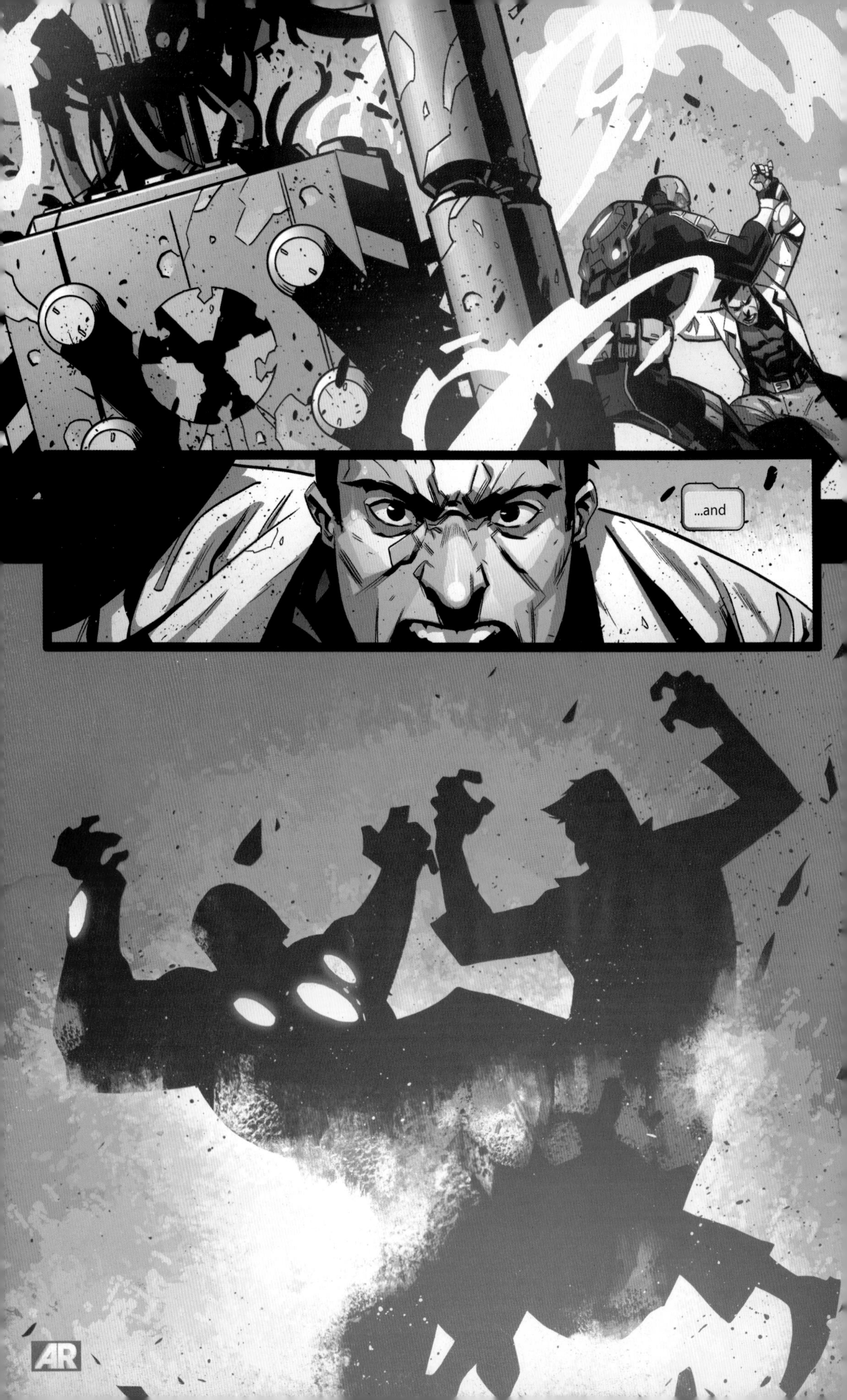
...and

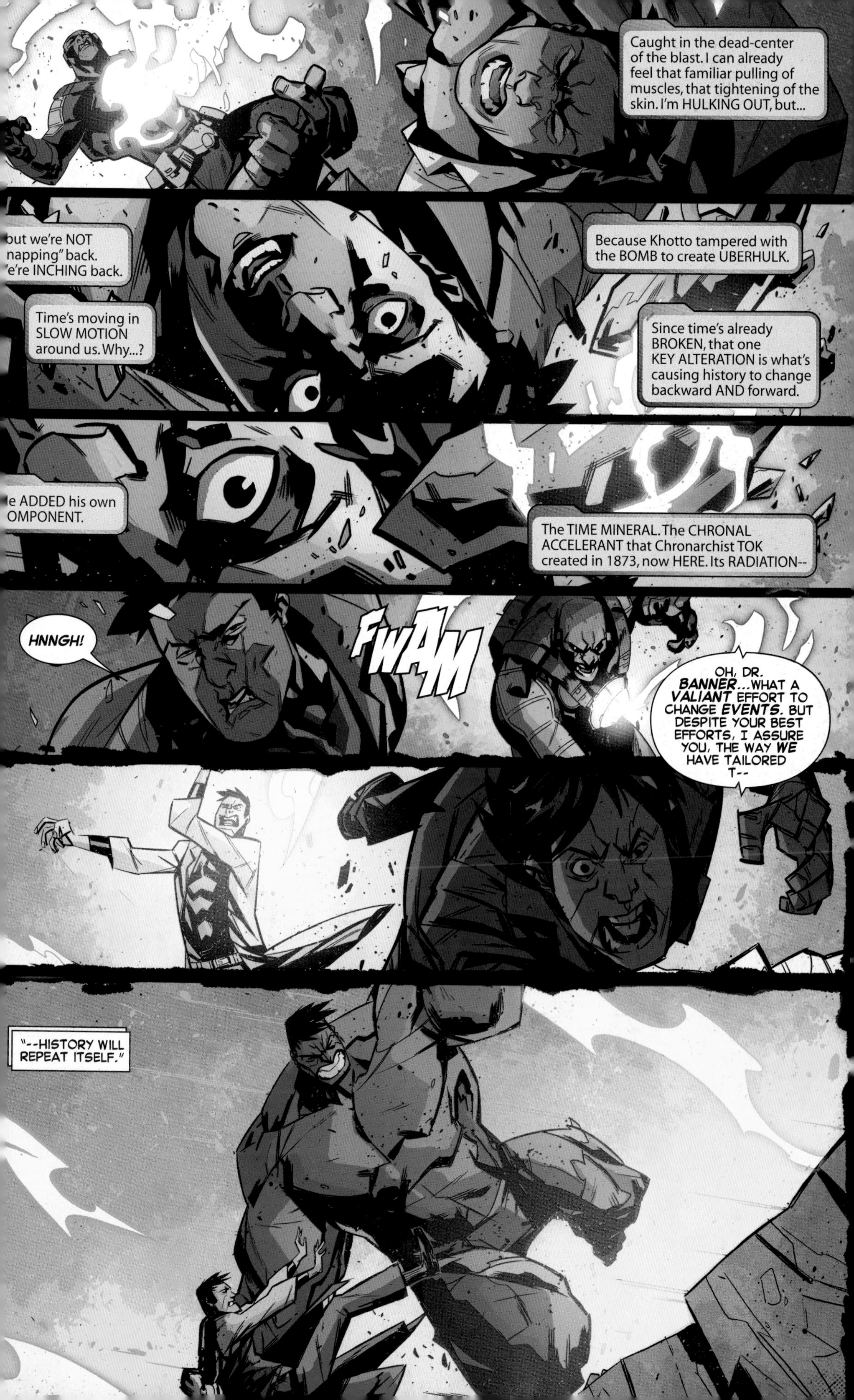
Caught in the dead-center of the blast. I can already feel that familiar pulling of muscles, that tightening of the skin. I'm HULKING OUT, but...
but we're NOT
napping" back.
e're INCHING back.
Because Khotto tampered with the BOMB to create UBERHULK.
Time's moving in SLOW MOTION around us. Why...?
Since time's already BROKEN, that one KEY ALTERATION is what's causing history to change backward AND forward.
e ADDED his own
OMPONENT.
The TIME MINERAL. The CHRONAL ACCELERANT that Chronarchist TOK created in 1873, now HERE. Its RADIATION--
HNNGH!
FWAM
OH, DR. BANNER...WHAT A VALIANT EFFORT TO CHANGE EVENTS. BUT DESPITE YOUR BEST EFFORTS, I ASSURE YOU, THE WAY WE HAVE TAILORED T--
"--HISTORY WILL REPEAT ITSELF."

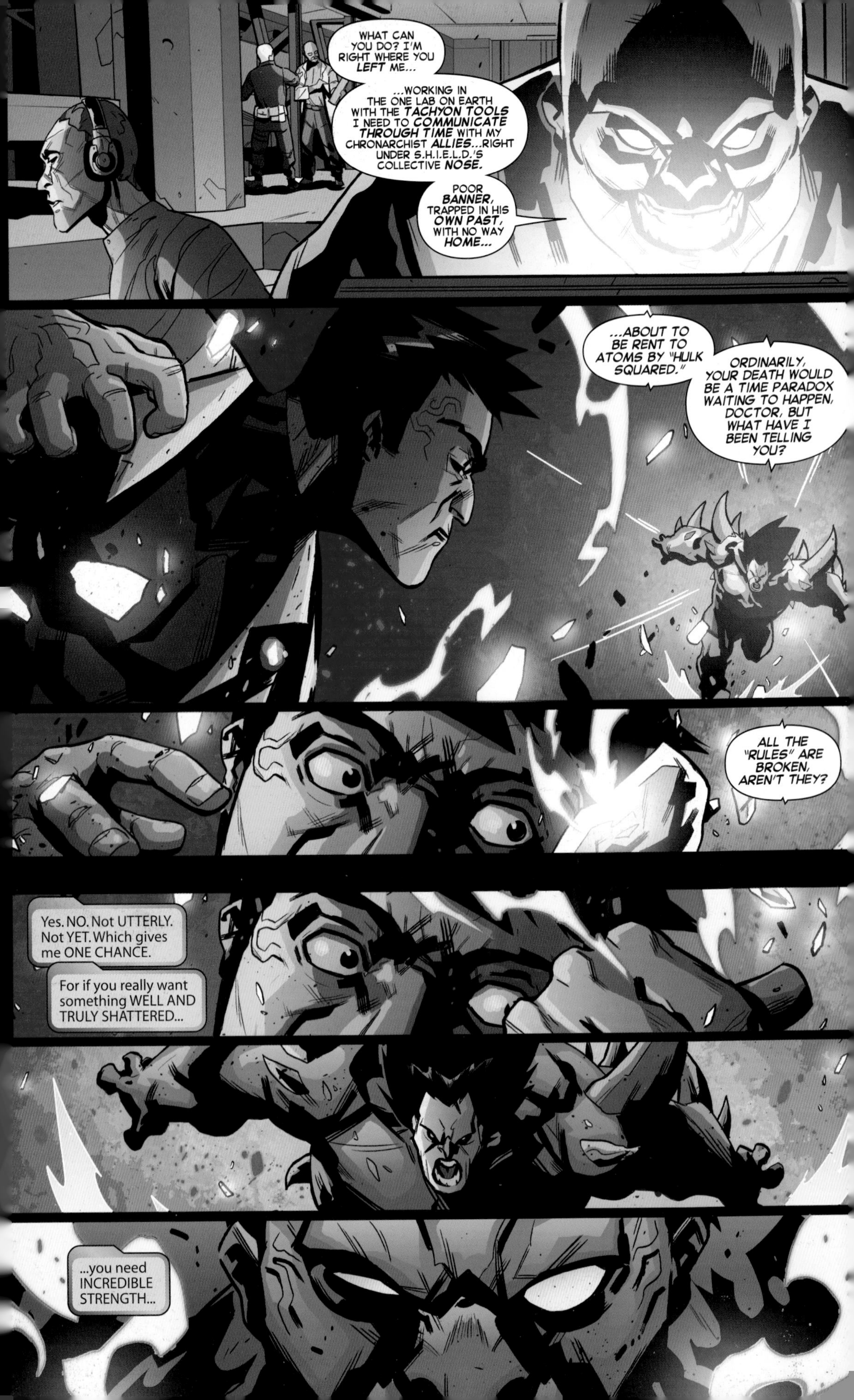
WHAT CAN YOU DO? I'M RIGHT WHERE YOU LEFT ME...
...WORKING IN THE ONE LAB ON EARTH WITH THE TACHYON TOOLS I NEED TO COMMUNICATE THROUGH TIME WITH MY CHRONARCHIST ALLIES...RIGHT UNDER S.H.I.E.L.D.'S COLLECTIVE NOSE.
POOR BANNER, TRAPPED IN HIS OWN PAST, WITH NO WAY HOME...
...ABOUT TO BE RENT TO ATOMS BY "HULK SQUARED."
ORDINARILY, YOUR DEATH WOULD BE A TIME PARADOX WAITING TO HAPPEN, DOCTOR, BUT WHAT HAVE I BEEN TELLING YOU?
ALL THE "RULES" ARE BROKEN, AREN'T THEY?
Yes. NO. Not UTTERLY. Not YET. Which gives me ONE CHANCE.
For if you really want something WELL AND TRULY SHATTERED...
...you need INCREDIBLE STRENGTH...

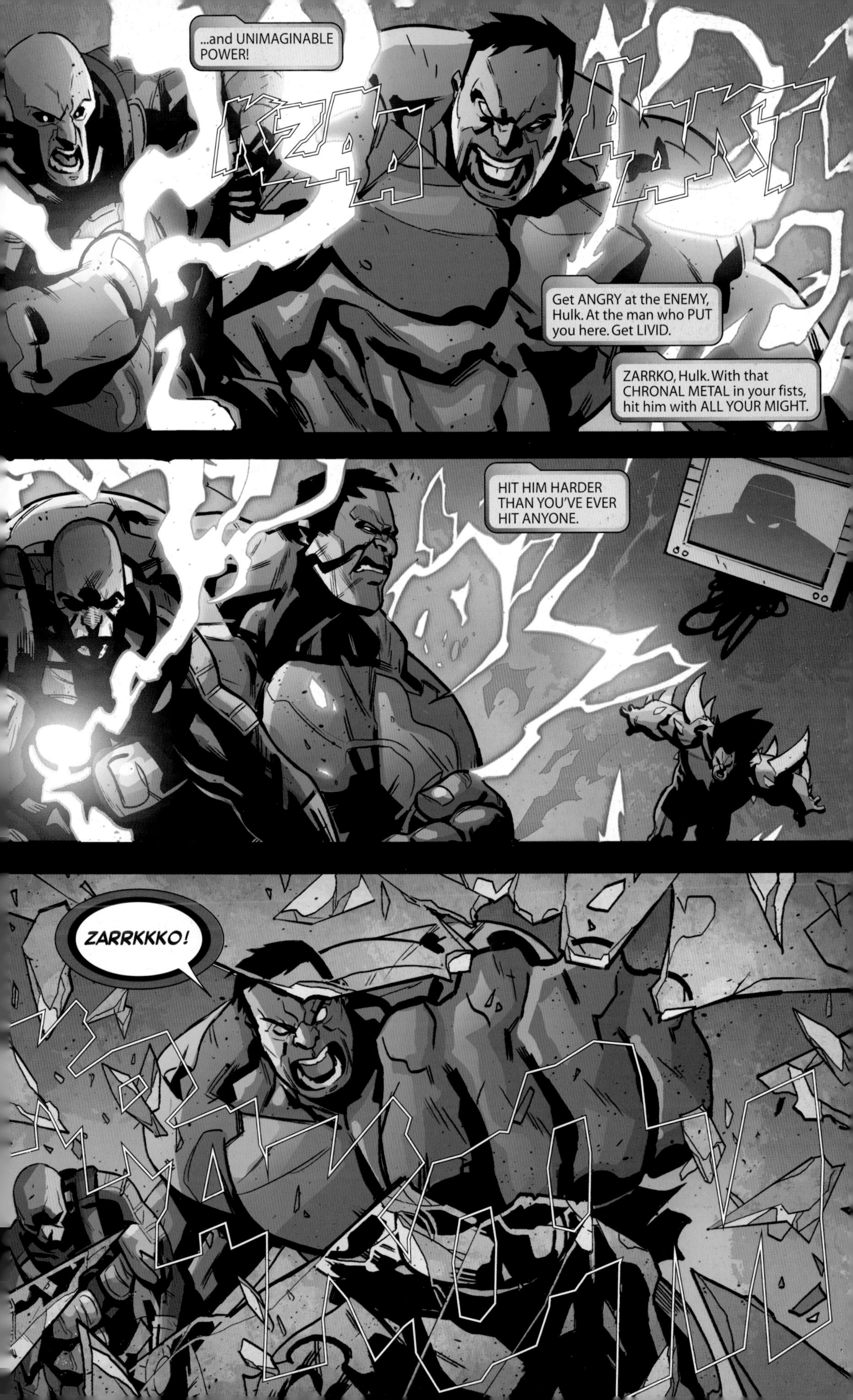
...and UNIMAGINABLE POWER!
Get ANGRY at the ENEMY, Hulk. At the man who PUT you here. Get LIVID.
ZARRKO, Hulk. With that CHRONAL METAL in your fists, hit him with ALL YOUR MIGHT.
HIT HIM HARDER THAN YOU'VE EVER HIT ANYONE.
ZARRKKKO!

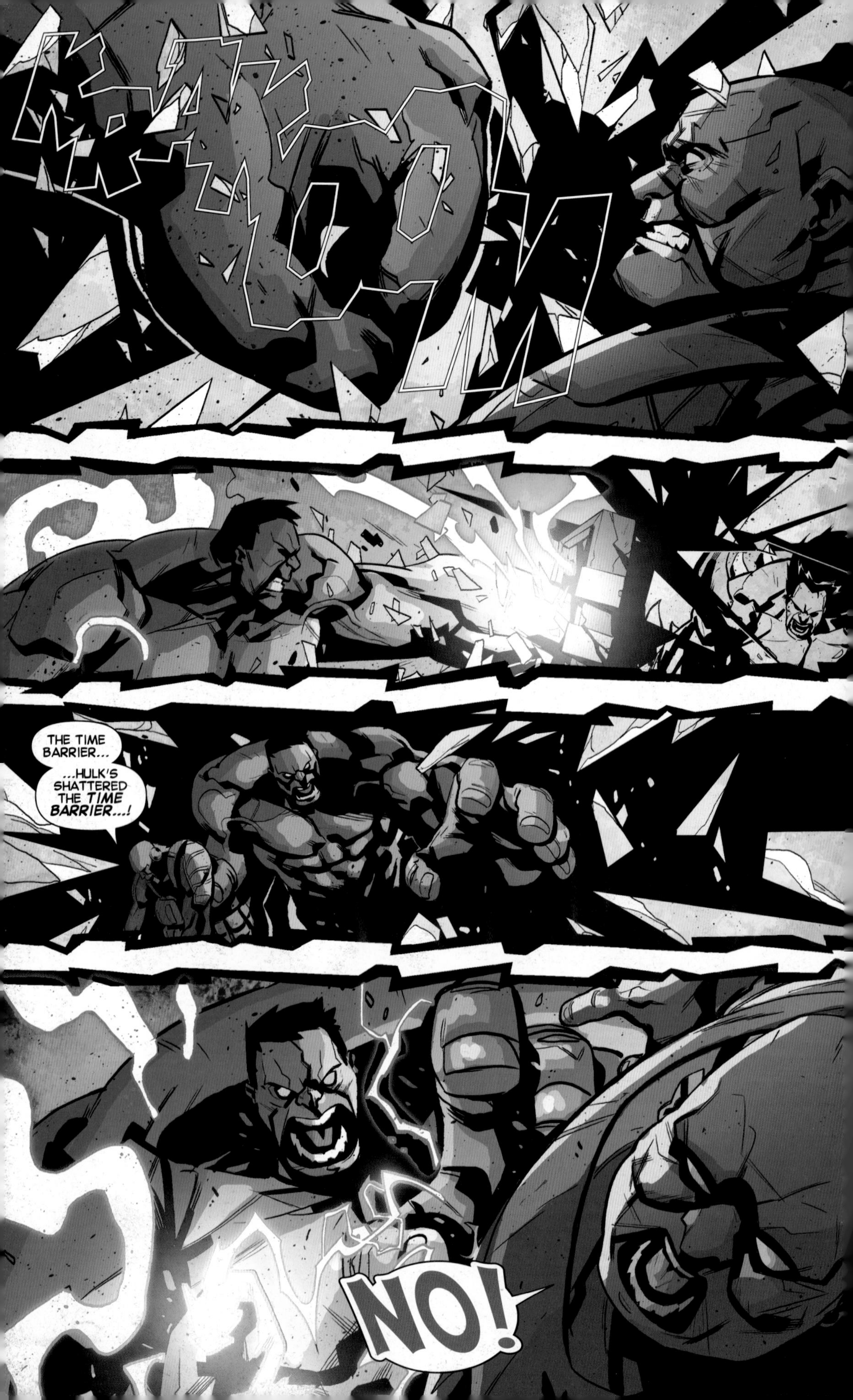
KRAKOOM
THE TIME BARRIER...
...HULK'S SHATTERED THE *TIME BARRIER*...!
NO!

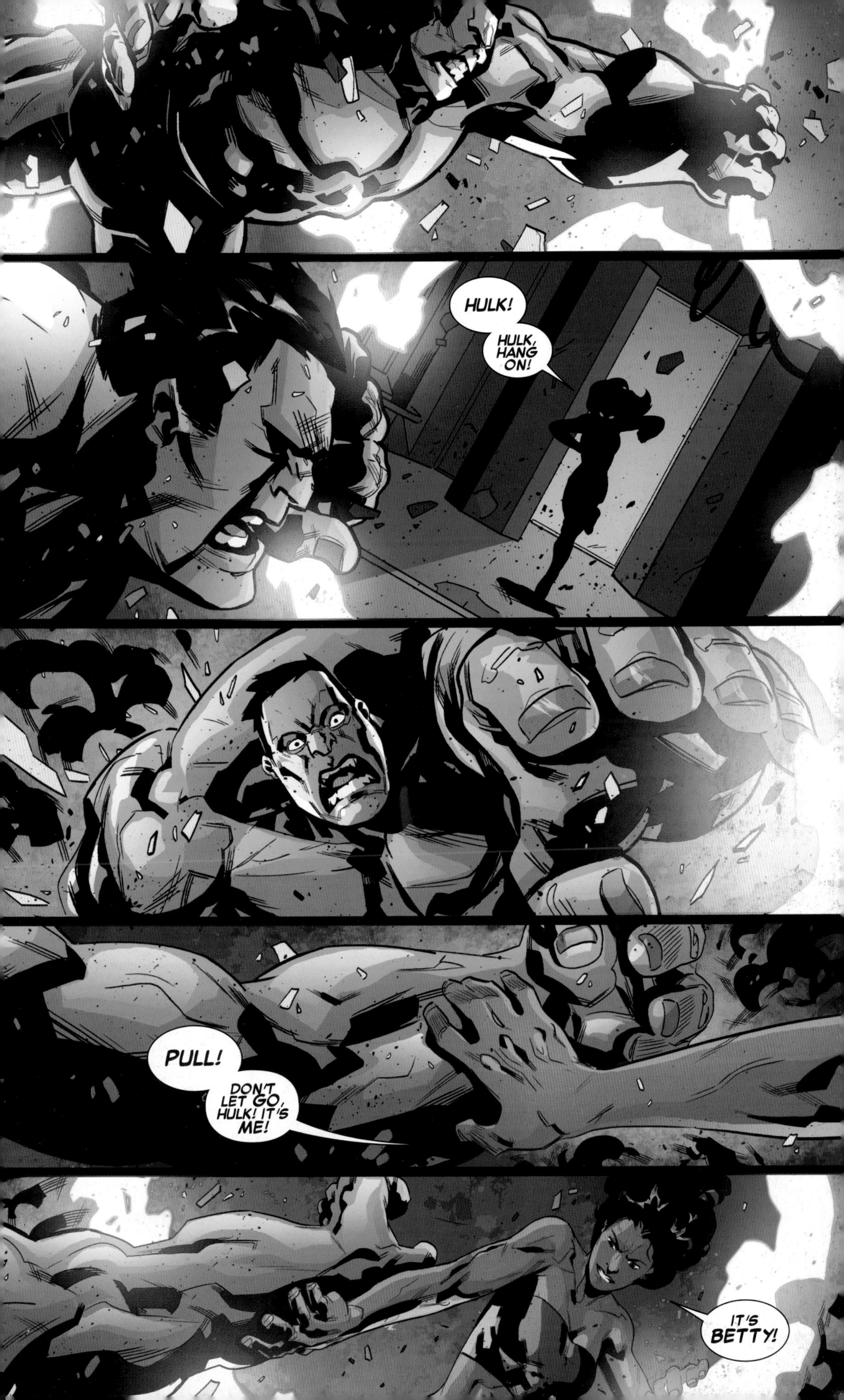
HULK!
HULK, HANG ON!
PULL!
DON'T LET GO, HULK! IT'S ME!
IT'S BETTY!

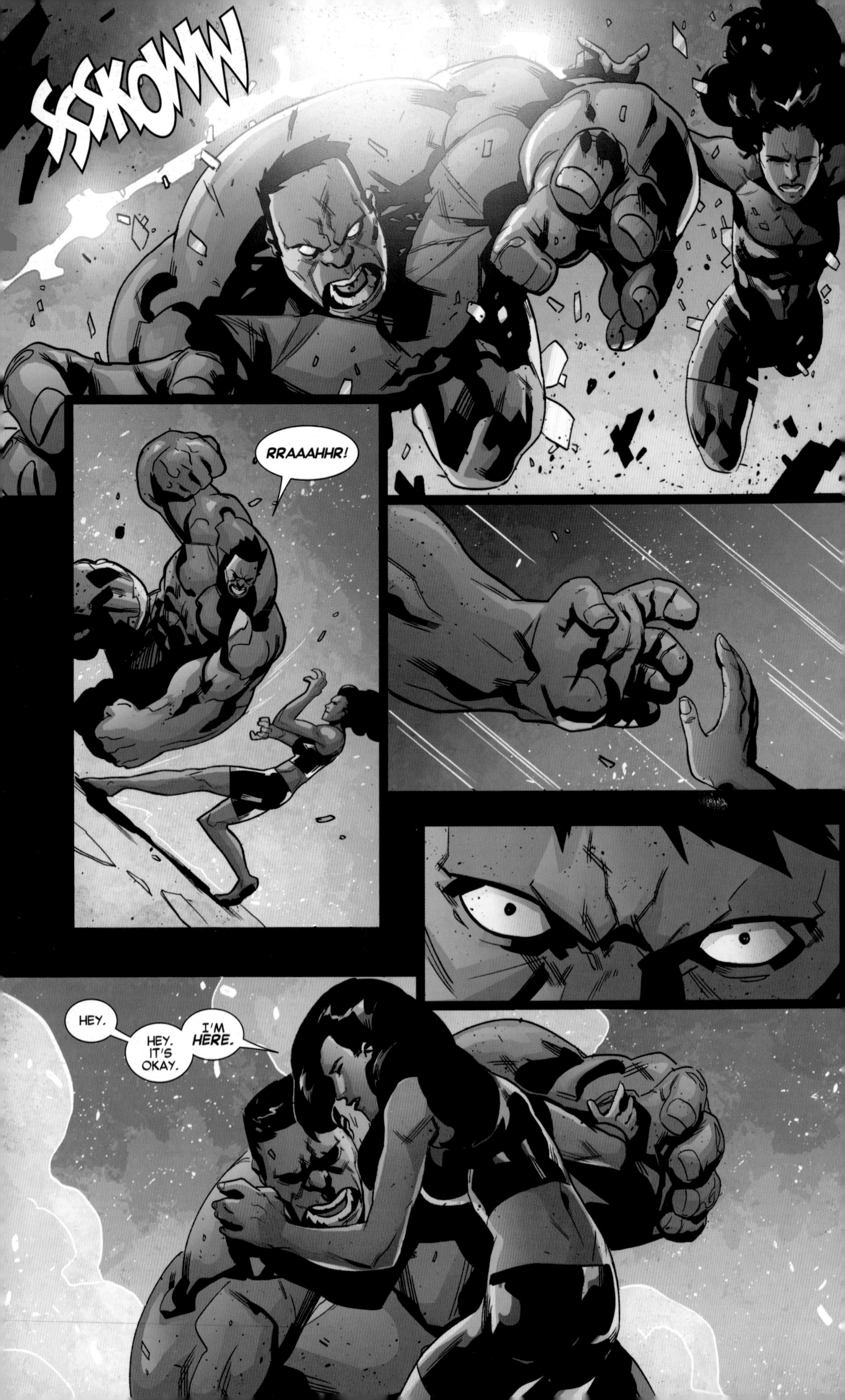
SSKOWW
RRAAAHHR!
HEY.
HEY. IT'S OKAY.
I'M HERE.

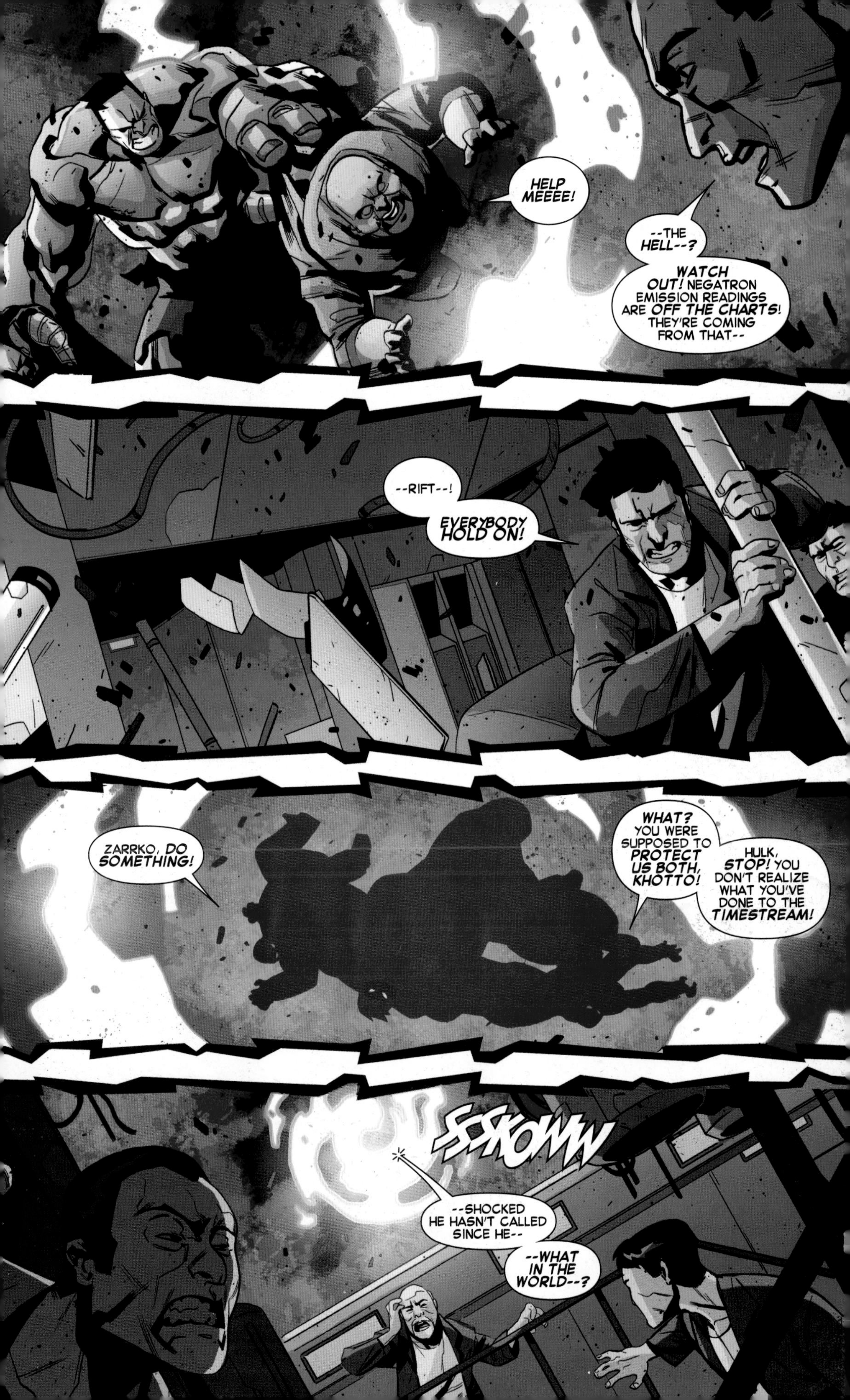
HELP MEEEE!
--THE HELL--?
WATCH OUT! NEGATRON EMISSION READINGS ARE OFF THE CHARTS! THEY'RE COMING FROM THAT--
--RIFT--!
EVERYBODY HOLD ON!
ZARRKO, DO SOMETHING!
WHAT? YOU WERE SUPPOSED TO PROTECT US BOTH, KHOTTO!
HULK, STOP! YOU DON'T REALIZE WHAT YOU'VE DONE TO THE TIMESTREAM!
SSKOWW
--SHOCKED HE HASN'T CALLED SINCE HE--
--WHAT IN THE WORLD--?

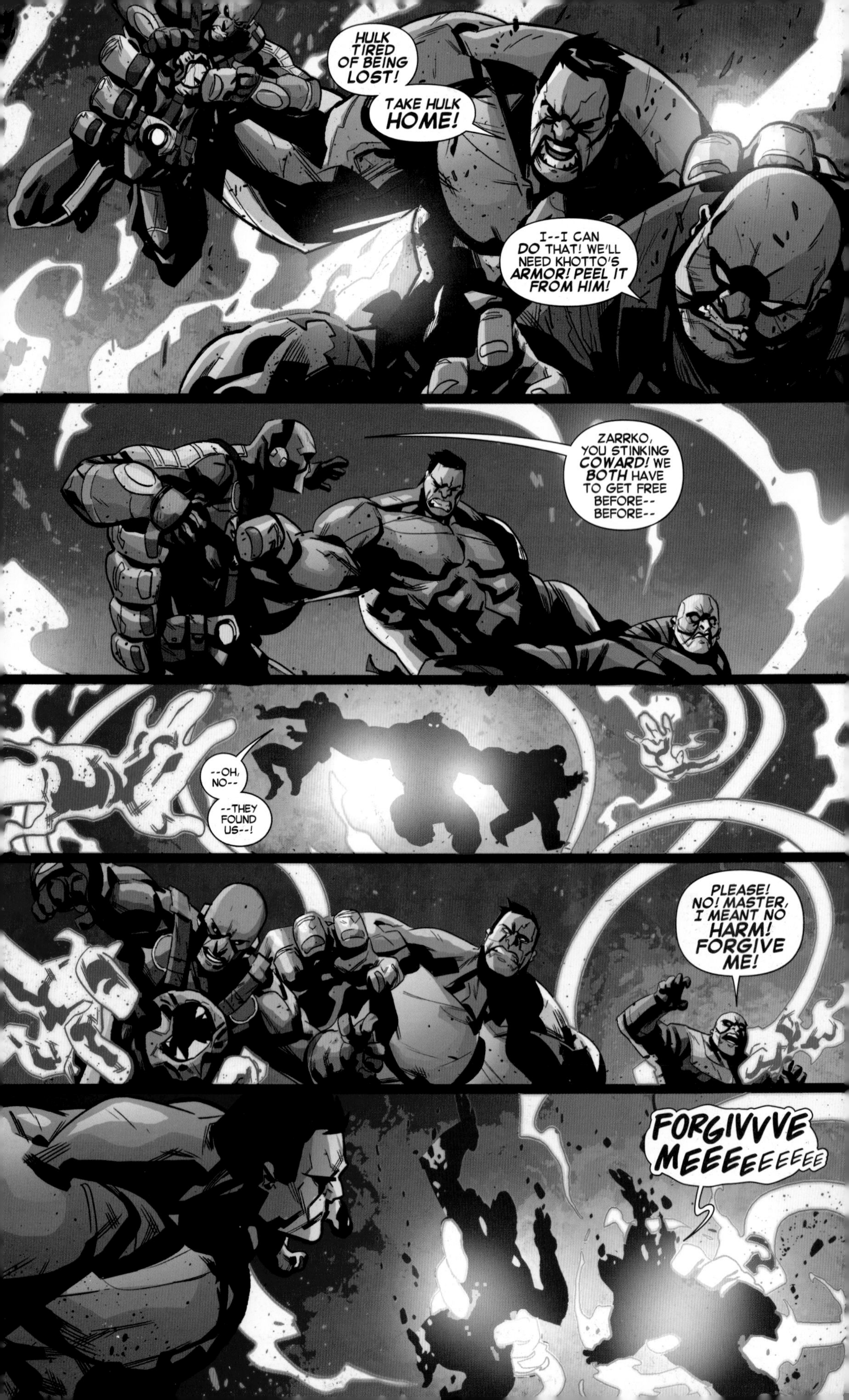
HULK TIRED OF BEING LOST!
TAKE HULK HOME!
I--I CAN DO THAT! WE'LL NEED KHOTTO'S ARMOR! PEEL IT FROM HIM!
ZARRKO, YOU STINKING COWARD! WE BOTH HAVE TO GET FREE BEFORE-- BEFORE--
--OH, NO--
--THEY FOUND US--!
PLEASE! NO! MASTER, I MEANT NO HARM! FORGIVE ME!
FORGIVVVE MEEEEEEEEE

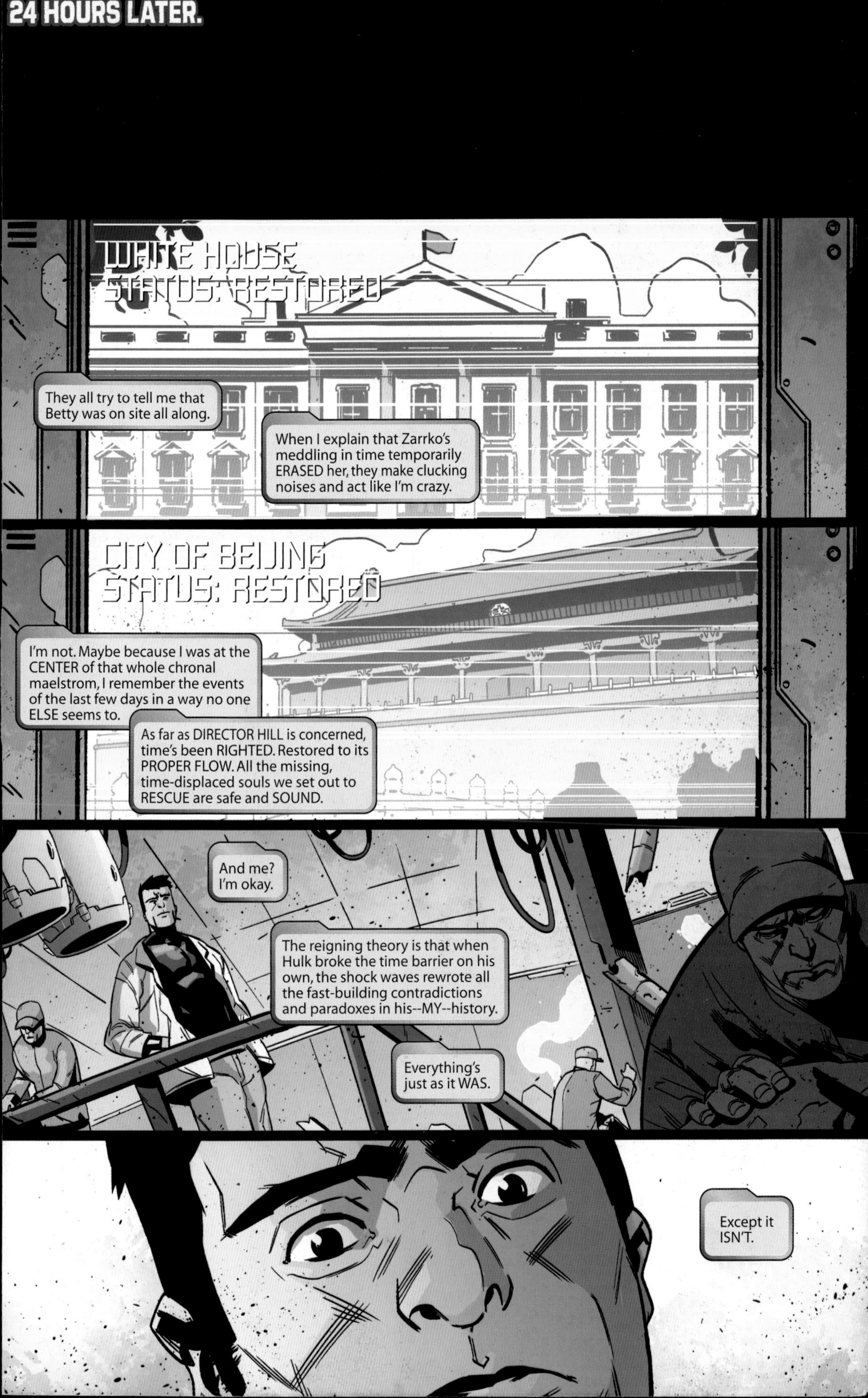
24 HOURS LATER.
WHITE HOUSE
STATUS: RESTORED
They all try to tell me that Betty was on site all along.
When I explain that Zarrko's meddling in time temporarily ERASED her, they make clucking noises and act like I'm crazy.
CITY OF BEIJING
STATUS: RESTORED
I'm not. Maybe because I was at the CENTER of that whole chronal maelstrom, I remember the events of the last few days in a way no one ELSE seems to.
As far as DIRECTOR HILL is concerned, time's been RIGHTED. Restored to its PROPER FLOW. All the missing, time-displaced souls we set out to RESCUE are safe and SOUND.
And me? I'm okay.
The reigning theory is that when Hulk broke the time barrier on his own, the shock waves rewrote all the fast-building contradictions and paradoxes in his--MY--history.
Everything's just as it WAS.
Except it ISN'T.

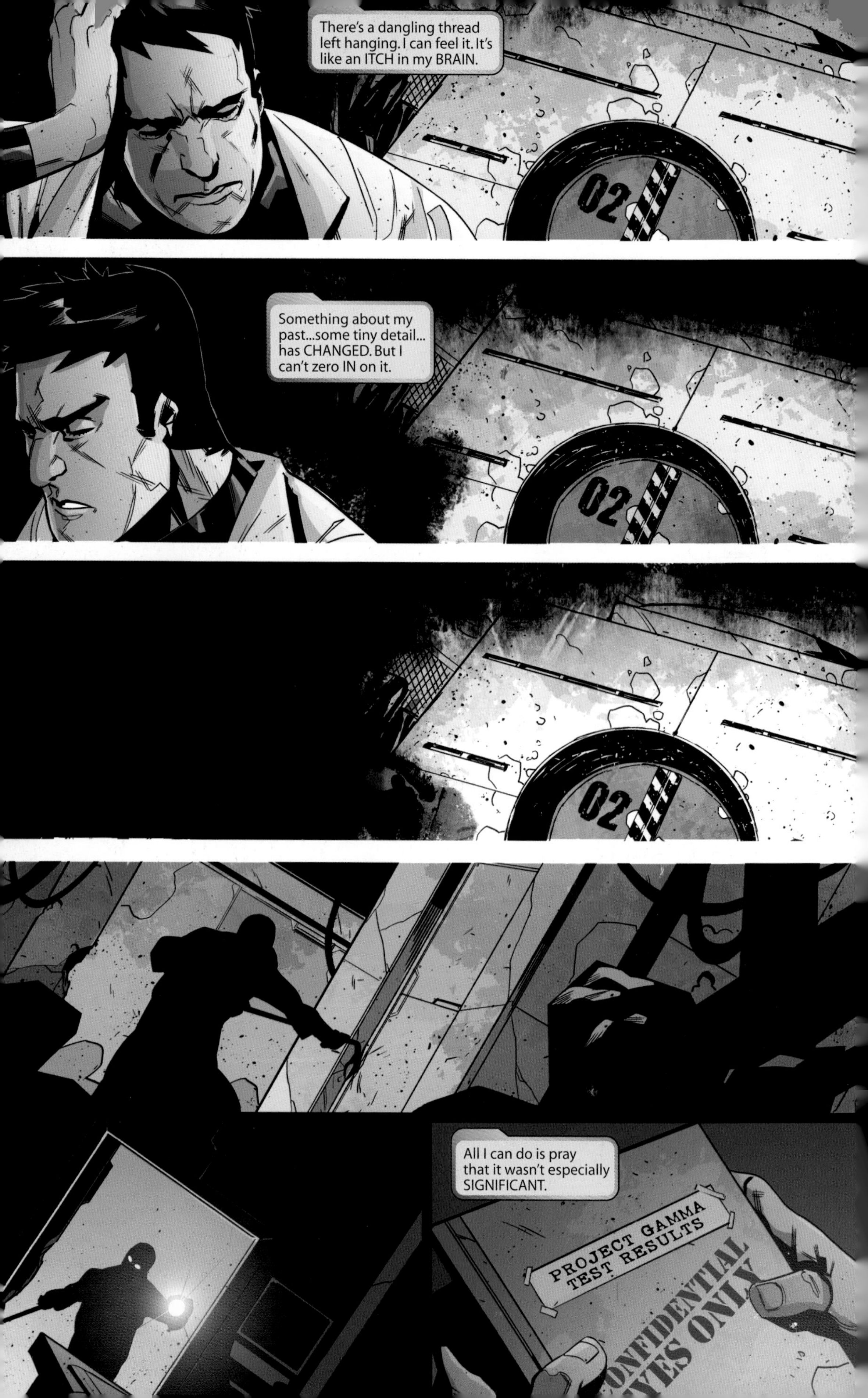
There's a dangling thread left hanging. I can feel it. It's like an ITCH in my BRAIN.
02
Something about my past...some tiny detail... has CHANGED. But I can't zero IN on it.
02
02
All I can do is pray that it wasn't especially SIGNIFICANT.
PROJECT GAMMA TEST RESULTS
CONFIDENTIAL
EYES ONLY

INDESTRUCTIBLE HULK Variant Cover Gallery

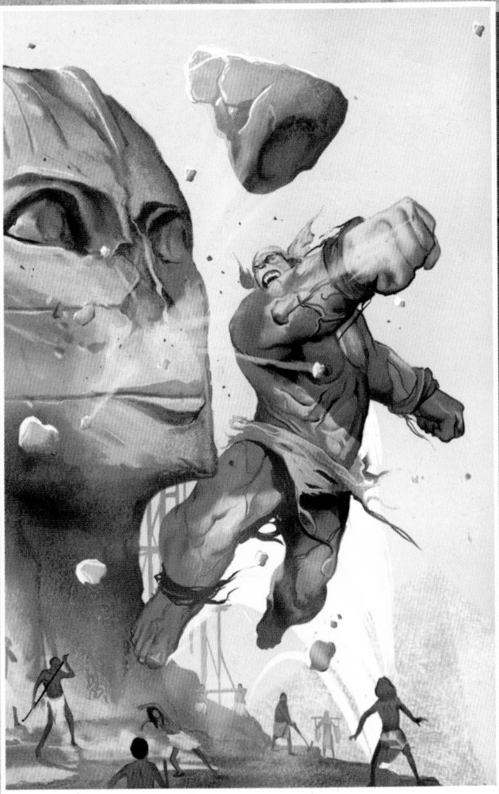

INDESTRUCTIBLE HULK#13
BY MICHAEL DEL MUNDO

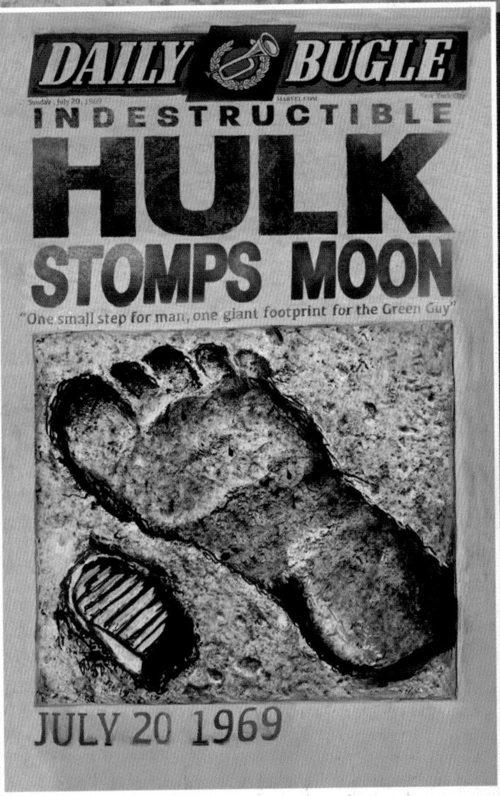
DAILY BUGLE
INDESTRUCTIBLE
HULK
STOMPS MOON
"One small step for man, one giant footprint for the Green Guy"
JULY 20 1969

INDESTRUCTIBLE HULK#14
BY MICHAEL DEL MUNDO

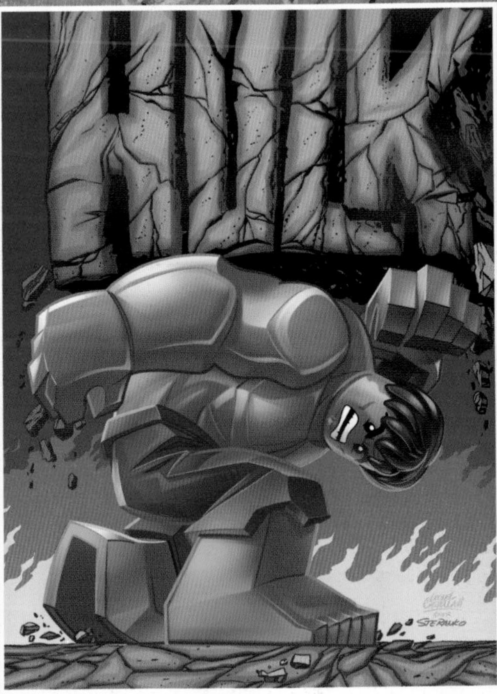
HULK

INDESTRUCTIBLE HULK#14
BY LEONEL CASTELLANI

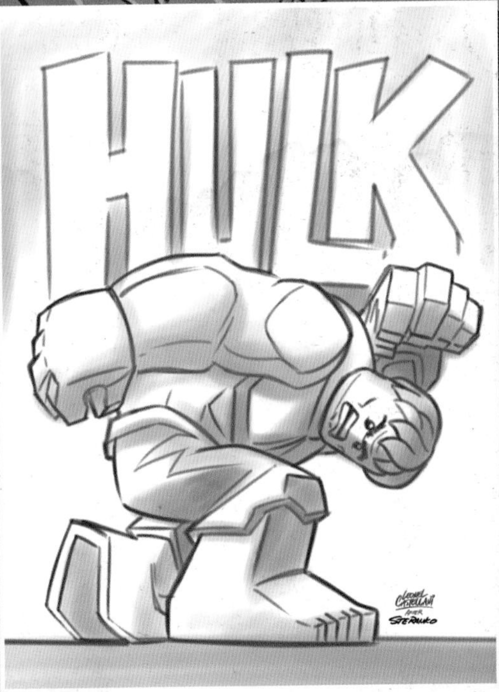
HULK

INDESTRUCTIBLE HULK#14
BY LEONEL CASTELLANI

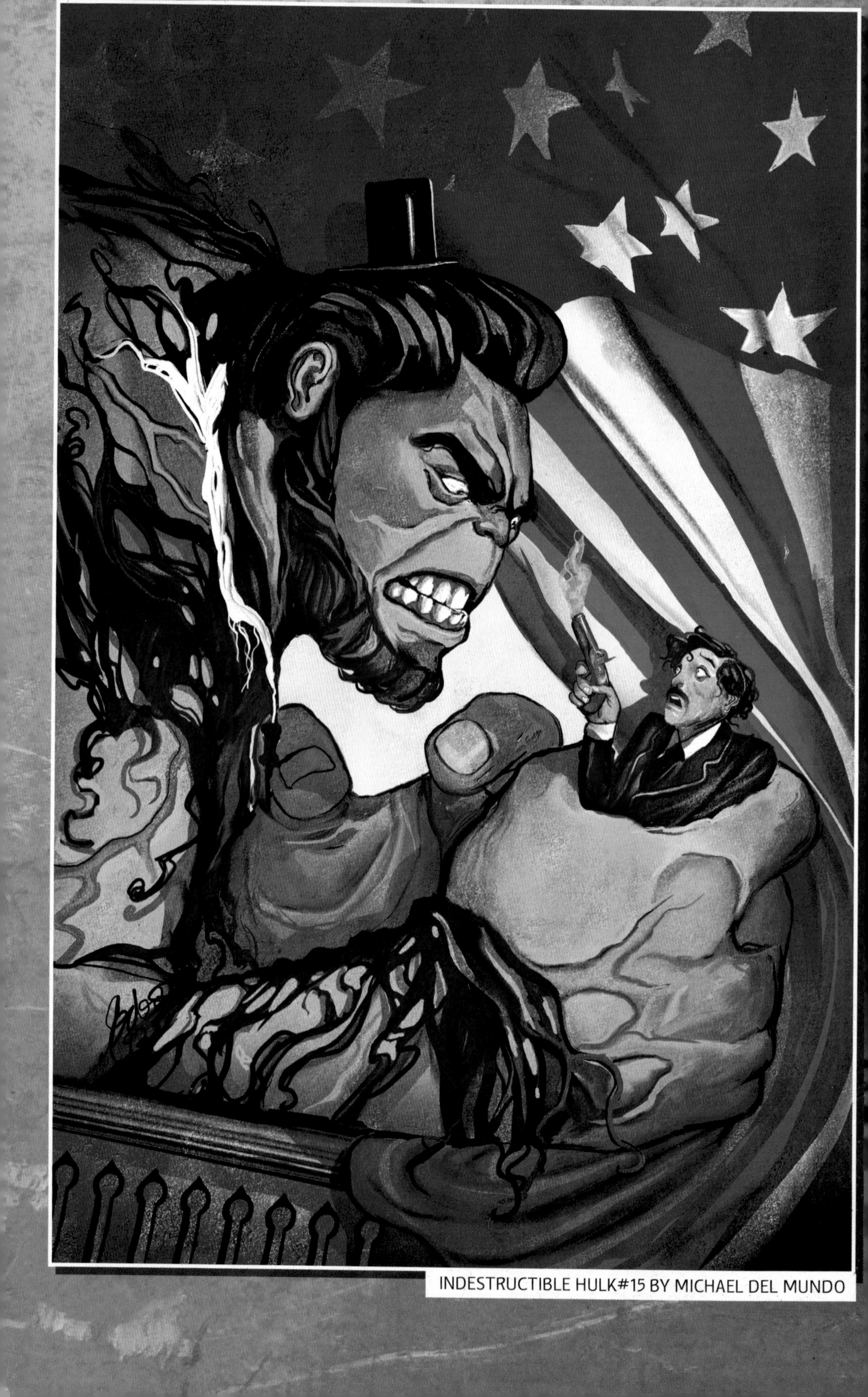

INDESTRUCTIBLE HULK#15 BY MICHAEL DEL MUNDO

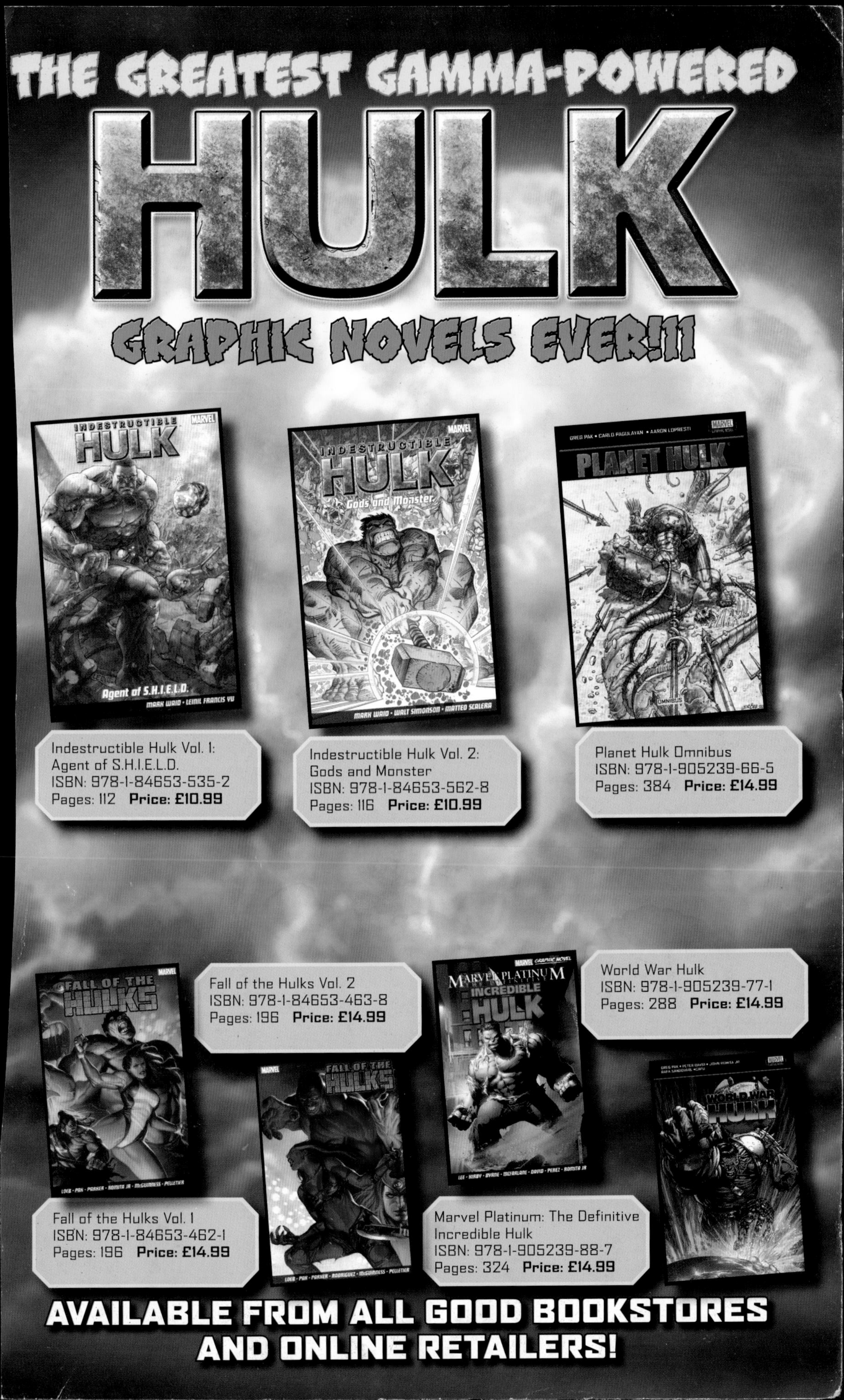
THE GREATEST GAMMA-POWERED
HULK
GRAPHIC NOVELS EVER!11
INDESTRUCTIBLE HULK
MARVEL
Agent of S.H.I.E.L.D.
MARK WAID • LEINIL FRANCIS YU
INDESTRUCTIBLE HULK
Gods and Monster
MARK WAID • WALT SIMONSON • MATTEO SCALERA
GREG PAK • CARLO PAGULAYAN • AARON LOPRESTI
PLANET HULK
OMNIBUS
Indestructible Hulk Vol. 1:
Agent of S.H.I.E.L.D.
ISBN: 978-1-84653-535-2
Pages: 112 Price: £10.99
Indestructible Hulk Vol. 2:
Gods and Monster
ISBN: 978-1-84653-562-8
Pages: 116 Price: £10.99
Planet Hulk Omnibus
ISBN: 978-1-905239-66-5
Pages: 384 Price: £14.99
FALL OF THE HULKS
LOEB • PAK • PARKER • ROMITA JR • McGUINNESS • PELLETIER
Fall of the Hulks Vol. 2
ISBN: 978-1-84653-463-8
Pages: 196 Price: £14.99
FALL OF THE HULKS
LOEB • PAK • PARKER • RODRIGUEZ • McGUINNESS • PELLETIER
MARVEL PLATINUM
INCREDIBLE HULK
LEE • KIRBY • BYRNE • McFARLANE • DAVID • PEREZ • ROMITA JR
World War Hulk
ISBN: 978-1-905239-77-1
Pages: 288 Price: £14.99
WORLD WAR HULK
Fall of the Hulks Vol. 1
ISBN: 978-1-84653-462-1
Pages: 196 Price: £14.99
Marvel Platinum: The Definitive
Incredible Hulk
ISBN: 978-1-905239-88-7
Pages: 324 Price: £14.99
AVAILABLE FROM ALL GOOD BOOKSTORES
AND ONLINE RETAILERS!

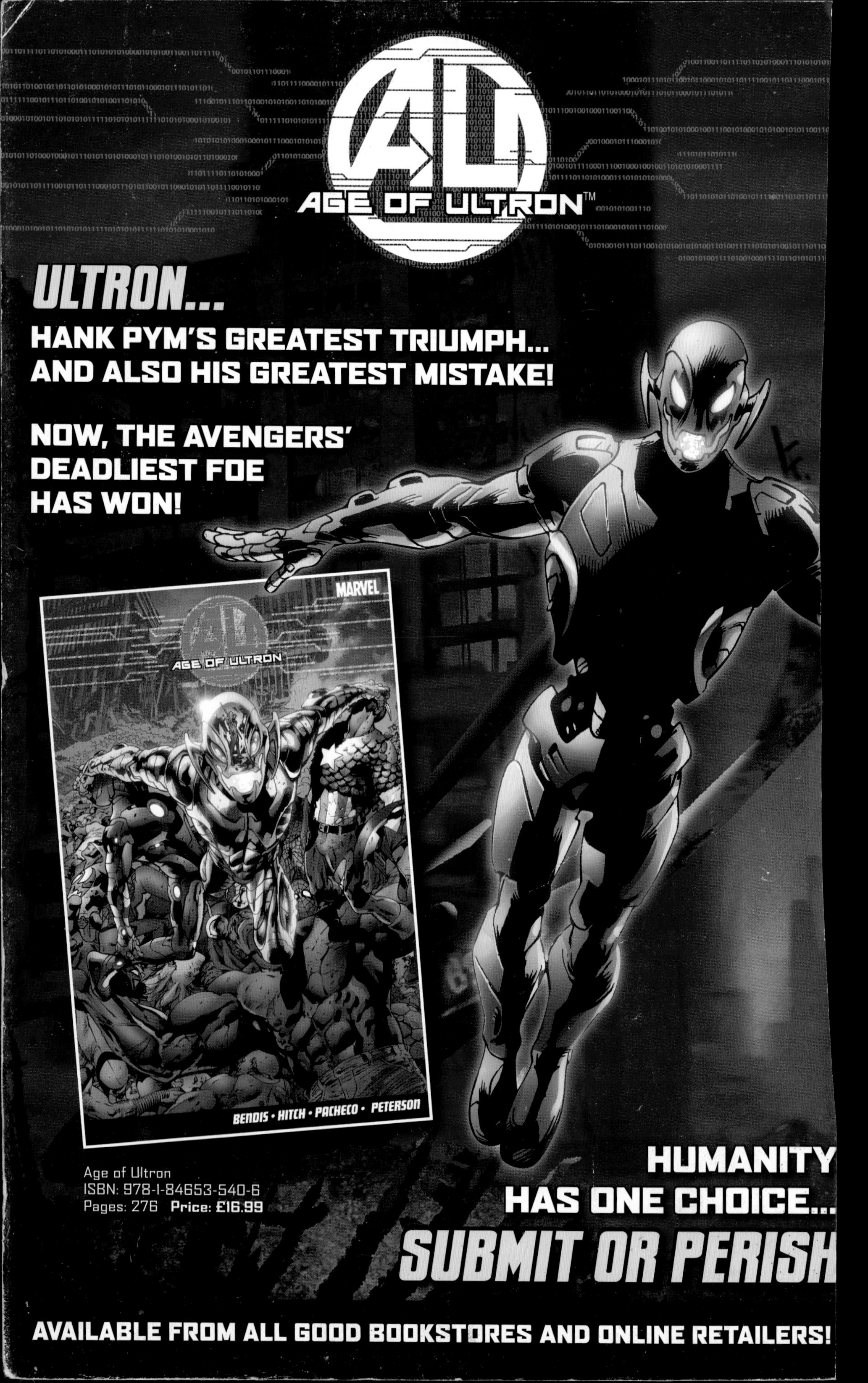
AGE OF ULTRON™
ULTRON...
HANK PYM'S GREATEST TRIUMPH...
AND ALSO HIS GREATEST MISTAKE!
NOW, THE AVENGERS' DEADLIEST FOE HAS WON!
MARVEL
AGE OF ULTRON
BENDIS • HITCH • PACHECO • PETERSON
Age of Ultron
ISBN: 978-1-84653-540-6
Pages: 276 Price: £16.99
HUMANITY HAS ONE CHOICE...
SUBMIT OR PERISH
AVAILABLE FROM ALL GOOD BOOKSTORES AND ONLINE RETAILERS!